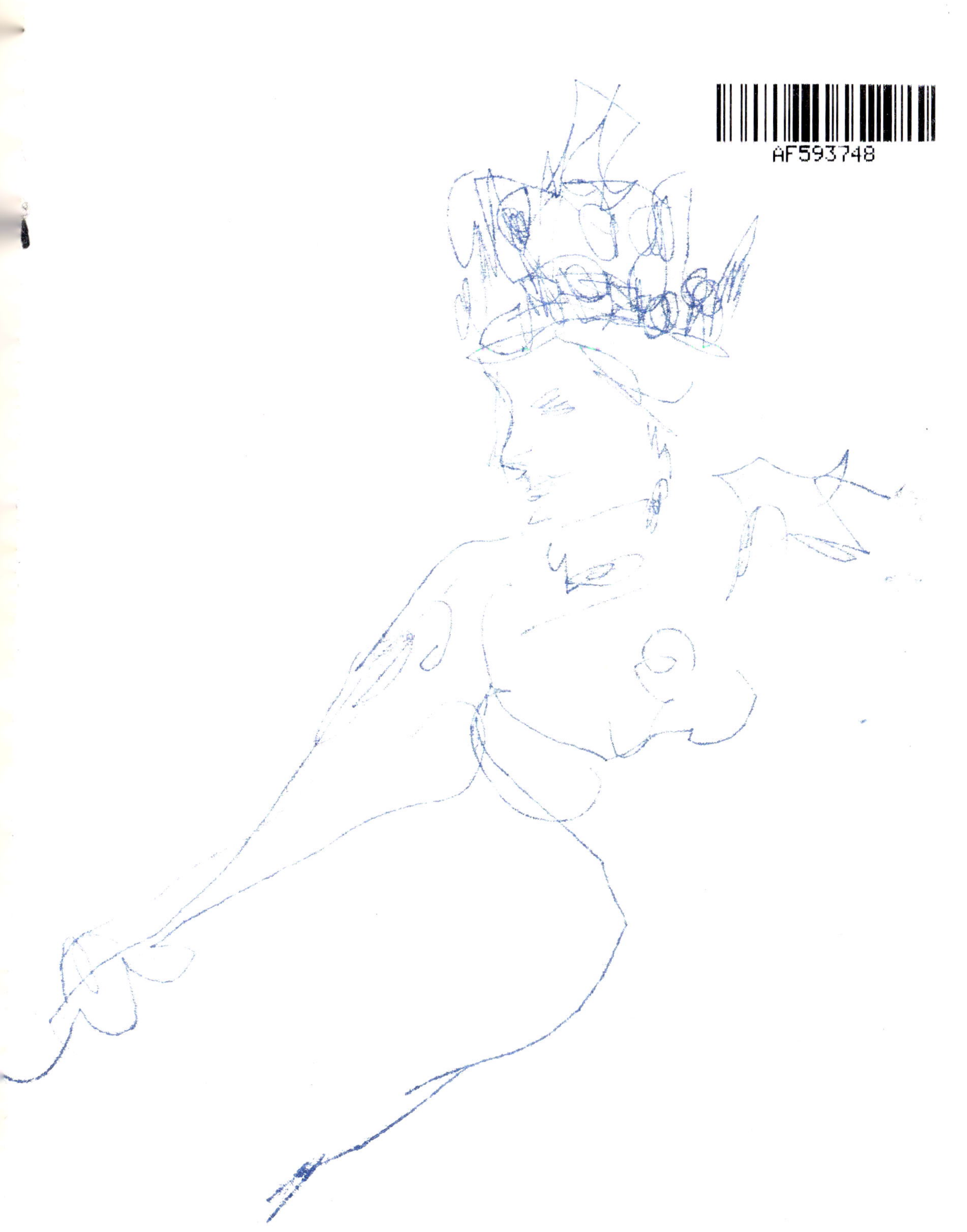

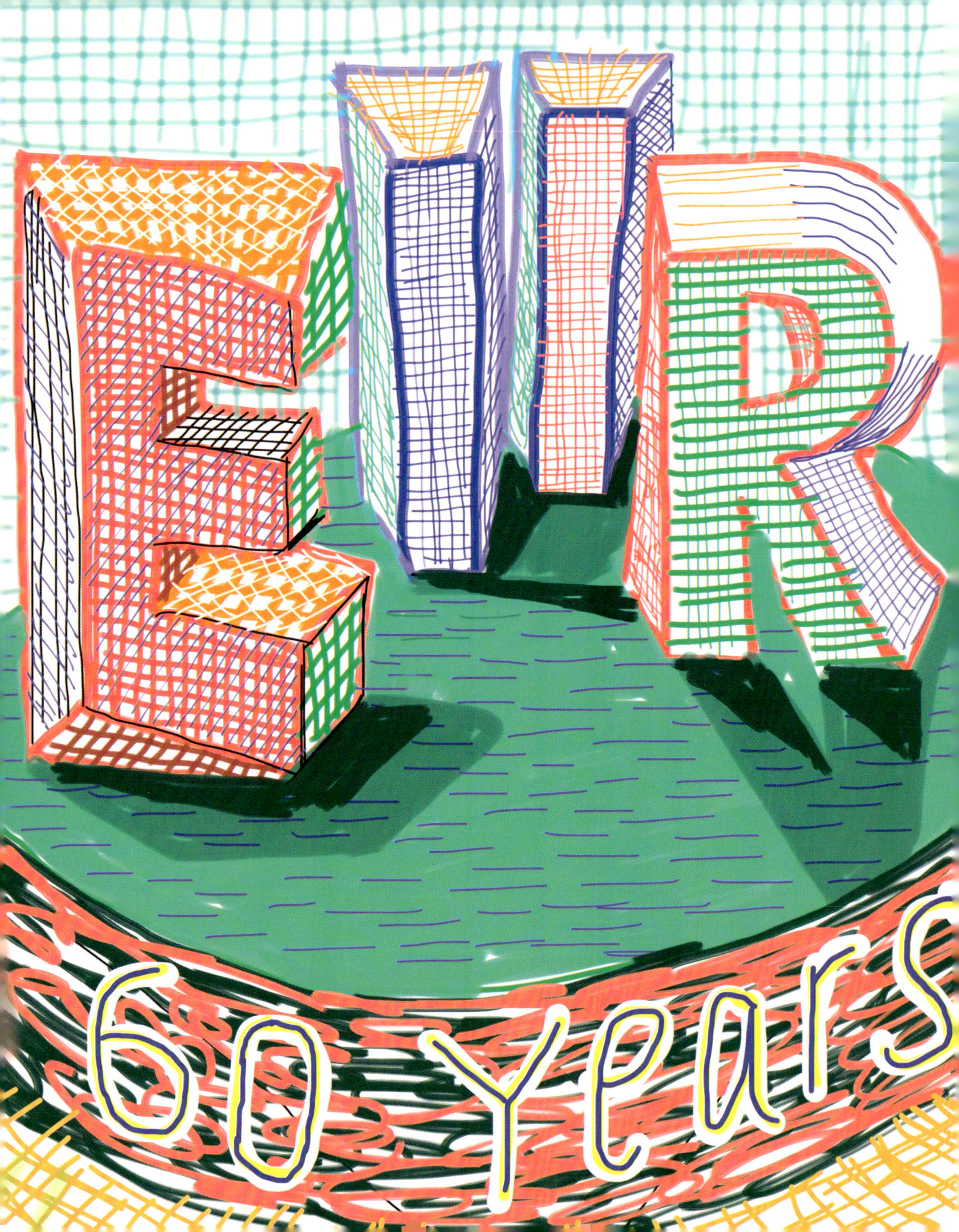
EIIR
60 years

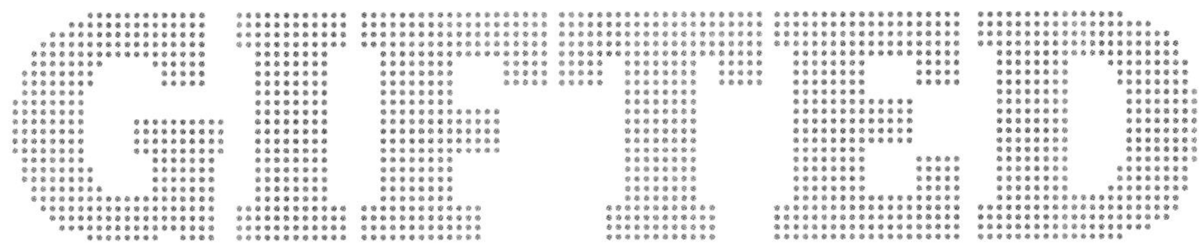

GIFTED

FROM THE ROYAL ACADEMY TO THE QUEEN

Royal Collection Trust

Introduction

Martin Clayton

In December 1768 King George III approved the Instrument of Foundation of the Royal Academy of Arts, the principal aims of which were to teach students 'the Arts of Design' and to mount annual exhibitions. The initial roll of thirty-six Academicians was rather cosmopolitan, including not just British artists such as Thomas Gainsborough and Joshua Reynolds (the first President of the Royal Academy), but also Italians (G.B. Cipriani, Francesco Bartolozzi and Francesco Zuccarelli), an American, Benjamin West, the Swiss Angelica Kauffman, the German Johan Zoffany, and the Swedish-born architect William Chambers, all of whom were then working in London.

Chambers was effectively the King's agent in the early years of the Academy – it was he who drafted the foundation document, and, as first Treasurer, he was the conduit through whom George III supported the fledgling organisation financially. Thus began an association between the Royal Academy and the monarchy that has now lasted for almost 250 years. Like all long-term relationships there have been periods of close engagement and others of a cooler distance, but the formal patronage of the Sovereign has ensured a continuity that few other organisations can rival.

George III made rooms available for the Academy in old Somerset House on the Strand, and it was there that Zoffany set his memorable group portrait of the Academicians attending a life class, painted for the King in 1771–2 and still in the Royal Collection. But Somerset House was in a state of decay, and from the middle of the 1770s the old building began to be demolished, to be replaced by the magnificent edifice, designed by Chambers, that stands on the site today.

Opposite: Johan Zoffany (1733–1810), *The Academicians of the Royal Academy* (detail), 1772, oil on canvas, RCIN 400747. Title page: David Hockney, *2012 Queen Elizabeth II Diamond Jubilee* (detail), 2012. Front page: Professor Tracey Emin, *HRH Royal Britania* (detail), 2012

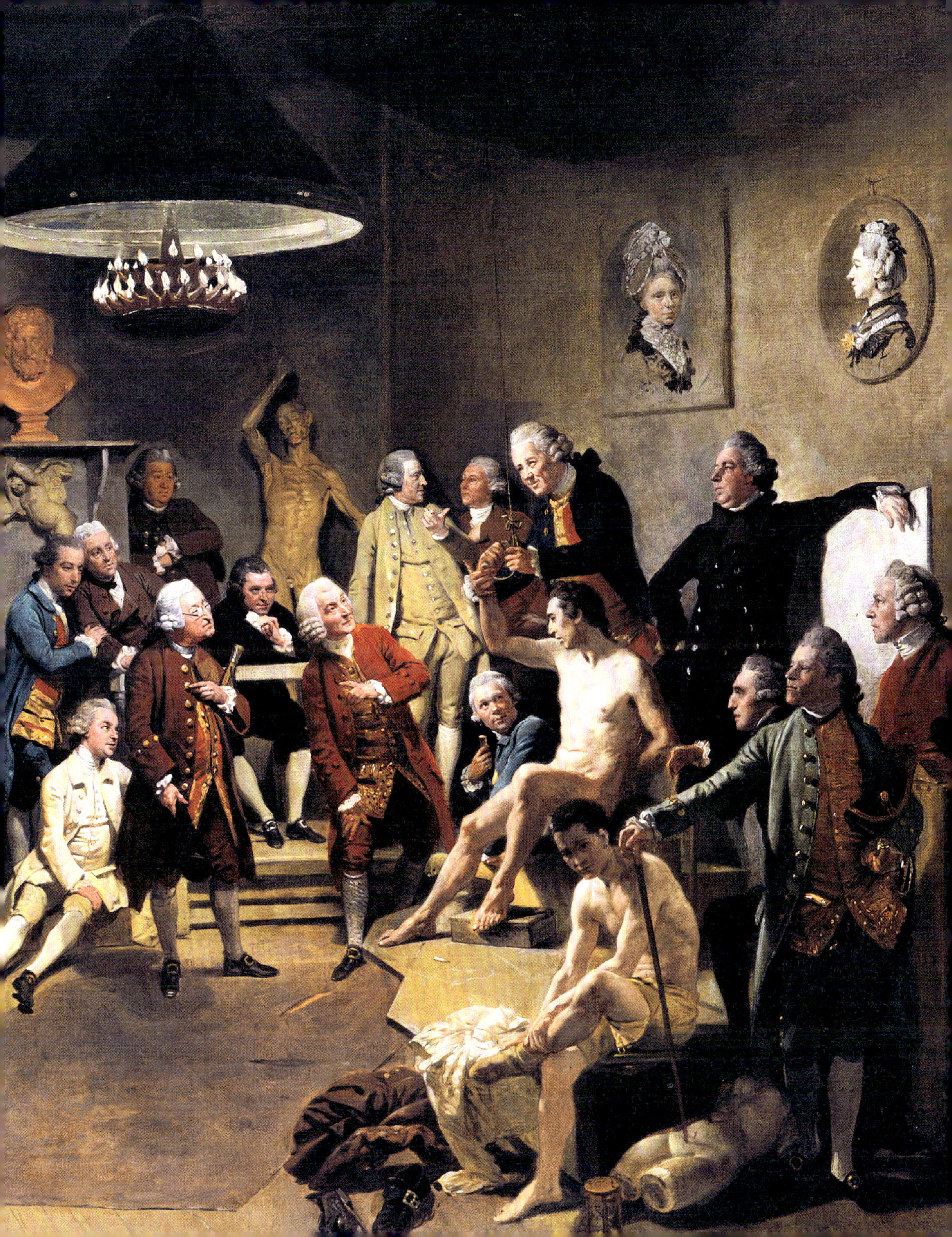

Again the Academy was allocated rooms in new Somerset House (today occupied by the Courtauld Gallery), and the King and his family keenly attended the Academy's annual exhibitions there. In time, the Prince of Wales (later Prince Regent, then George IV) was himself a generous benefactor of the Academy. He lent the School of Painting more than one of Raphael's tapestry cartoons, then hanging at Hampton Court, for study purposes, and he made gifts of, for example, a two-ton bronze lamp, the chain and medal of office of the President, and many casts of classical sculpture. In the Royal Library today is the Academy's elaborate letter of thanks to the Prince Regent for a cast of the Niobids presented in 1819, signed by West (then President), Thomas Lawrence, J.M.W. Turner, Henry Fuseli, John Flaxman, David Wilkie and many others. And the Prince's engagement with the Academy was not just as a distant patron, for he was a regular attendee at the Academy's convivial annual dinners.

The last public appearance of William IV was to open the Academy's new rooms in Trafalgar Square, annexed to the National Gallery, in April 1837 (the final move to Burlington House on Piccadilly came in 1868). William was succeeded by Queen Victoria, who with Prince Albert became an enthusiastic visitor to the annual exhibitions at the Academy, where she bought celebrated paintings such as William Powell Frith's *Ramsgate Sands* and Frederick Leighton's *Cimabue's Madonna Carried in Procession*. After Albert's death in 1861, the Prince of Wales, like his great-uncle George IV, often attended the dinner held prior to the opening of the annual exhibition. But the fulfilment of his duties at the Academy, both as Prince of Wales and later as Edward VII, was more ceremony than substance, and indeed the earlier part of the twentieth century saw the Academy dwindle in importance as a mainstay of British cultural life. George V fulfilled his duties as Patron of the Academy but little more; the future Edward VIII did not frequent the annual dinners of the Academicians as previous Princes of Wales had done. While George VI had little personal interest in artistic matters, his consort Queen Elizabeth was an active collector; however her mentor Kenneth Clark, concurrently Director of the National Gallery and Surveyor of the King's Pictures, was (as he later claimed) considered a 'dangerous revolutionary' in Royal Academy circles, and Queen Elizabeth therefore found herself, perhaps by accident, somewhat detached from the Academy.

Alfred Munnings was elected President in 1944, trenchantly reactionary in matters of art. A more immediate challenge than keeping the Modernists at bay was the state of the Academy's finances following the stringencies of the War. The first post-war loan exhibition to be held at the Academy, *The King's Pictures* in the winter of 1946–7 – more than 500 paintings assembled from across the Royal Collection – was a huge success and the financial saviour of the Academy. Five years later some 200 drawings were loaned from the Royal Library to the Academy's great exhibition marking the quincentenary of the birth of Leonardo da Vinci. And the election of Gerald Kelly as Munnings' successor in 1949 saw a growing personal *rapprochement* between the Academy and the crown. Kelly had spent a large part of the War working (rather slowly) at Windsor on the state portraits of the King and Queen, and there he had come to know the young Princesses Elizabeth and Margaret Rose. On the accession of Her Majesty as Queen Elizabeth II in 1952, Kelly took the decision to go beyond the traditional presentation of a loyal address from the Royal Academy upon the Coronation (a tradition practised by many official bodies across the United Kingdom and Commonwealth): he invited his fellow Academicians each to furnish a work on paper as a Coronation Gift to The Queen.

The four boxes of mounted drawings and prints presented in 1953, and still held in the Royal Library, form a snapshot of 'official' British art at mid-century, with 66 works by, among many others, Kelly and Munnings, Frank Brangwyn, William Russell Flint, Augustus John and Laura Knight. Conspicuous by their absence were the British *avant-garde* – no Ben Nicholson, Henry Moore, Barbara Hepworth, Graham Sutherland or John Piper; only Stanley Spencer (who had resigned as an Academician in 1935, accepting re-election in 1950) represented what we might now consider British Modernism.

But this inspired gift marked the start of a sustained engagement between the Royal Academy and The Queen. In March 1955, Her Majesty visited the Academy Schools and Library, the first sovereign ever to do so, and in December 1968 she attended the Royal Academy's Bicentenary Dinner, the first time the monarch had dined officially at the Academy. That dinner was held two years into the tenure as President of Thomas Monnington, little considered now as an artist but an effective and tolerant leader of the Royal Academy. During Monnington's presidency there were elected as Associates or full Academicians such 'non-academic' artists as Peter Blake, Sandra Blow, John Bratby, Elisabeth Frink, Ernö Goldfinger and Eduardo Paolozzi.

In 1976, the architect and designer Hugh Casson was elected as President. From the 1950s Casson had been employed on interior schemes for the new Royal Yacht *Britannia*, on the Royal Train, and at Buckingham Palace and Windsor Castle, and his wit and charm – combined with his skill as a designer – had ensured that he had become a friend of The Queen and The Duke of Edinburgh (and of Queen Elizabeth, The Queen Mother). In the summer of 1977 the first loan exhibition was held in the Private Rooms of the Academy, entitled *This Brilliant Year*, ostensibly documenting Queen Victoria's Golden Jubilee in 1887, but also indirectly marking The Queen's Silver Jubilee; that autumn a memorable exhibition of 50 of Leonardo's anatomical drawings from the Royal Library graced the main galleries; and in the same year the Academy followed up its Coronation Gift with an equally generous gift of 77 drawings, watercolours and prints to mark the Silver Jubilee. The contrast between that gift and the Coronation Gift showed just how far the Academy's membership and outlook had evolved in the intervening 24 years.

Into the twenty-first century, the Royal Academy has continued to grow in its ambitions and to expand its aesthetic reach. It is now unquestionably one of the powerhouses of the British art scene, and embraces every possible style, from the traditionally figurative to the coolest abstraction. The reactionary days of the 1940s seem a very distant memory. And thus the gift of over a hundred works on paper to mark The Queen's Diamond Jubilee in 2012 has been one of the most welcome, even transformative additions to the Royal Collection in modern times.

It is of course invidious to cite individual works from within the gift, but a few examples might give some sense of its range: from the expansiveness of Will Alsop's *Somewhere – Sometime – Someplace* to the meticulous control of Tess Jaray's *Terrace*; from the traditional landscape of Ken Howard's *Florentine Farmhouse* or Anthony Eyton's *Uluru (Ayer's Rock)* to the visionary mood of Hughie O'Donoghue's *Voyage of the Plassy* or Barbara Rae's *Bealach na Bà;* from the humour of Richard Wilson's *Hang on a minute lads, I've got a great idea!* or Grayson Perry's *Design for Kenilworth AMI* to the lyricism of Richard Long's *A Day's*

Walk Across Dartmoor or Christopher Le Brun's *The Complete Journey*; from the geometric clarity of Alan Stanton's *Belgrade Theatre* to the organic sumptuousness of Anish Kapoor's *Untitled*. And of course the range of media is far broader than the Academicians of the Coronation Gift, sixty years ago, could have imagined – acrylics, screenprints, collages, monotypes, inkjet prints, even an iPad drawing.

While most of the contributions to the gift were selected simply as fine examples of the artists' work, a few were clearly chosen for their relevance to the monarchy – an imagined portrait of The Queen by Tracey Emin; the site of the Coronation in John Maine's *Westminster Abbey Sacrarium*; Union flags in Gillian Ayres' *Festive 1* and Tom Phillips' *Sixteen Appearances of the Union Jack*, and the Triskelion of the Isle of Man in Bryan Kneale's *The Legs of Man*; Michael Manser's plans for The Queen's Suite at Heathrow airport, and Michael Hopkins' design for Buckingham Palace ticket office. And a couple celebrate that other great event of the summer of 2012, the London Olympics – Zaha Hadid's visualisation of the Olympic Aquatic Centre, and Anne Desmet's tiny wood-engraving of the Olympic Stadium.

Taken as a whole, the Royal Academy's Diamond Jubilee Gift to The Queen is a unique phenomenon. It is a tribute to the vitality of the Royal Academy after almost a quarter of a millennium, and an adornment to the Royal Collection, rich in the drawings of Leonardo and Holbein, Poussin and Canaletto, and now enhanced by a cross-section of the best in contemporary British graphic art.

Unless otherwise stated, all works are on white paper; sheet size is given, height before width.

Overleaf: Two of the silk-covered solander boxes in which the Diamond Jubilee Gift was presented to The Queen, pictured at the official announcement of the Gift in December 2012

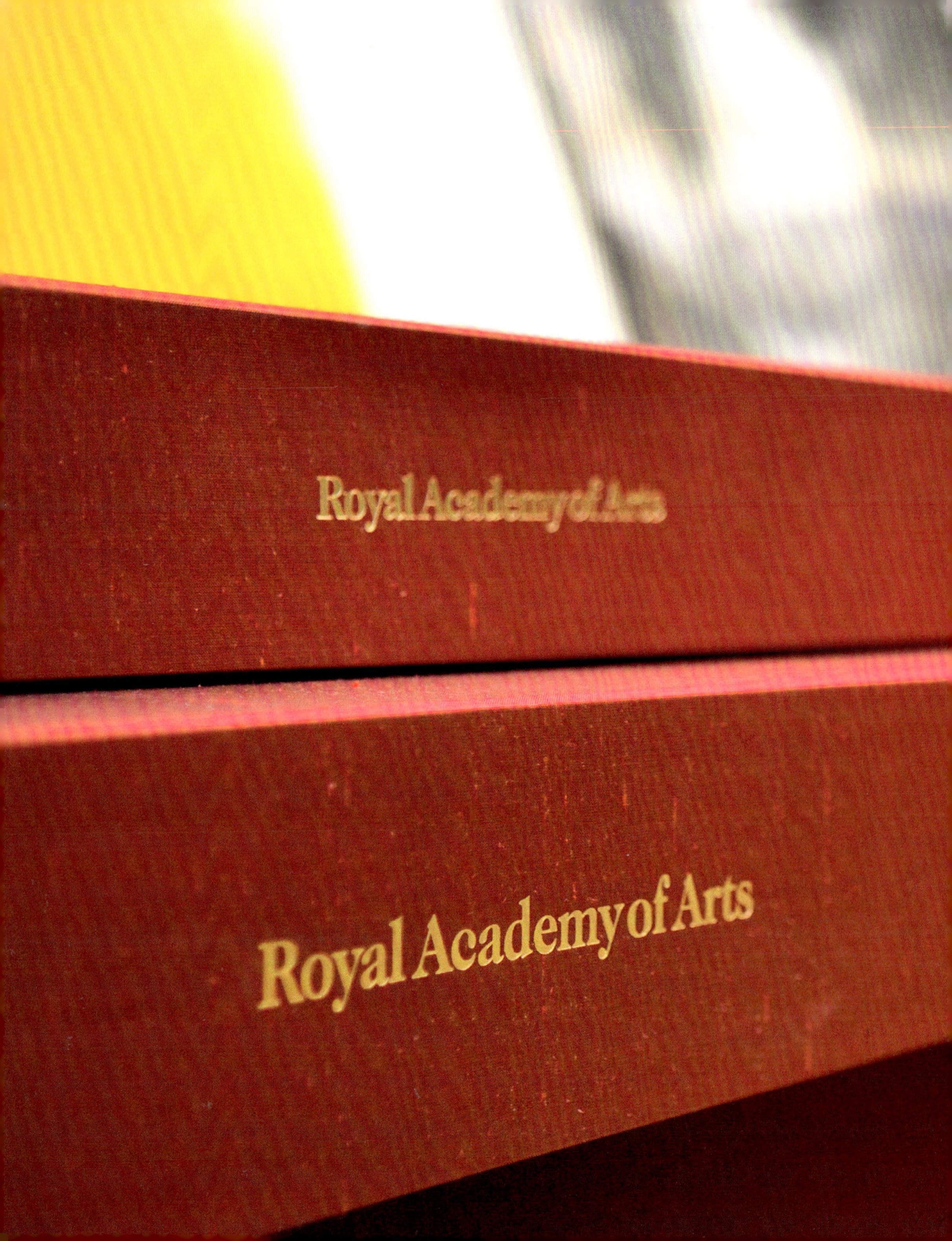

Royal Academy of Arts

Royal Academy of Arts

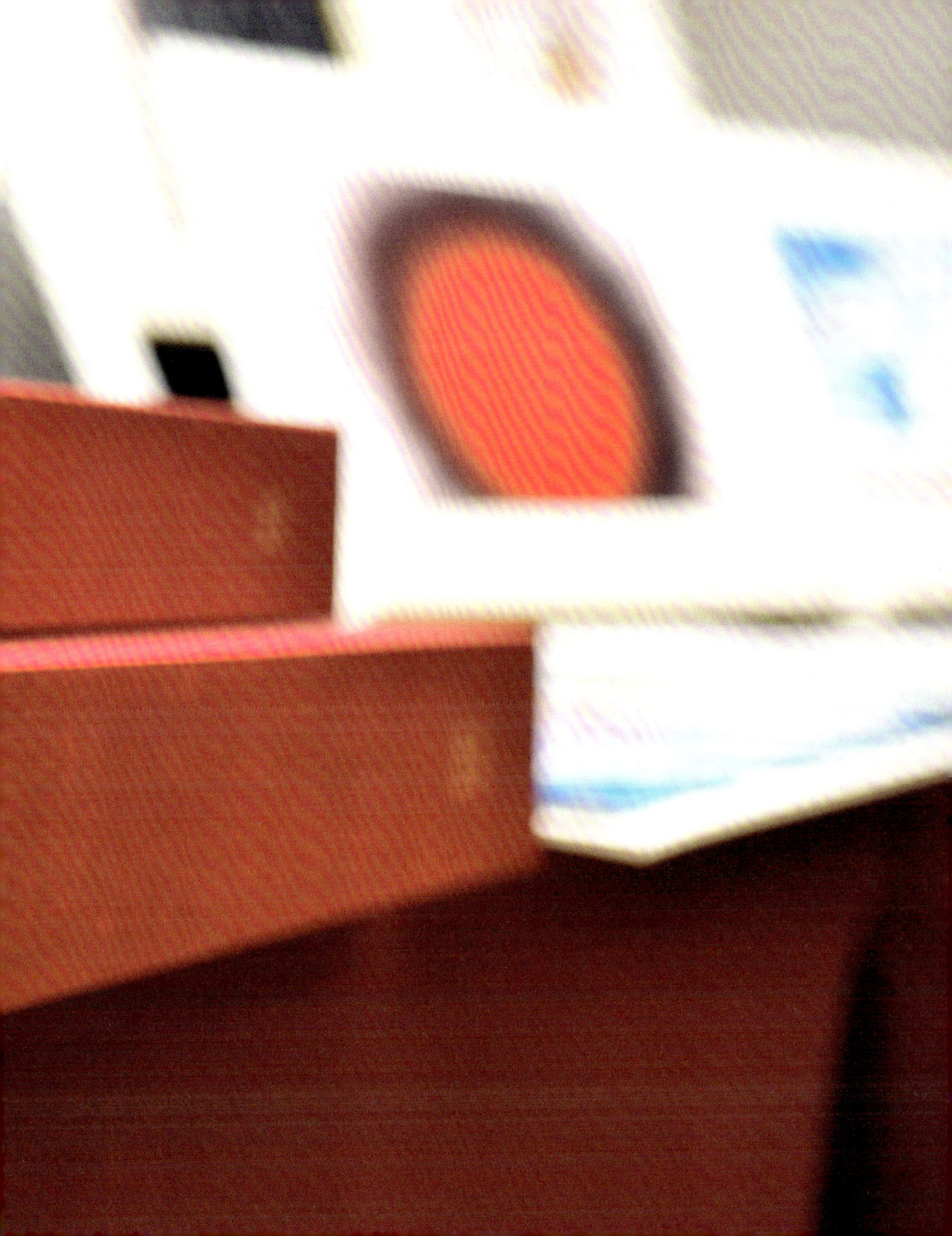

Professor Ivor Abrahams RA (b. 1935)
Oxford Gardens Suite, no. 4, 1977
Screenprint with embossing and varnish
26.7 x 38.2 cm
RCIN 212700

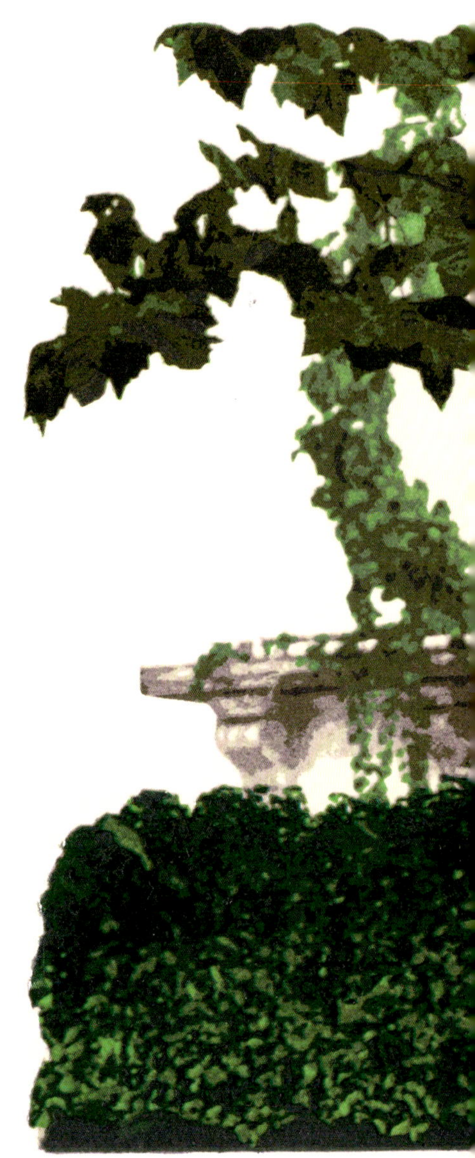

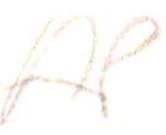

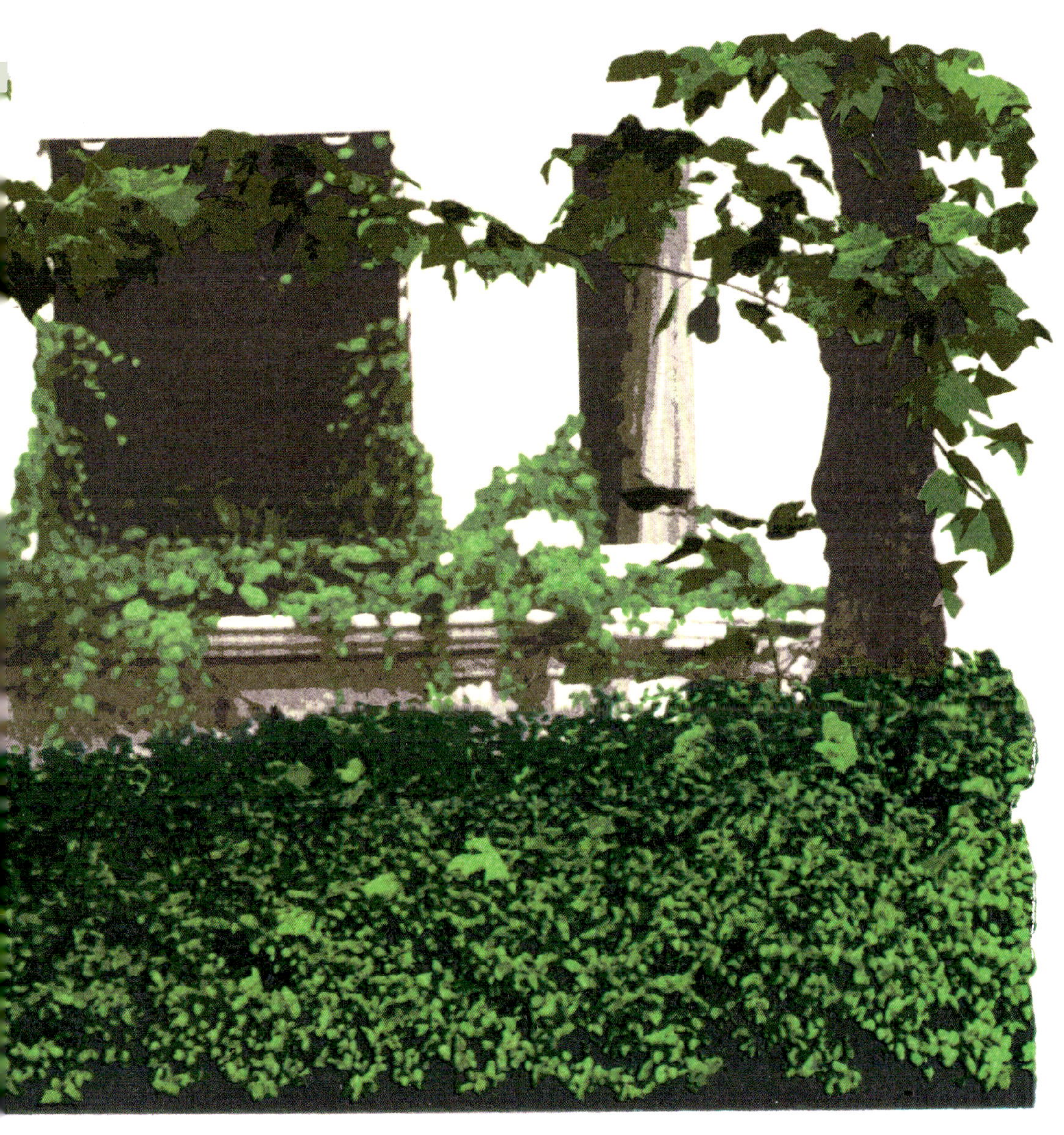

Professor Norman Ackroyd CBE RA (b. 1938)

The Flannan Isles – Roareim, 2012

Aquatint

40.7 x 58.0 cm (sheet)

32.4 x 50.3 cm (plate)

RCIN 212701

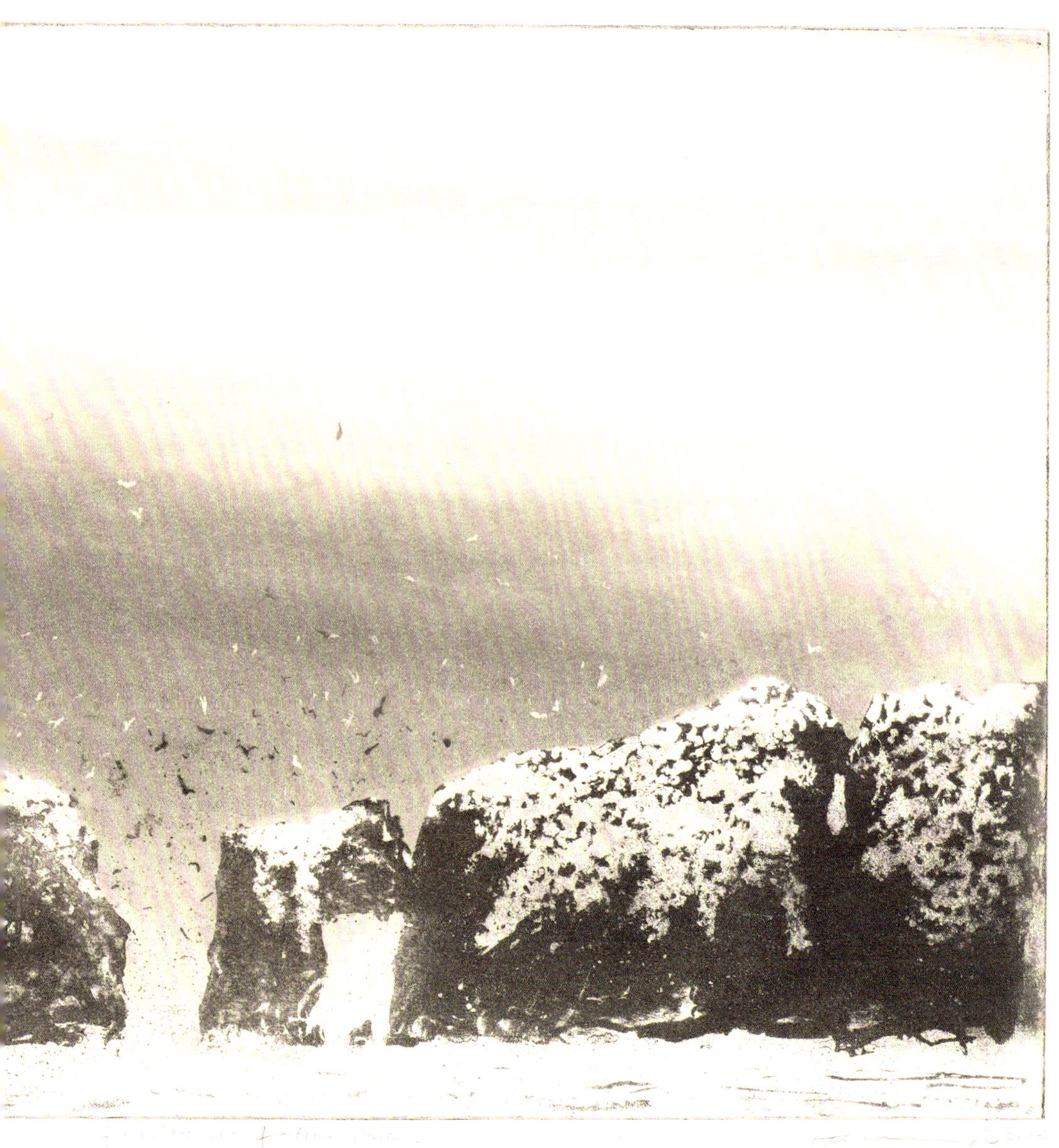

Professor Will Alsop OBE RA (b. 1947)
Somewhere – Sometime – Someplace, 2013
Acrylic
60.7 x 80.9 cm
RCIN 212797

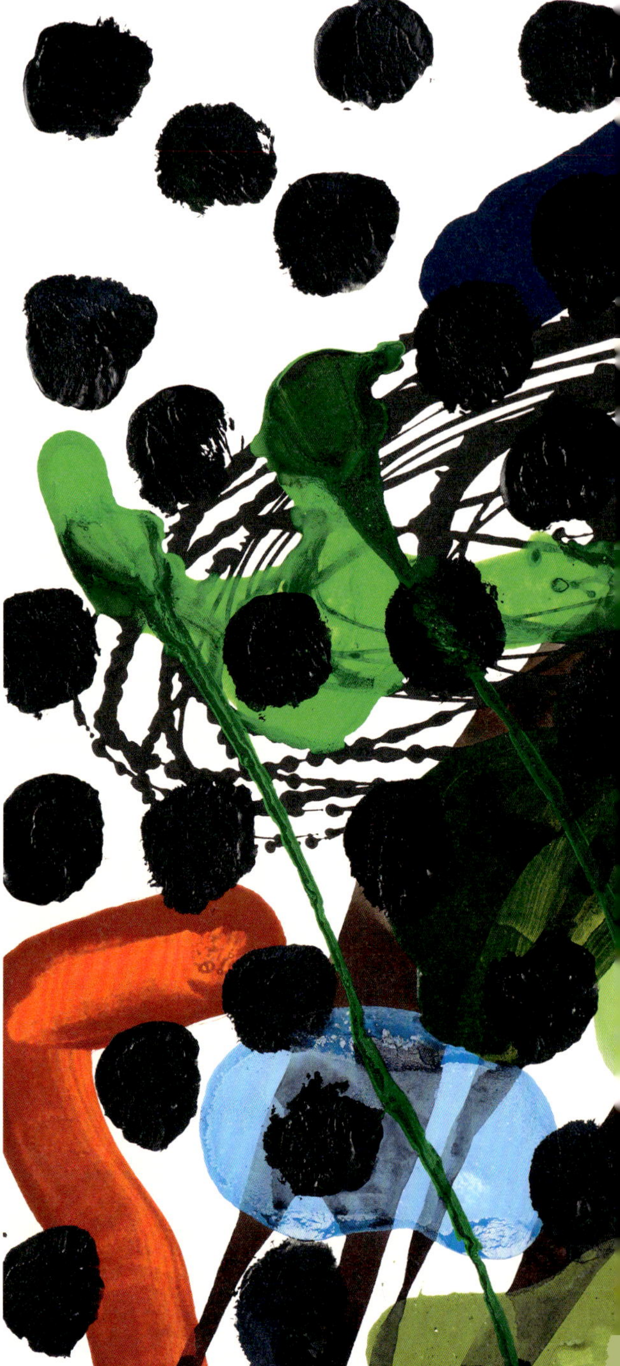

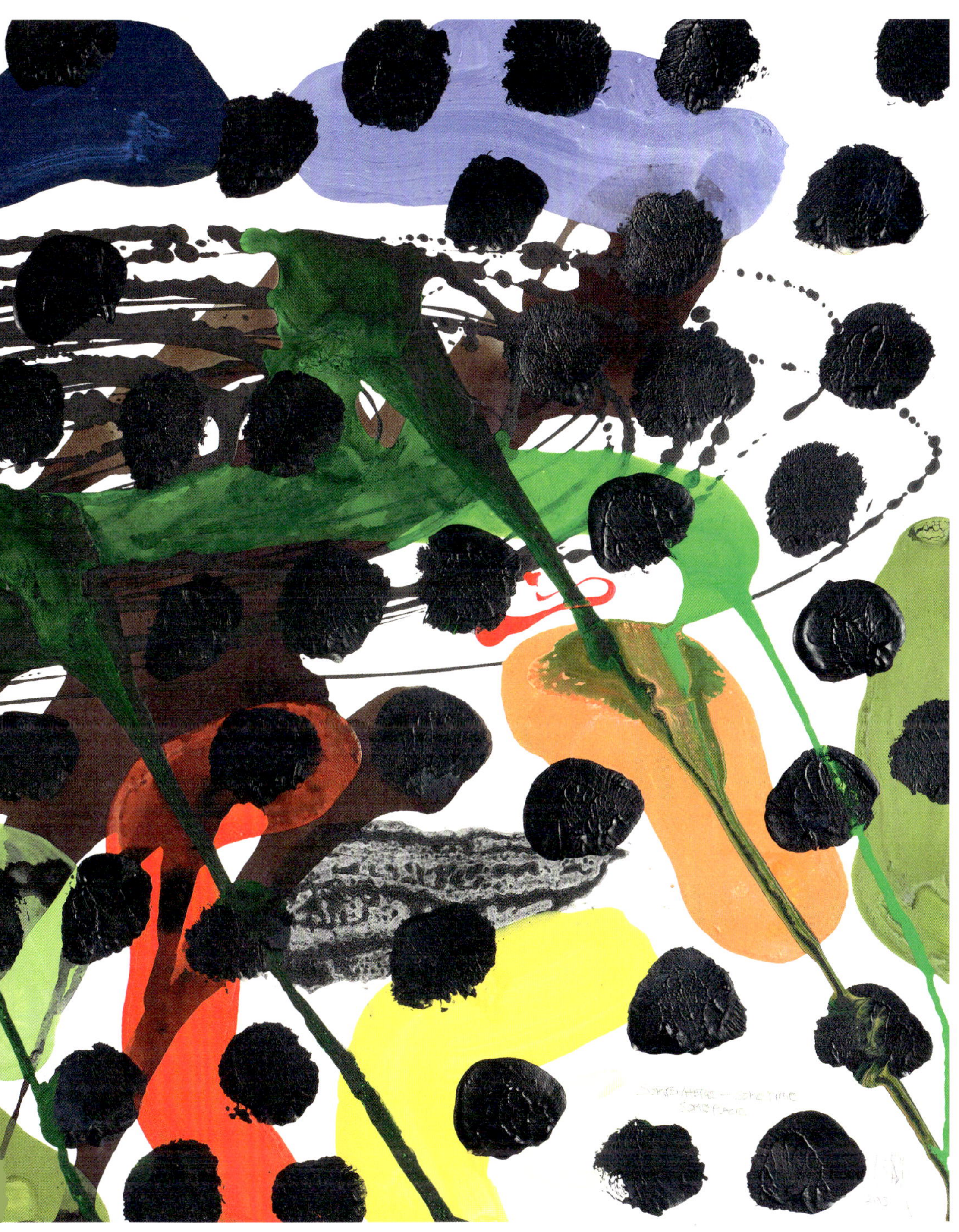
SOMEWHERE – SOMETIME
SOMEPLACE

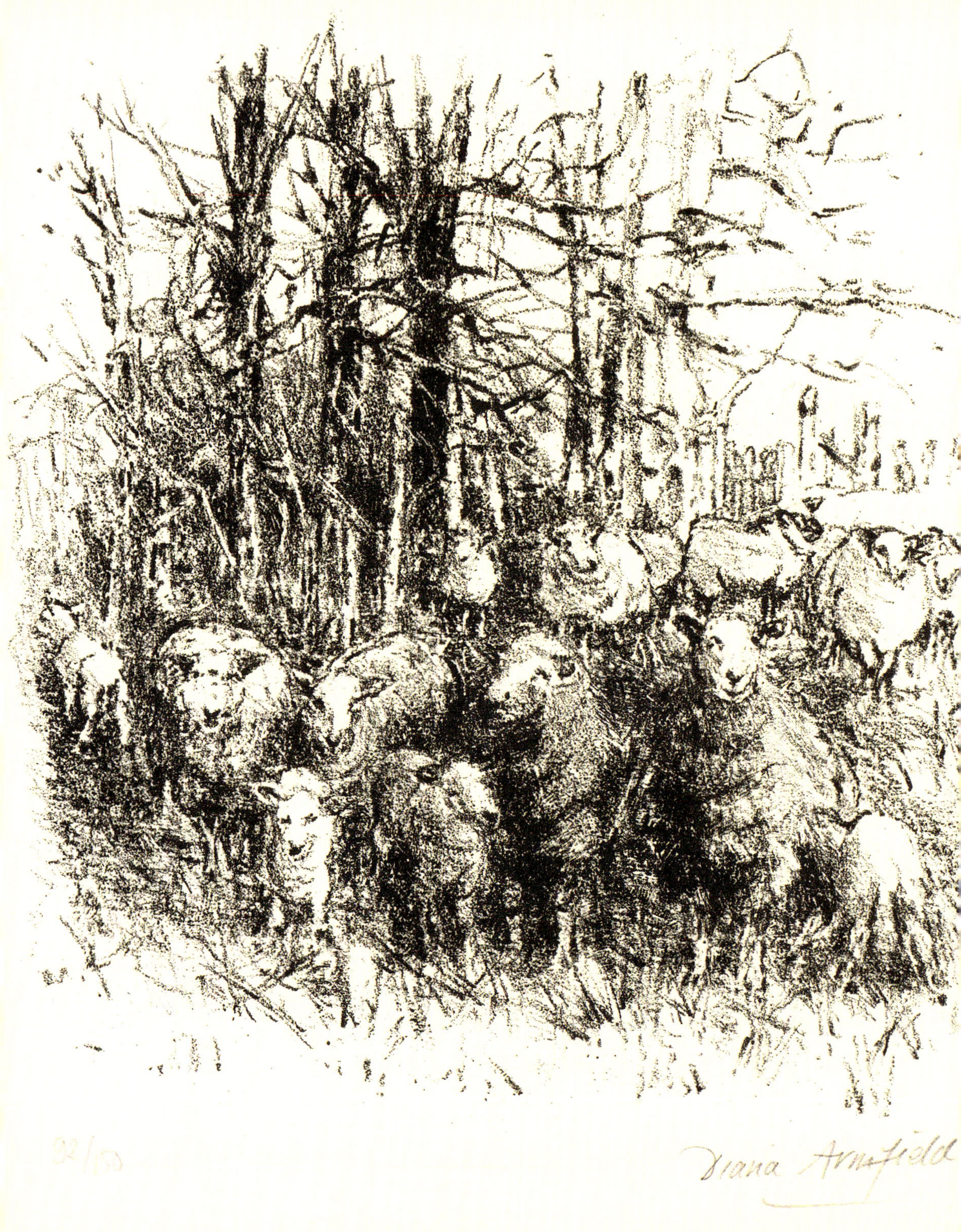
Diana Armfield

Diana Armfield RA (b. 1920)
Sheep Sheltering: Winter at Llwynhir, 2008
Lithograph
28.2 x 29.1 cm
RCIN 212702

Gillian Ayres CBE RA (b. 1930)
Festive I, 2004
Acrylic
57.2 x 78.1 cm
RCIN 212703

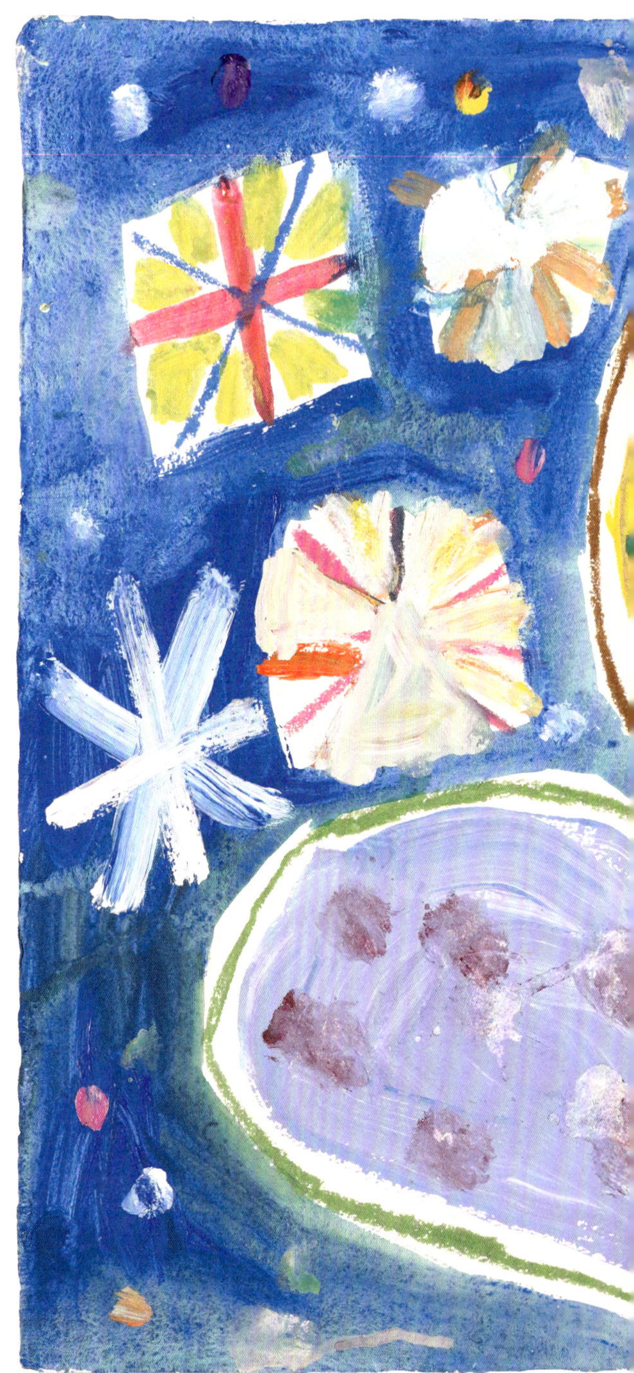

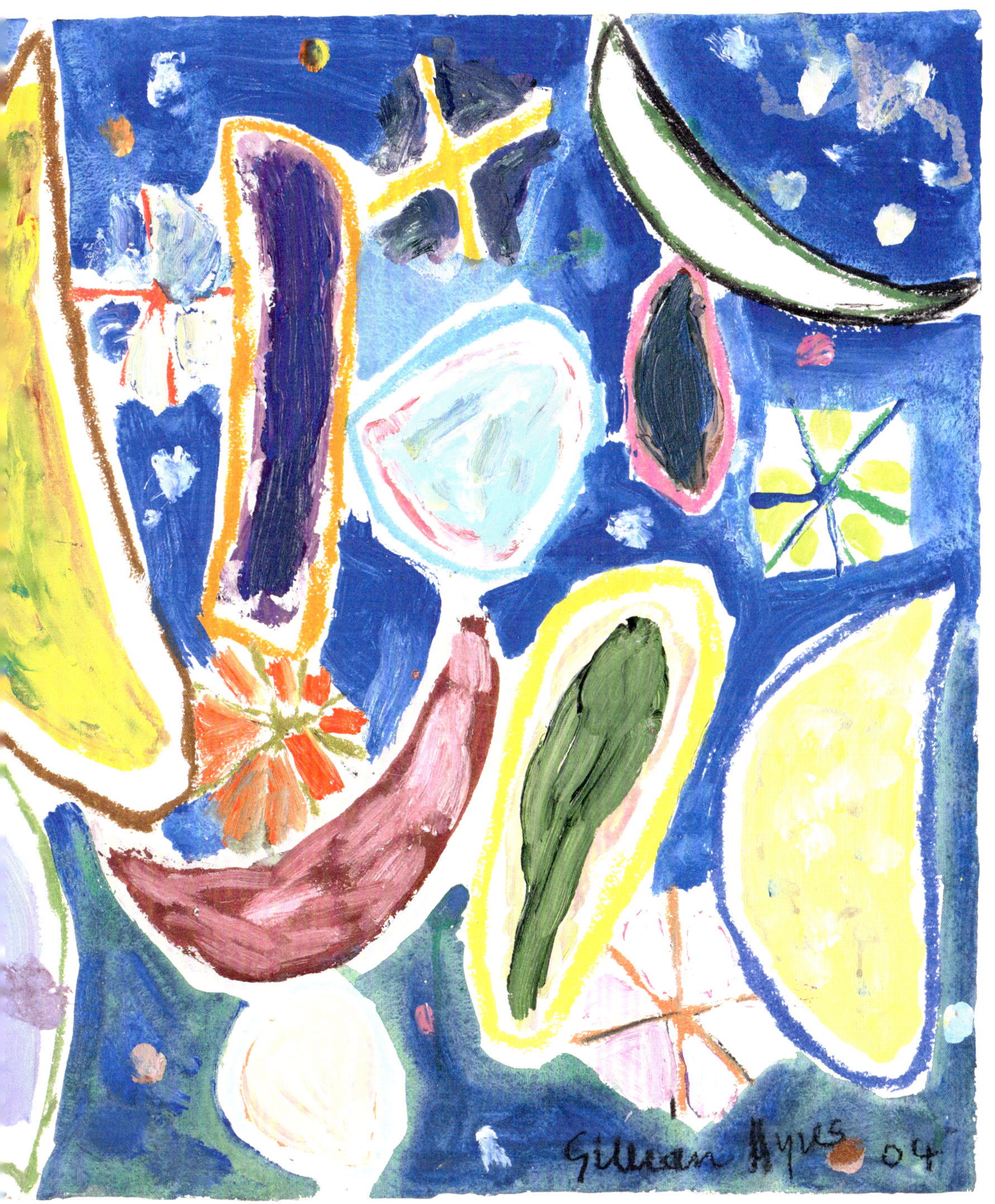
Gillian Ayres 04

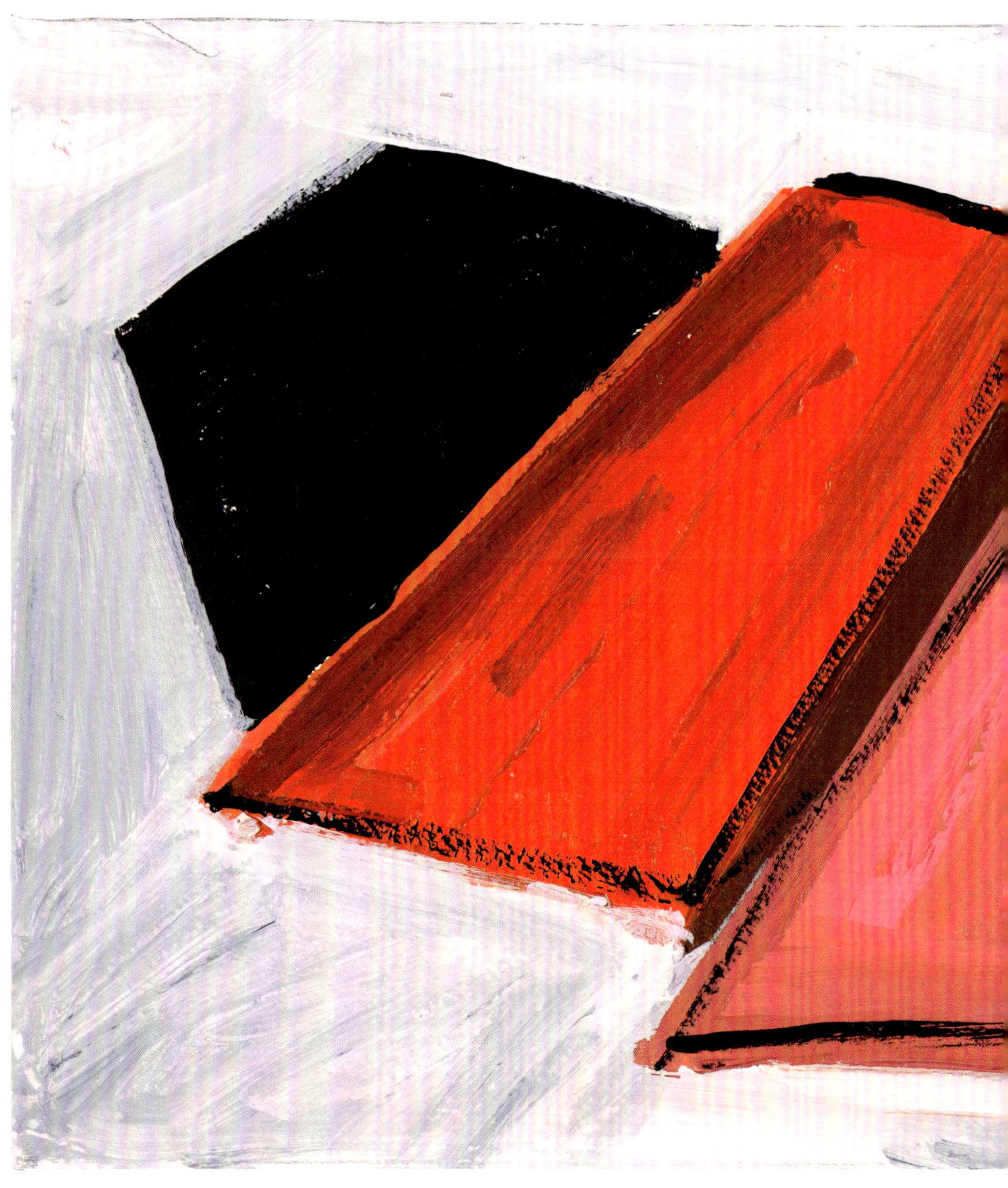

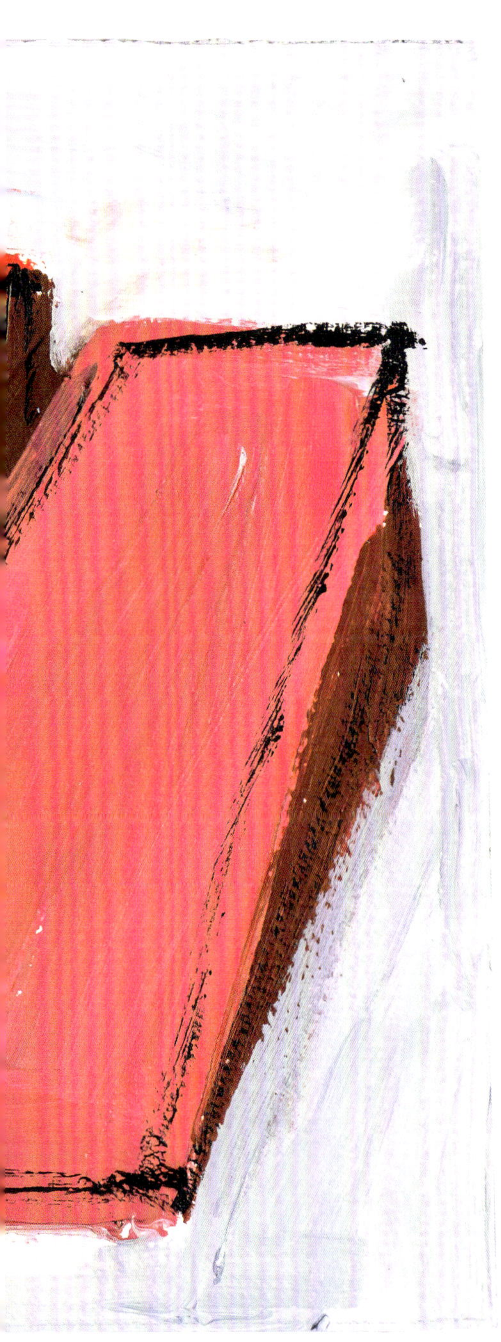

Phyllida Barlow RA (b. 1944)
untitled: awnings (4), 2013
Acrylic
22.9 x 30.5 cm
RCIN 212995

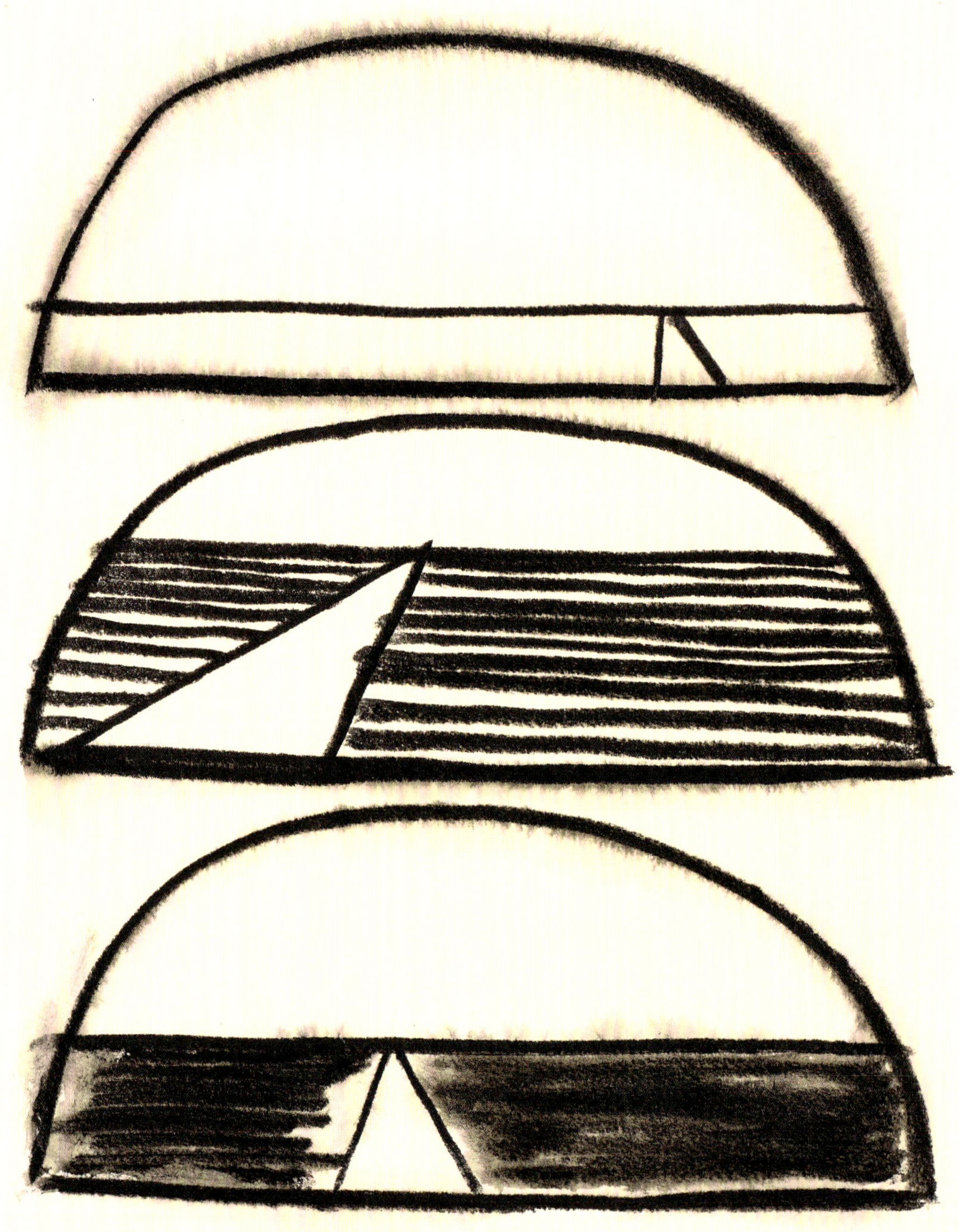

Basil Beattie RA (b. 1935)
Janus Series, 2009
Charcoal
36.0 x 27.9 cm
RCIN 212704

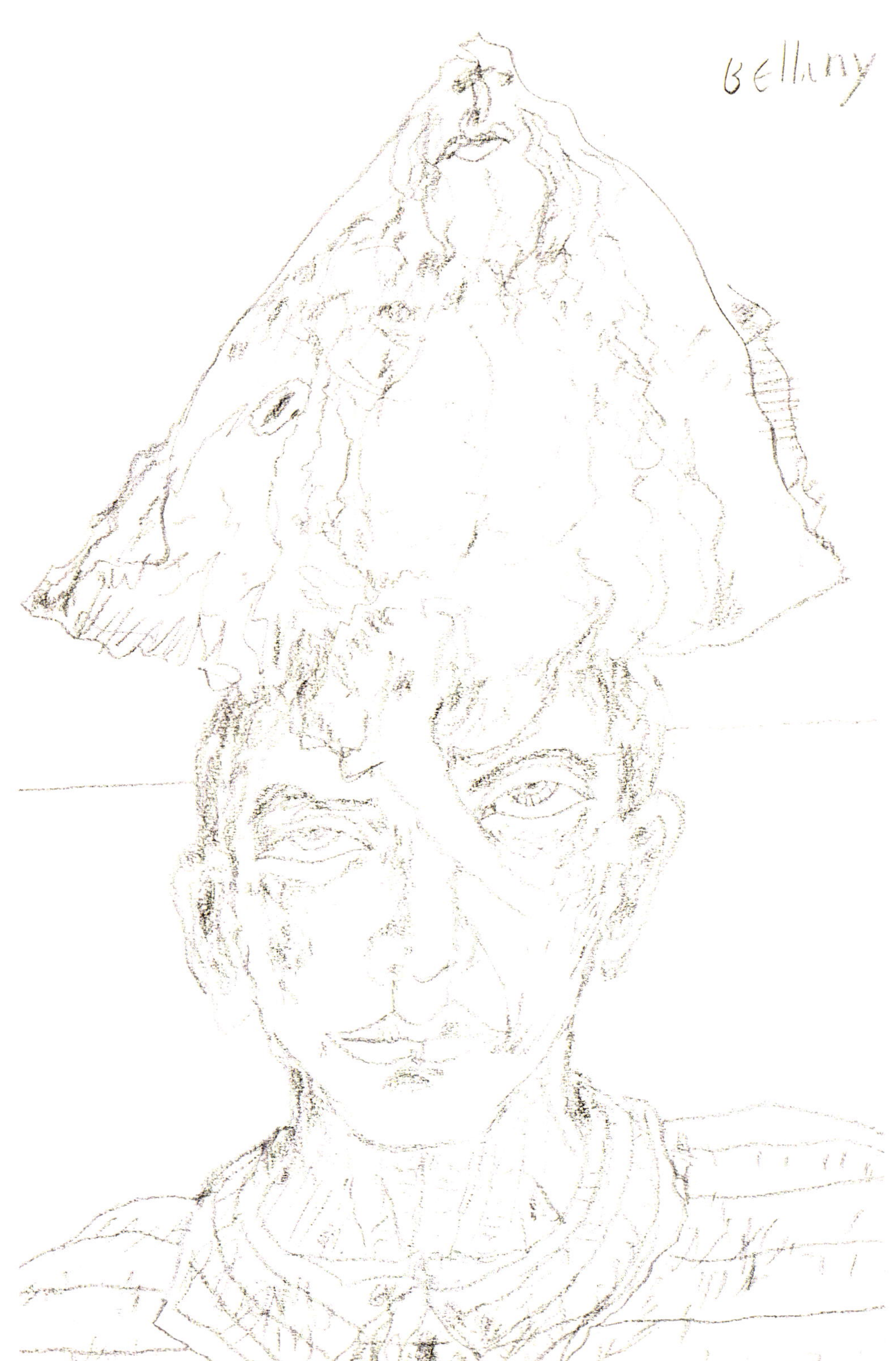
Bellany

Dr John Bellany CBE RA (1942–2013)
Untitled, *c.*2008
Charcoal
59.7 x 42.0 cm
RCIN 212705

Tony Bevan RA (b. 1951)

Self-portrait, 2012

Crayon

43.2 x 38.0 cm

RCIN 212706

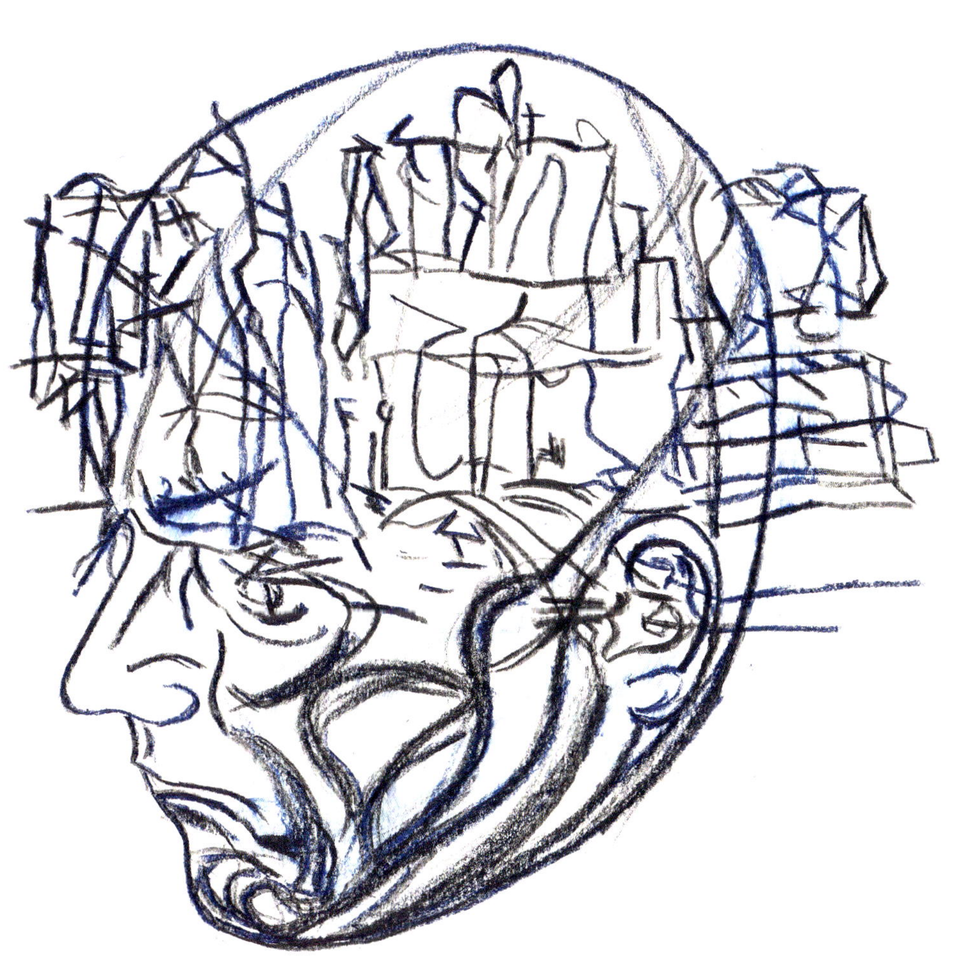

Dame Elizabeth Blackadder DBE RA (b. 1931)
Hellebores, 2013
Pencil and watercolour
50.5 x 30.9 cm
RCIN 212798

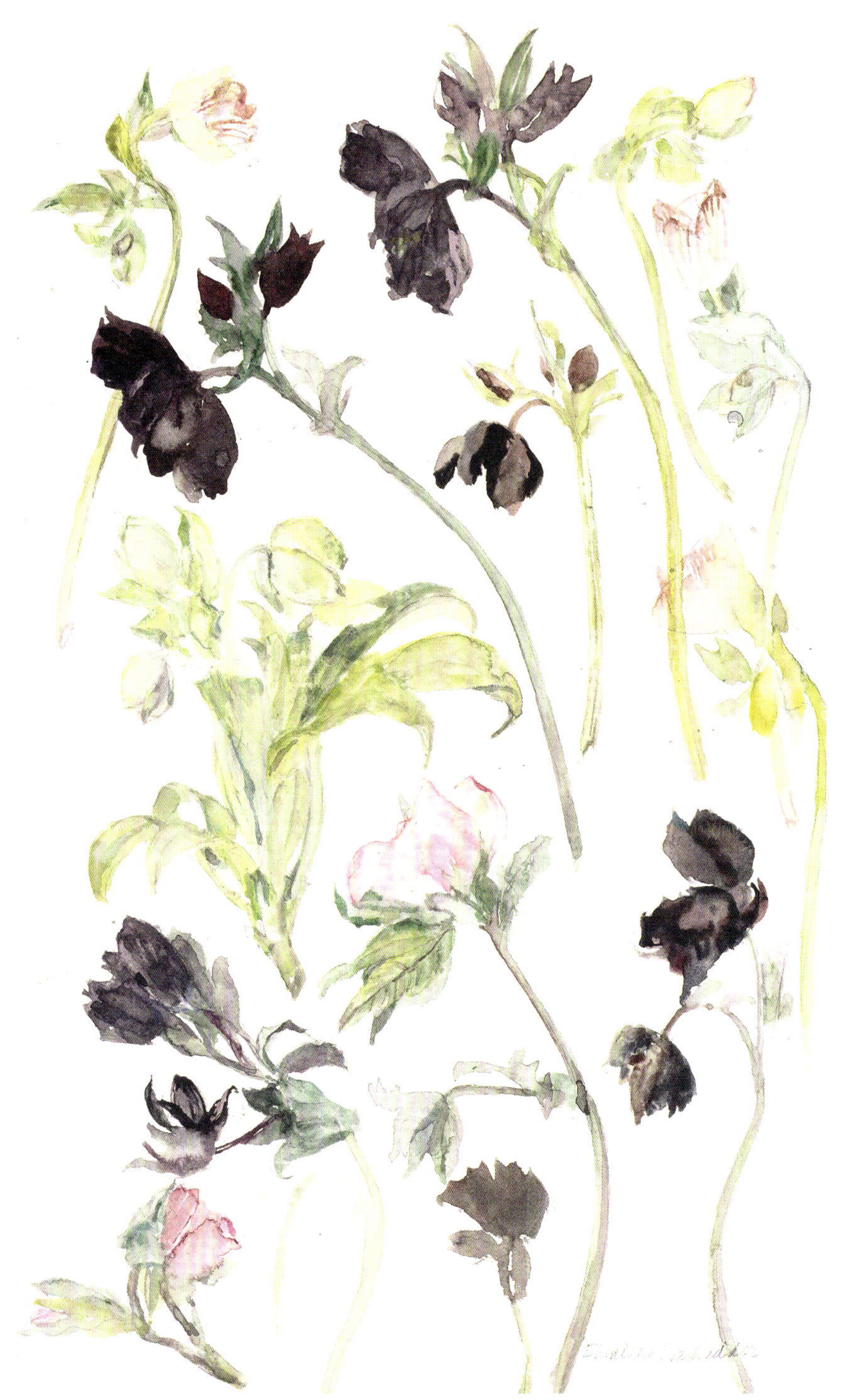

Olwyn Bowey RA (b. 1936)
Susie, 2007
Pencil, charcoal and watercolour
35.5 x 46.5 cm
RCIN 212707

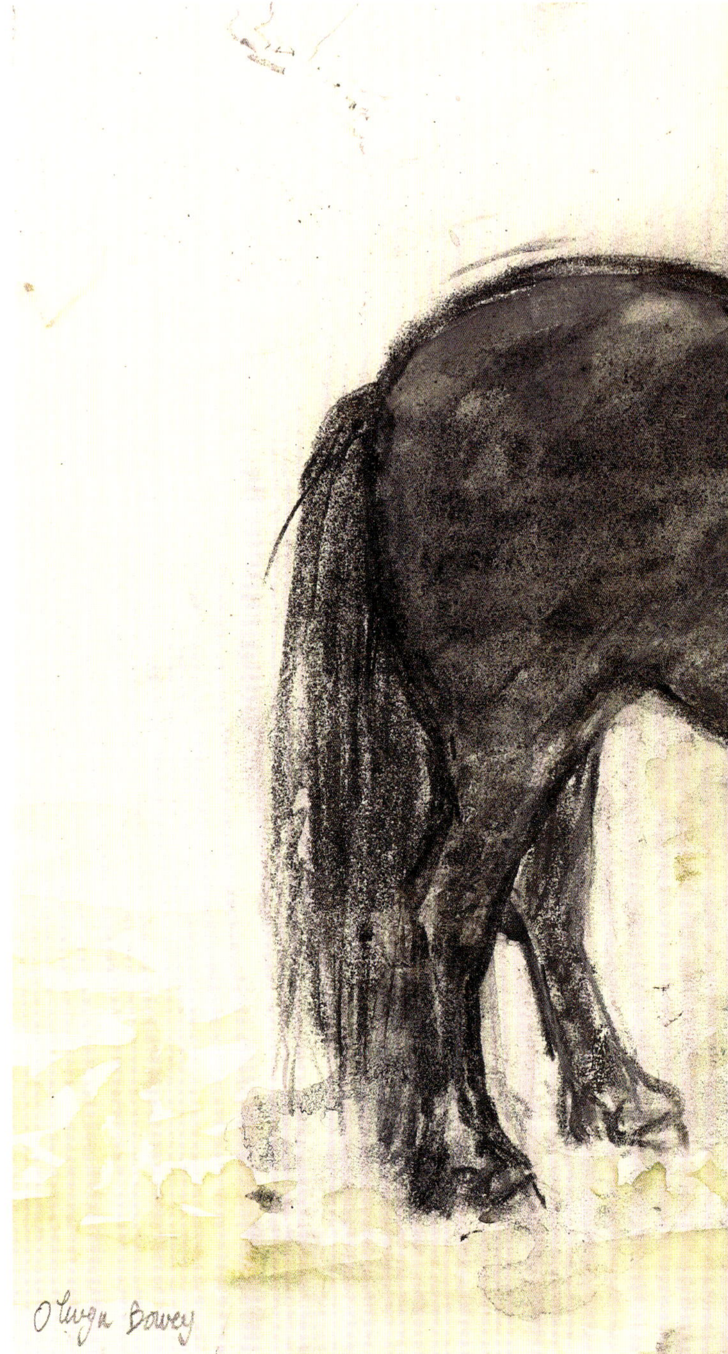

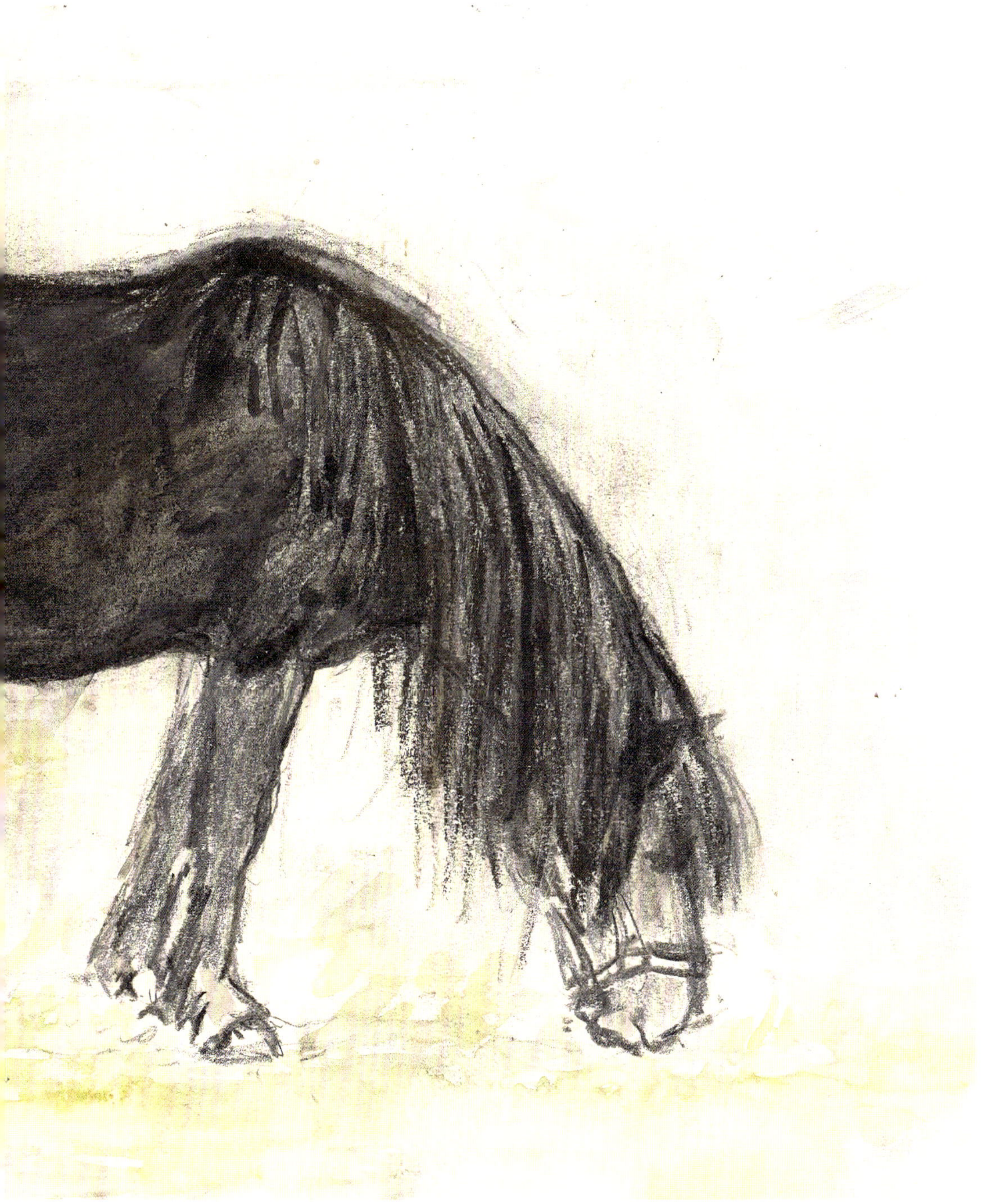

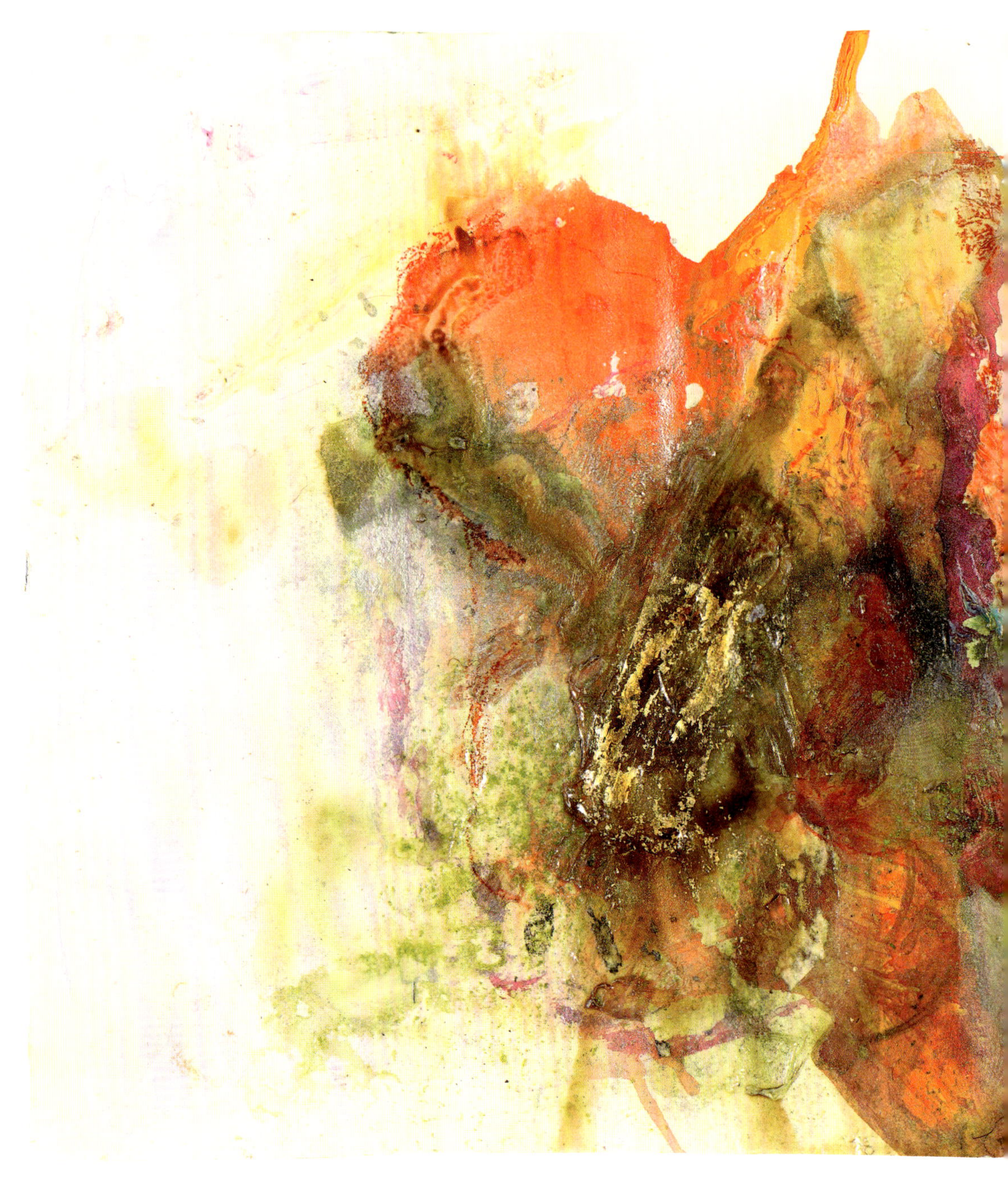

Frank Bowling OBE RA (b. 1936)

Revisiting "Night Journey", 2012

Mixed media

37.6 x 55.9 cm

RCIN 212708

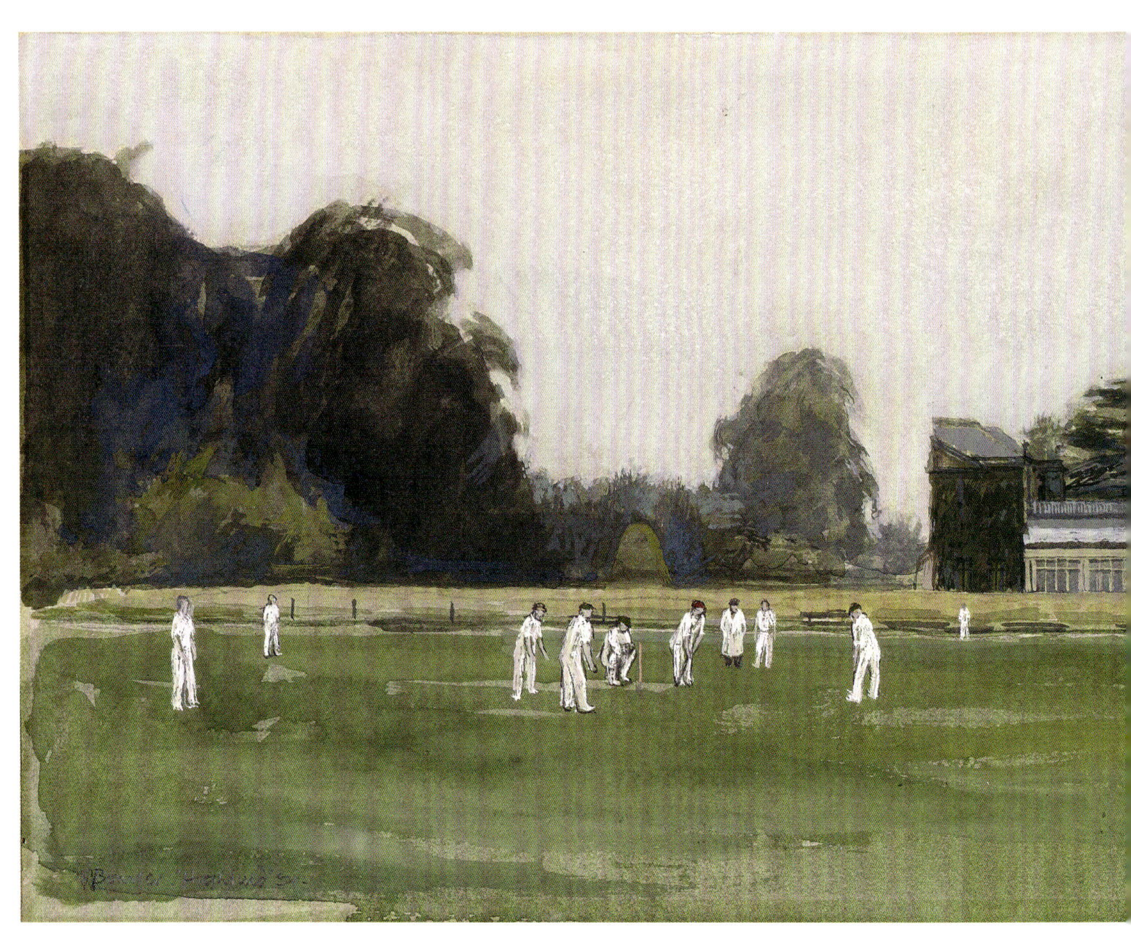

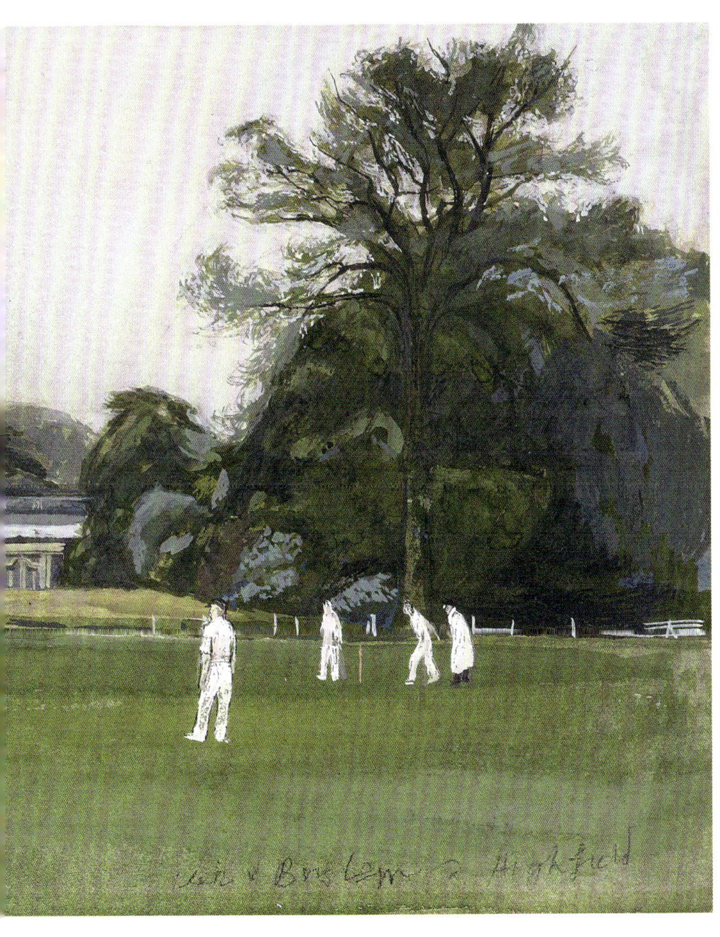

William Bowyer RA (b. 1926)
Highfield, Leek CC v Burslem CC, 1954
Pencil and gouache
23.0 x 39.0 cm (sheet)
16.5 x 36.0 cm (sight)
RCIN 212795

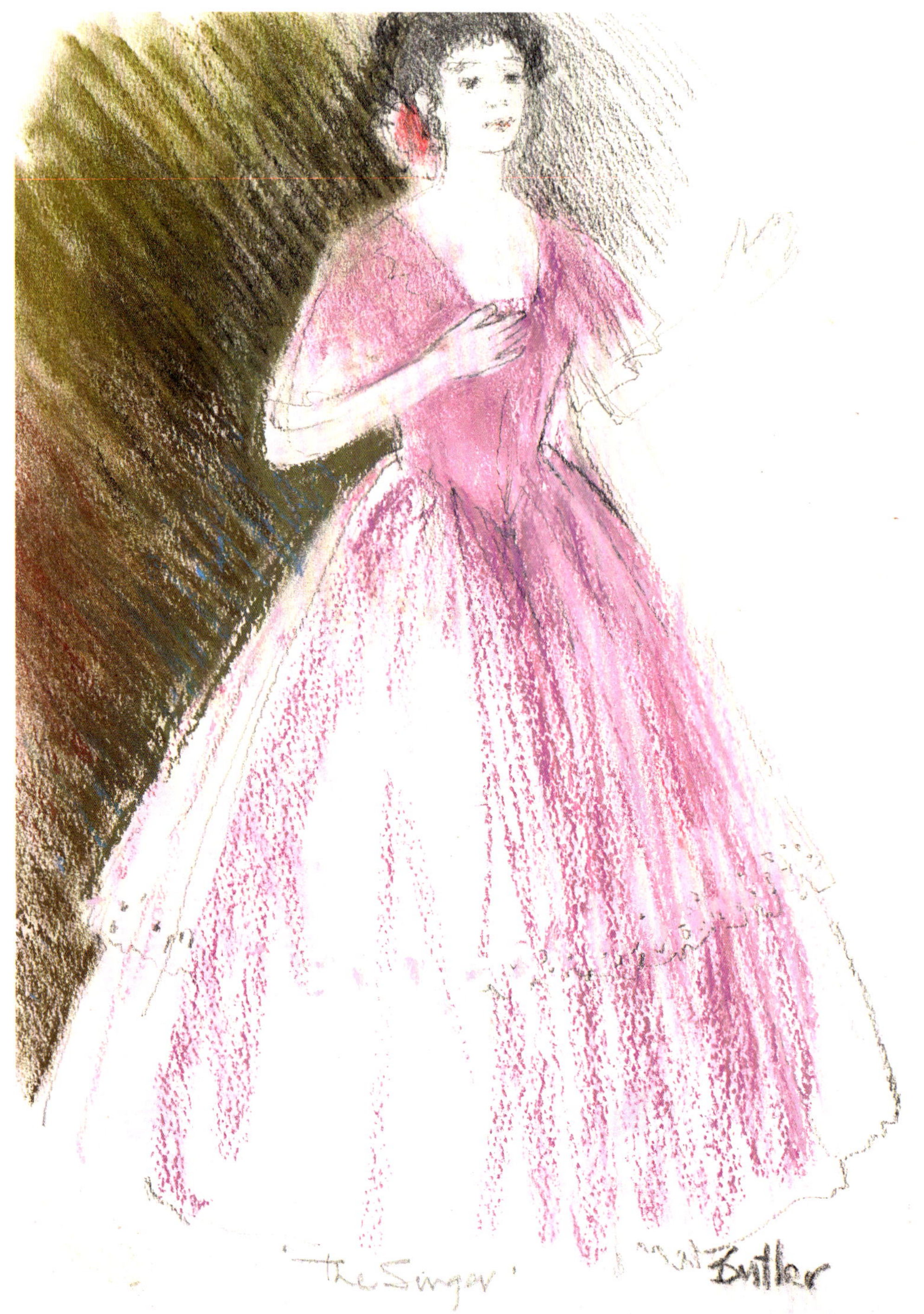
'The Singer'
Butler

James Butler MBE RA (b. 1931)

The Singer, 2012

Pencil and pastel

39.3 x 28.5 cm

RCIN 212709

Jeffery Camp RA (b. 1923)
St James's Park, 1994
Lithograph
30.7 x 40.7 cm
RCIN 212796

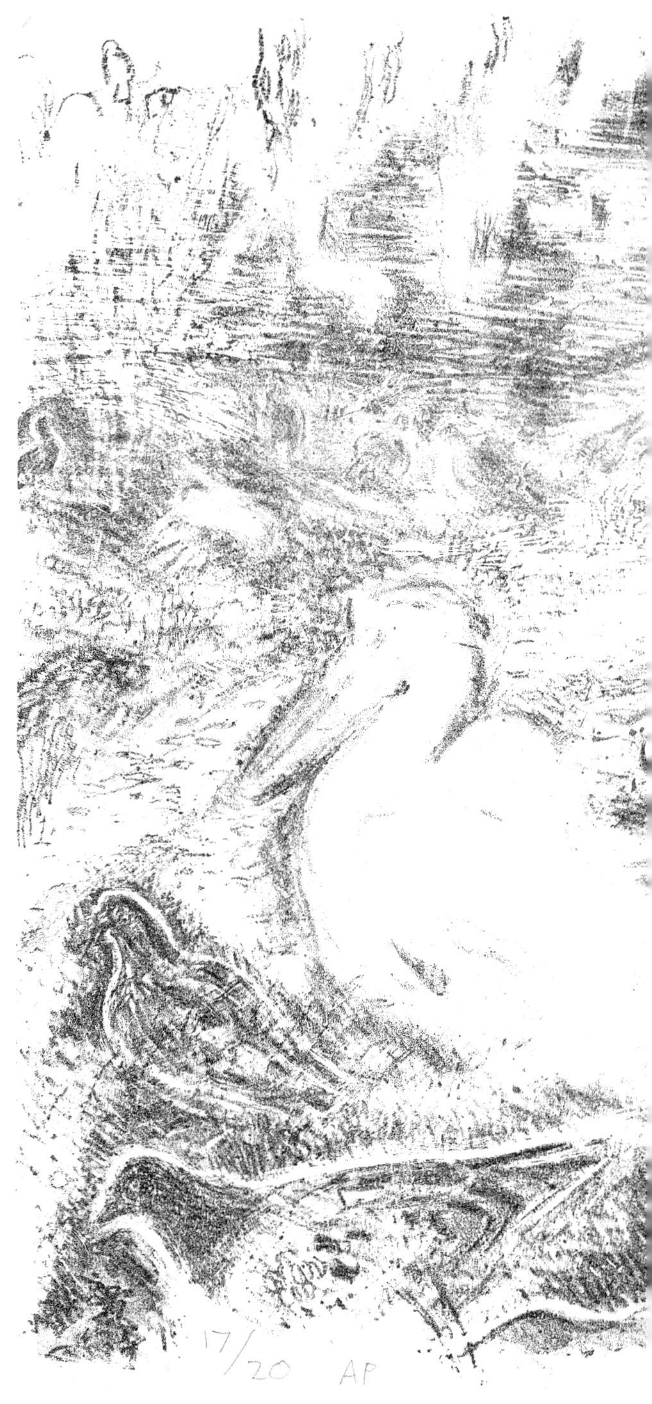

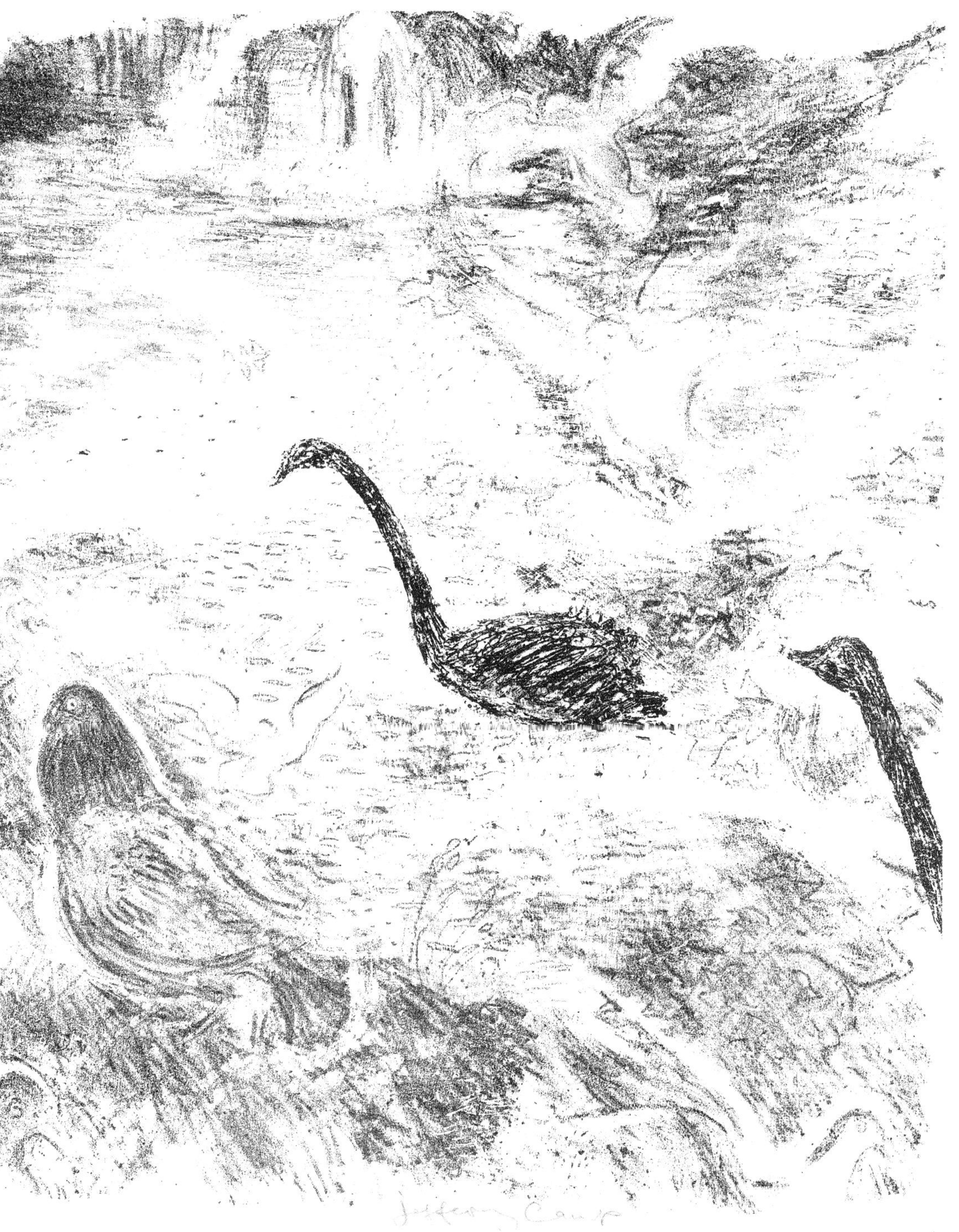
Jeffery Camp

Sir Anthony Caro OM CBE RA (b. 1924)
Seated Figure, 1983
Black chalk on pale buff paper
60.7 x 45.7 cm
RCIN 212710

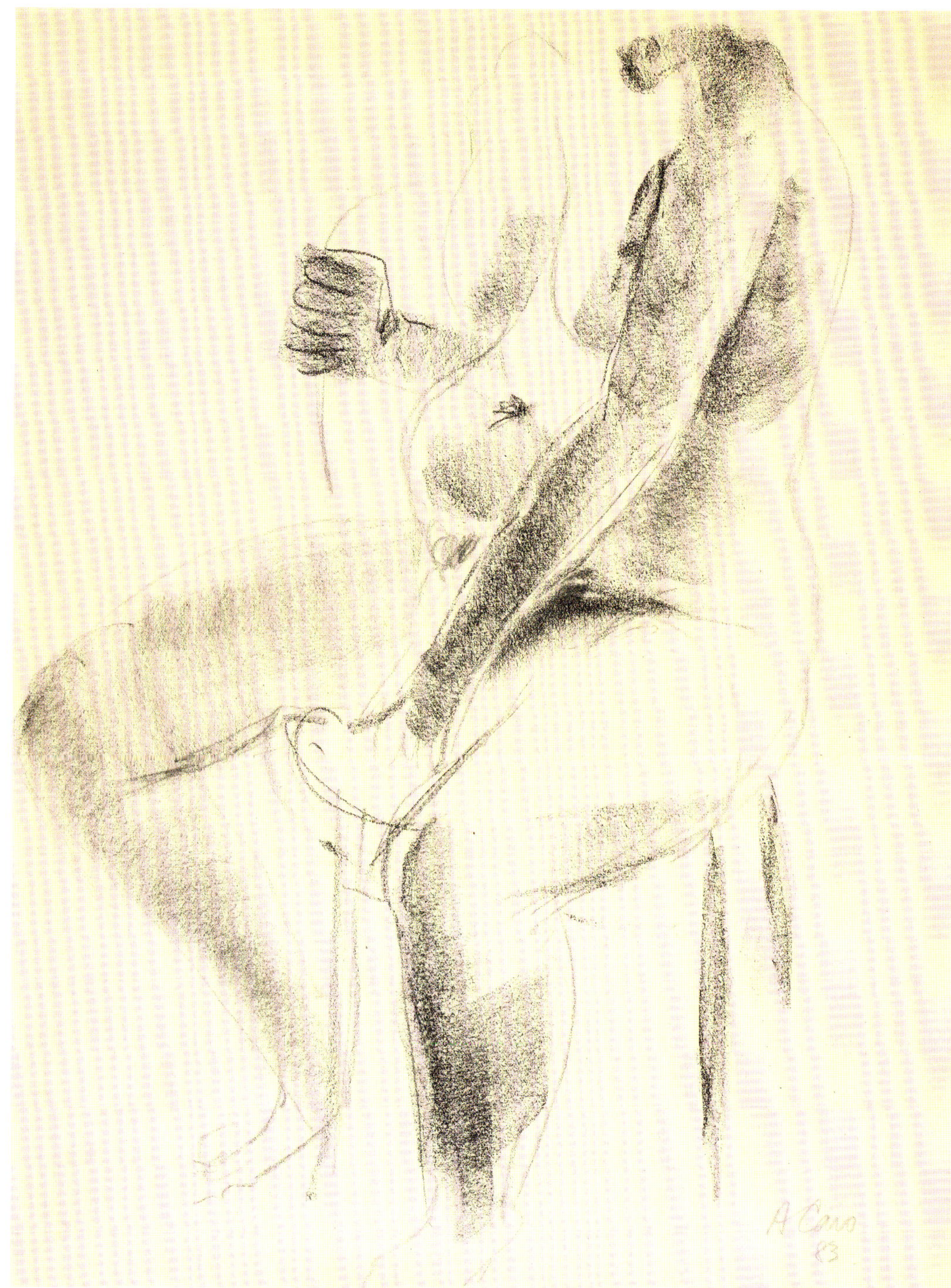
A Caro
83

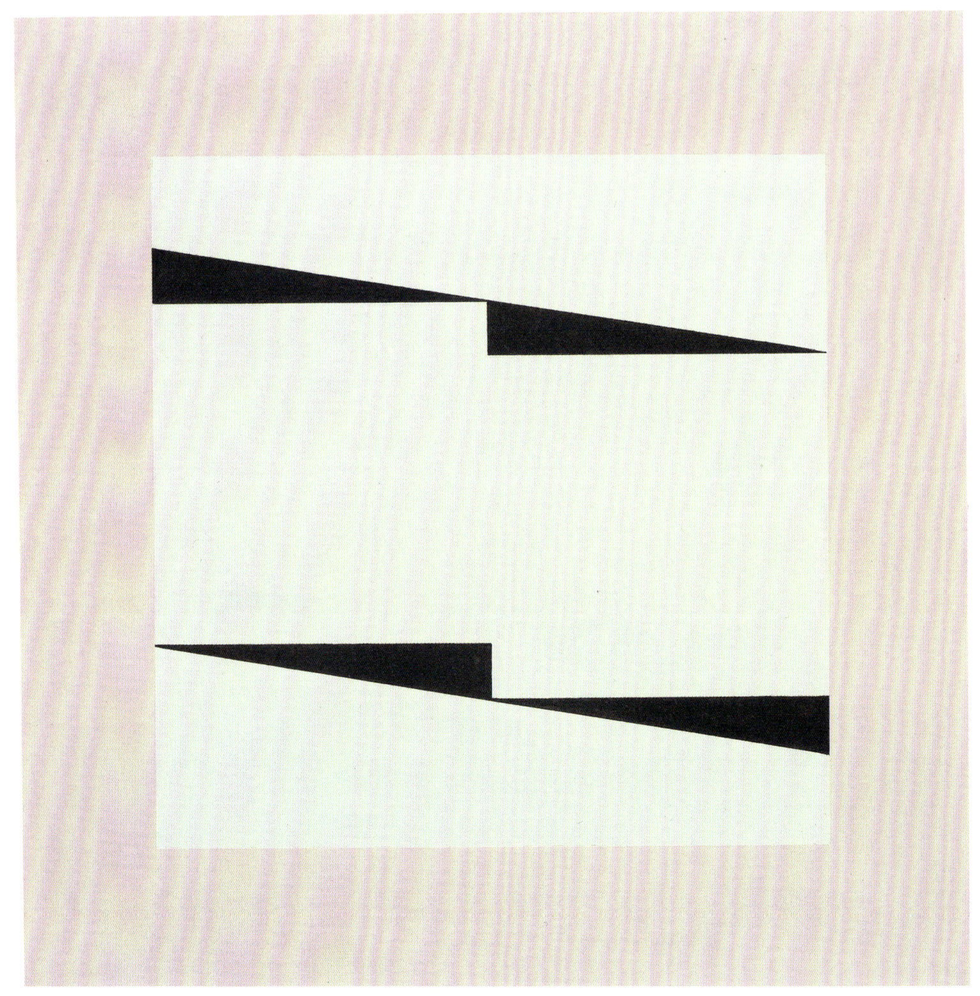

John Carter RA (b. 1942)

Stepped Forms, 2012

Acrylic

33.8 x 34.0 cm

RCIN 212711

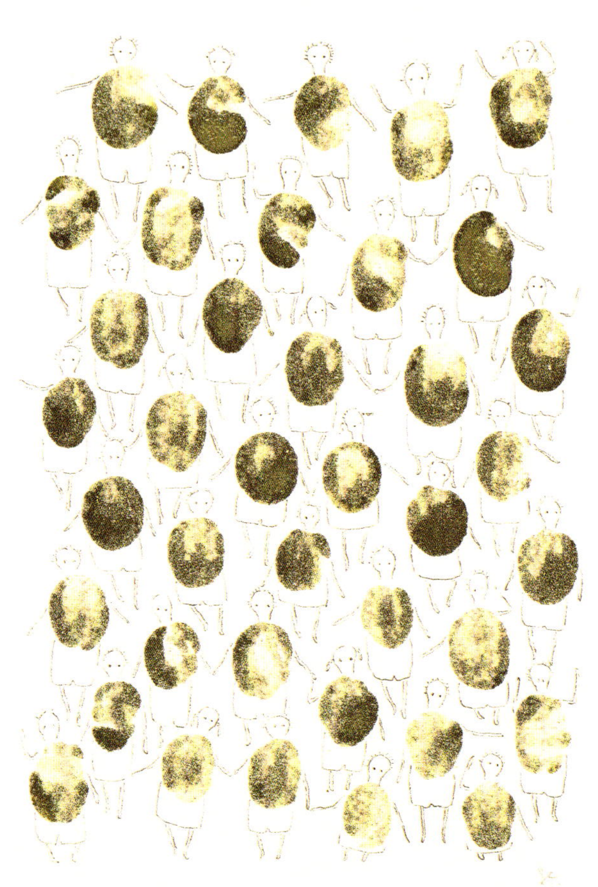

Stephen Chambers RA (b. 1960)
The Golden Beehive (Little) #1, 2013
Gold paint and pen and ink
36.1 x 28.0 cm
RCIN 212712

Professor Sir David Chipperfield CBE RA (b. 1953)

East Wing – Section through the North and South Dome Rooms, Neues Museum, Berlin, 2009

Inkjet print

33.9 x 54.1 cm

RCIN 212713

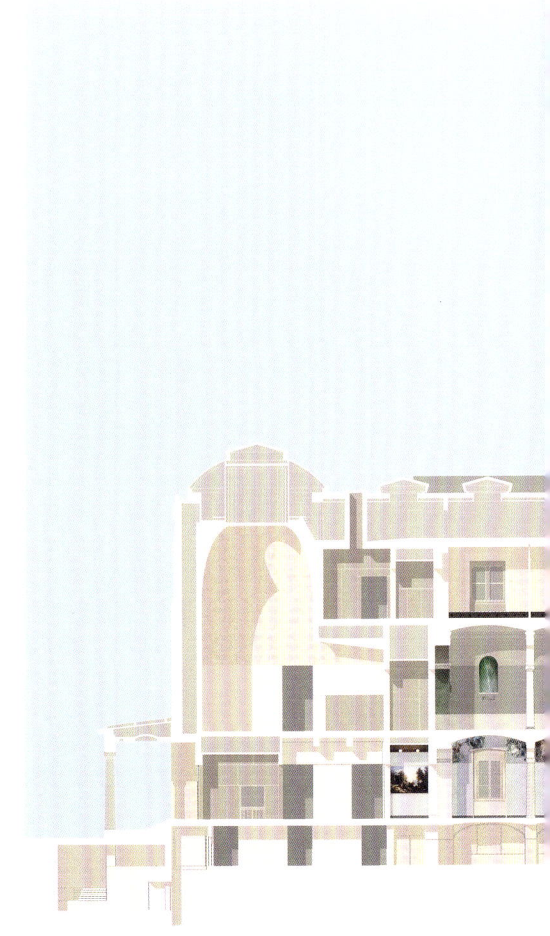

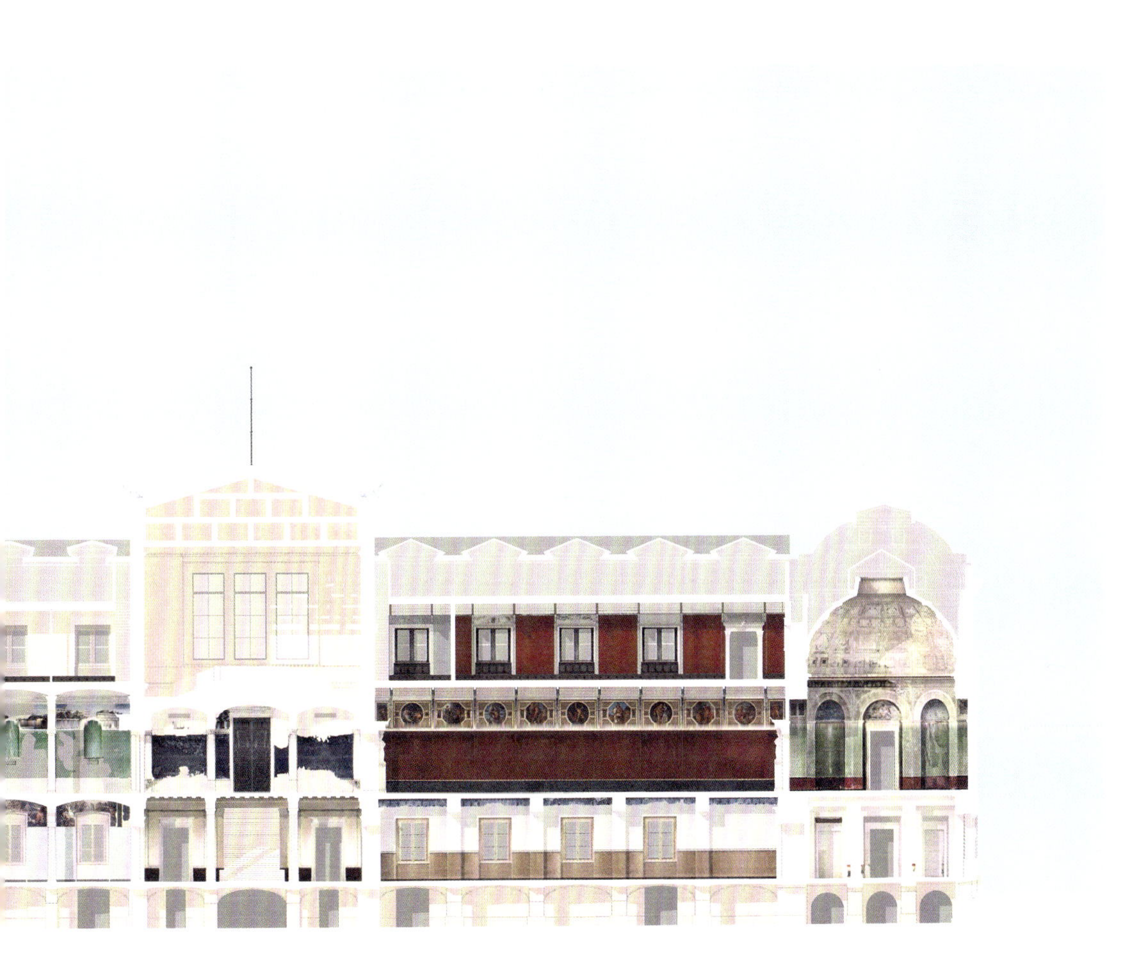

Ann Christopher RA (b. 1947)
The Space Between, 2012
Crayon, graphite and pastel over etching
42.5 x 41.5 cm (sheet)
27.2 x 27.2 cm (plate)
RCIN 212714

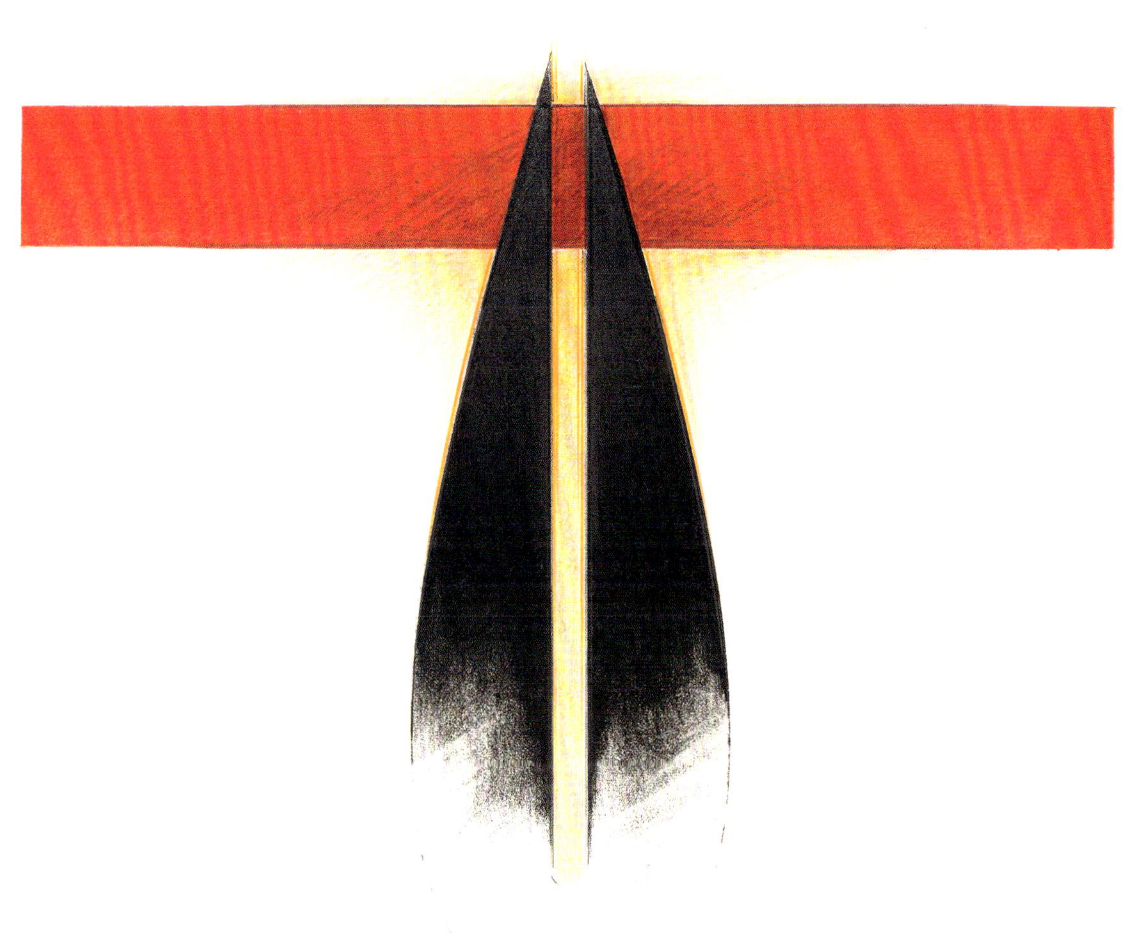

Geoffrey Clarke RA (b. 1924)
Head, 1956
Sugar-lift aquatint
32.8 x 33.5 cm (sheet)
23.7 x 24.4 cm (plate)
RCIN 212799

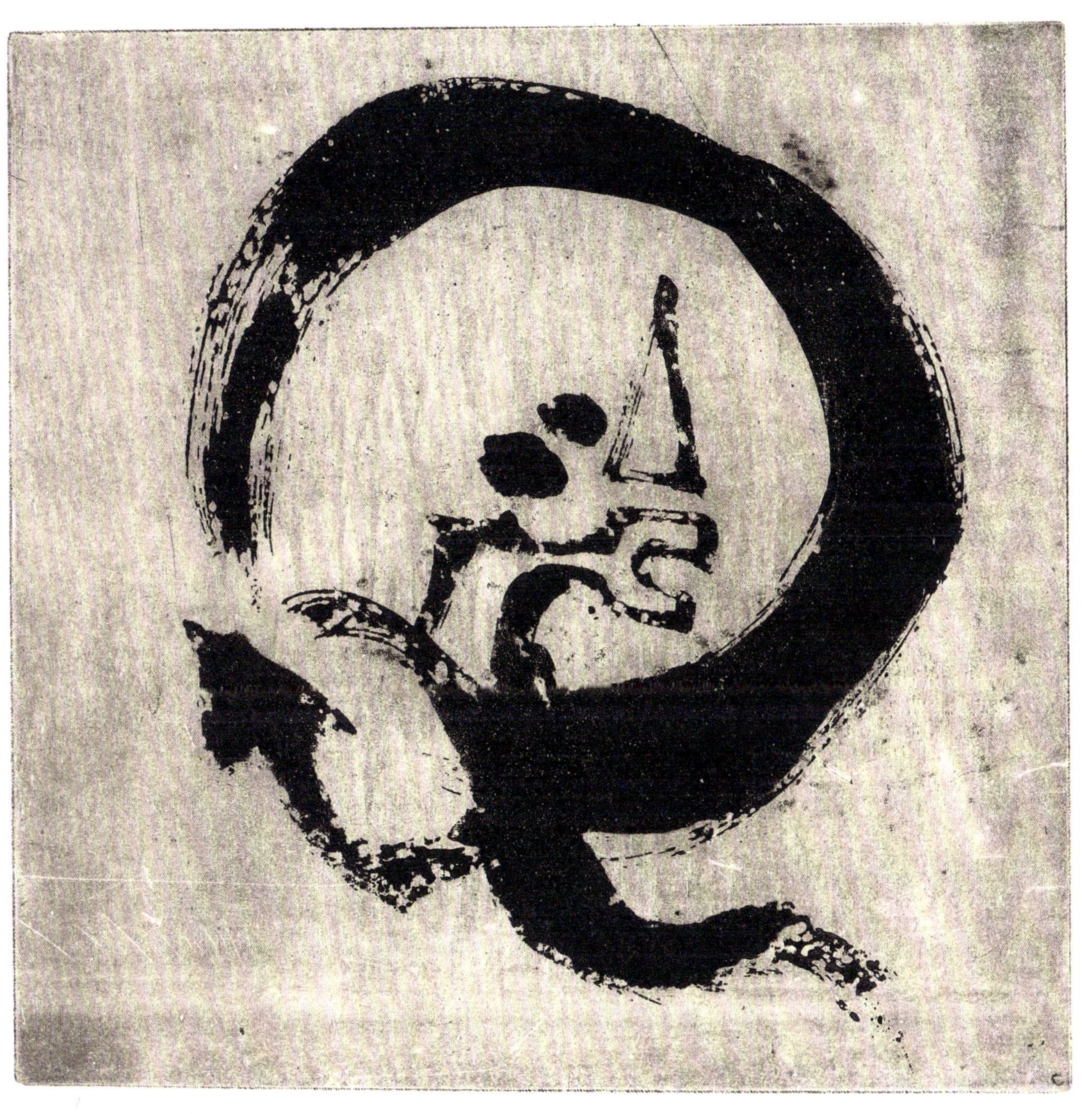

Professor Maurice Cockrill RA (b. 1935)

Treasure, 2012

Ink, gouache and collage
on Japanese rice straw paper

65.5 x 49.4 cm

RCIN 212715

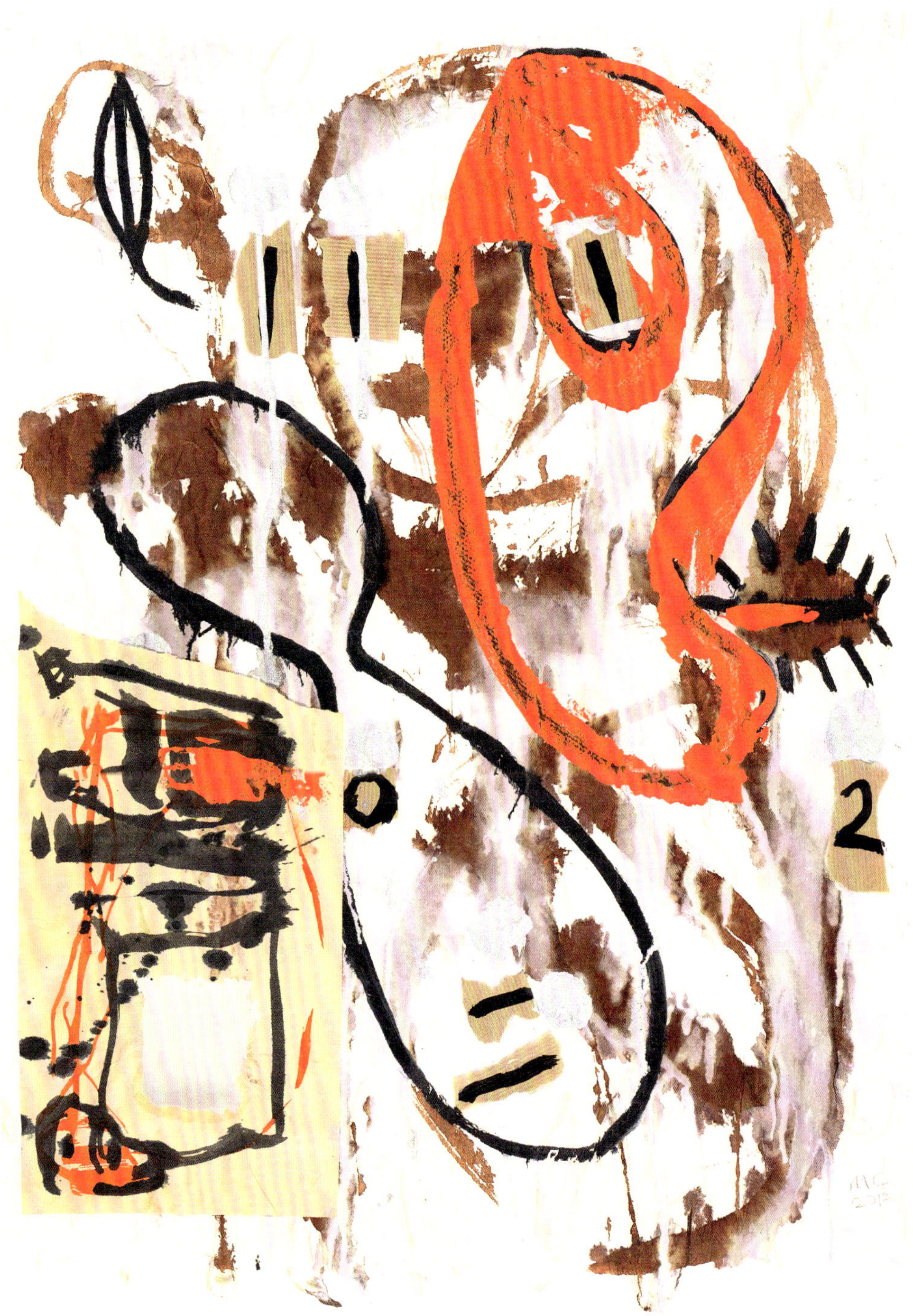
2

Professor Sir Peter Cook RA (b. 1936)

Comfo-Veg Room, 2012

Inkjet print

50.8 x 49.0 cm

RCIN 212716

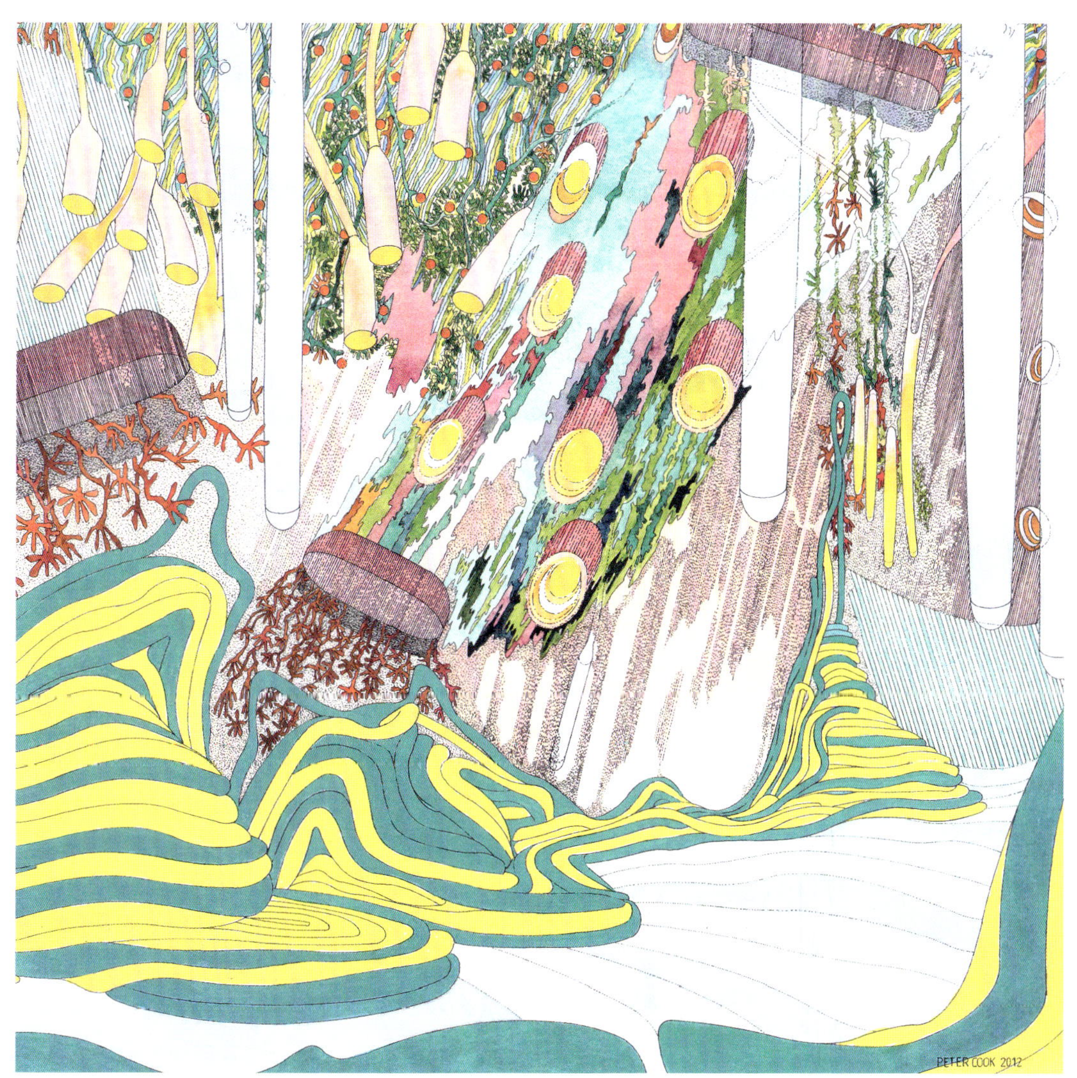
PETER COOK 2012

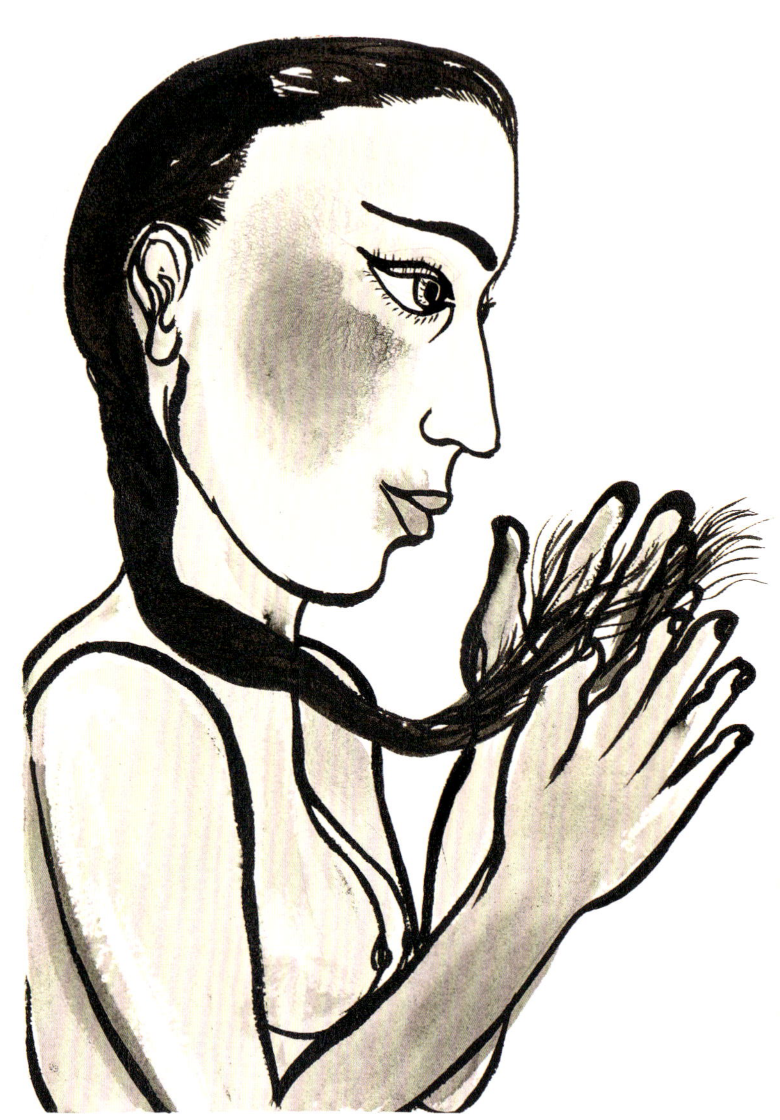

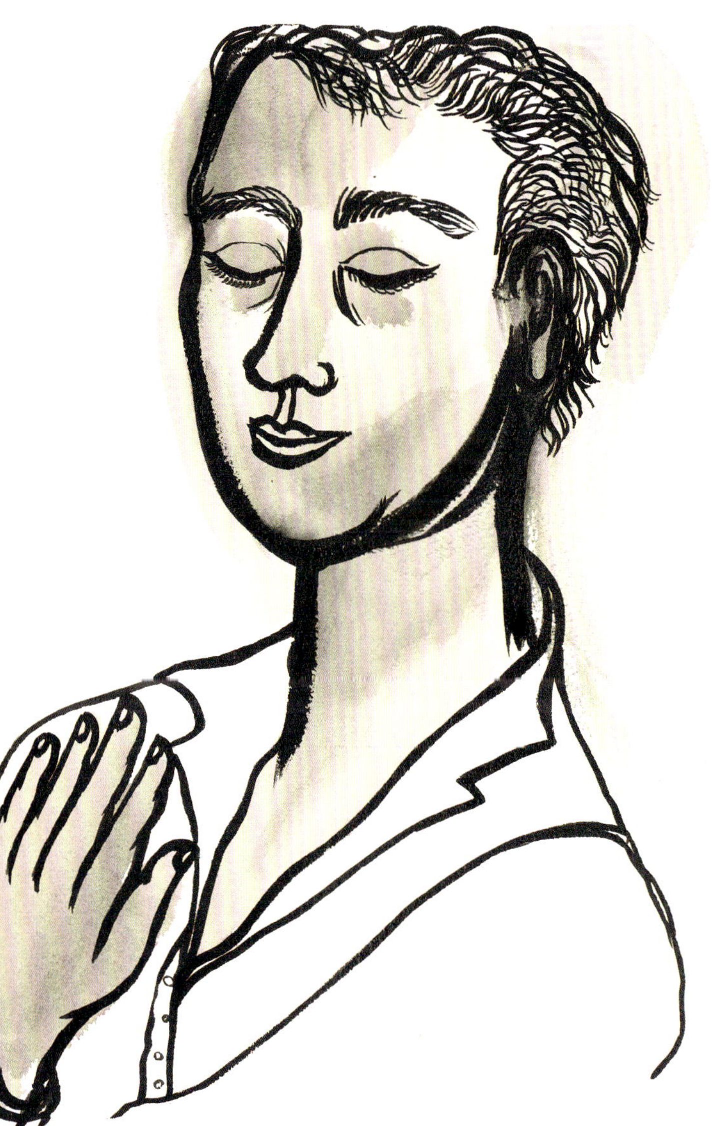

Eileen Cooper RA (b. 1953)
From the 'Couples' Series, 2011
Pencil, ink and wash
38.5 x 28.5 cm and 39.8 x 28.2 cm
RCIN 212717.a–b

Stephen Cox RA (b. 1946)
Study for Sculpture: Front View, 2003
Compressed charcoal
57.3 x 38.2 cm
RCIN 212718

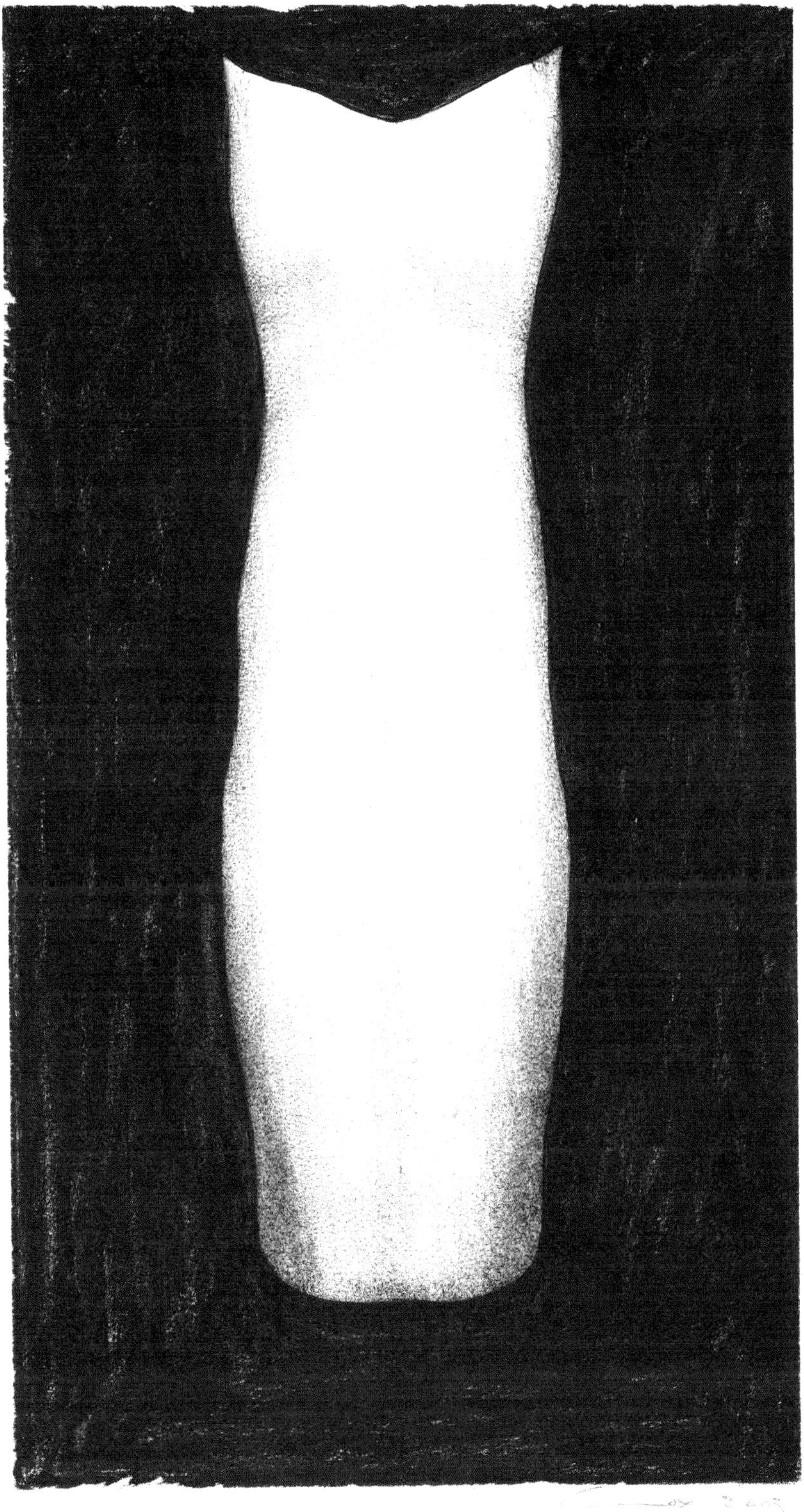

Michael Craig-Martin CBE RA (b. 1941)

Hope, 2012

Inkjet print

57.7 x 44.4 cm (sheet)

40.5 x 37.8 cm (image)

RCIN 212719

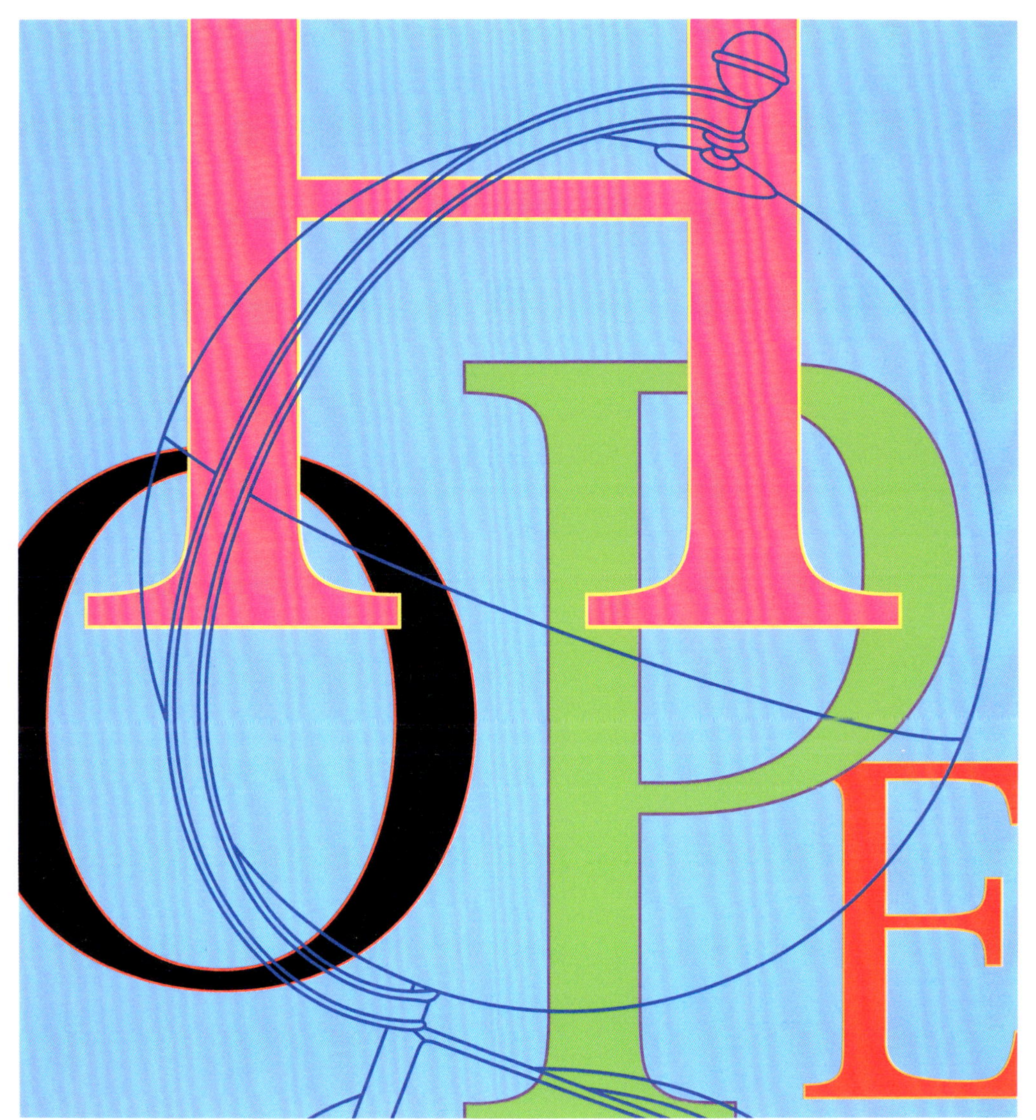
HOPE

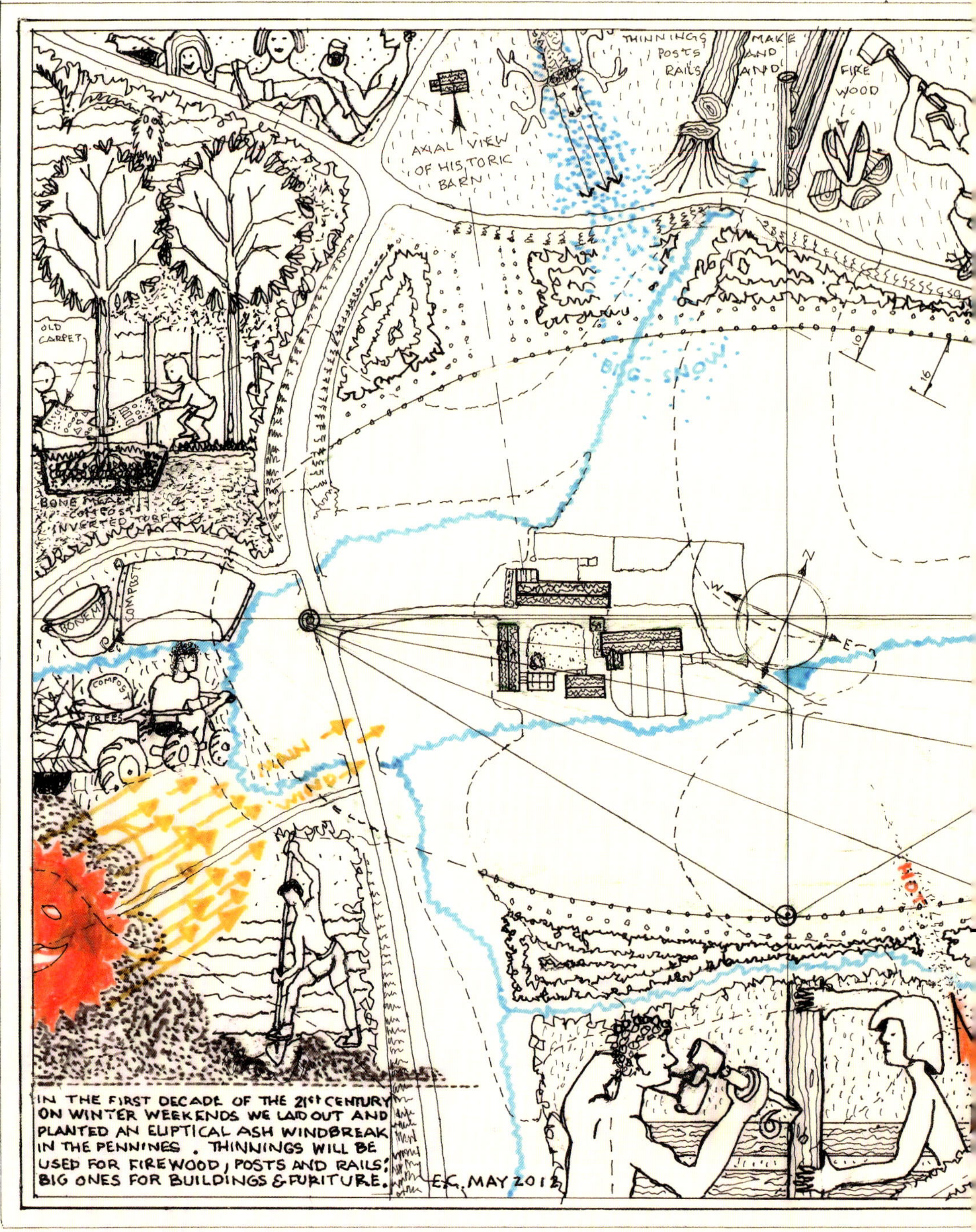

THINNINGS POSTS RAILS AND
MAKE AND
FIRE WOOD
AXIAL VIEW OF HISTORIC BARN
BIG SNOW
OLD CARPET
BONE MEAL
COMPOST
INVERTED TURF
BONE MEAL
COMPOST
COMPOST
TREES
MAIN WIND
N
W
E
10
16
HOT
IN THE FIRST DECADE OF THE 21st CENTURY ON WINTER WEEKENDS WE LAID OUT AND PLANTED AN ELIPTICAL ASH WINDBREAK IN THE PENNINES. THINNINGS WILL BE USED FOR FIREWOOD, POSTS AND RAILS; BIG ONES FOR BUILDINGS & FURITURE.
E.G. MAY 2012

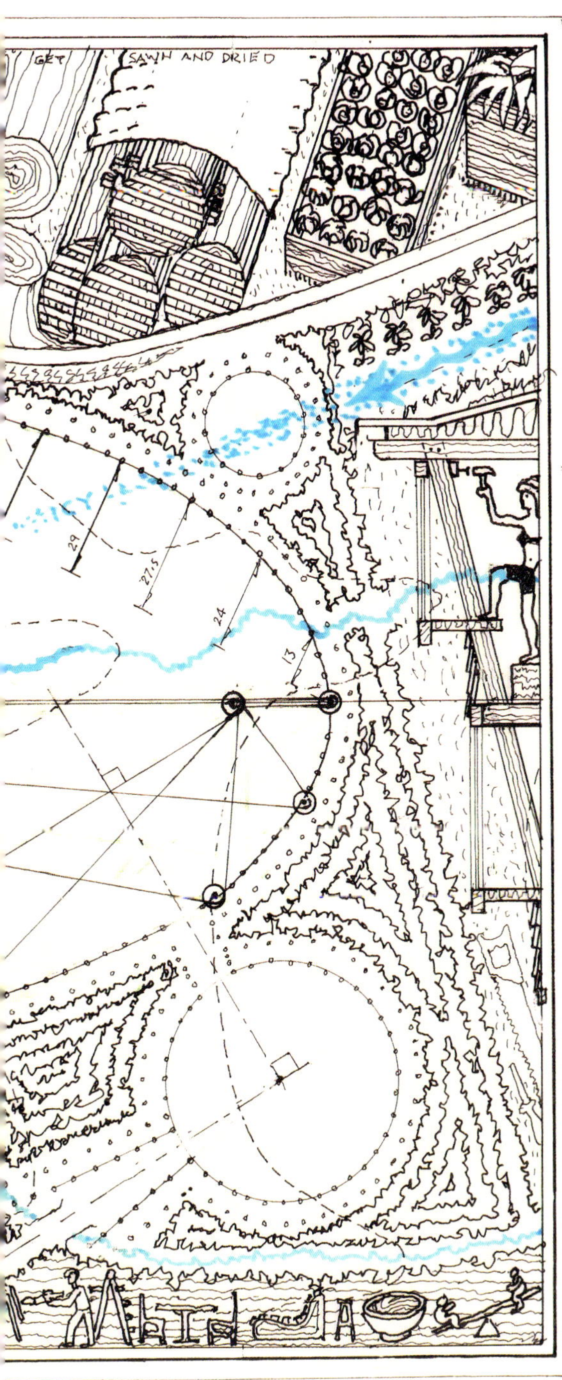

Edward Cullinan CBE RA (b. 1931)

Trees at Gib Tor, 2012

Pen and ink, felt pen and coloured pencil on tracing paper

27.9 x 35.8 cm

RCIN 212720

Frederick Cuming Hon DLitt RA (b. 1930)

Studio Evening Moonrise, 2012

Screenprint

46.5 x 38.3 cm

RCIN 212993

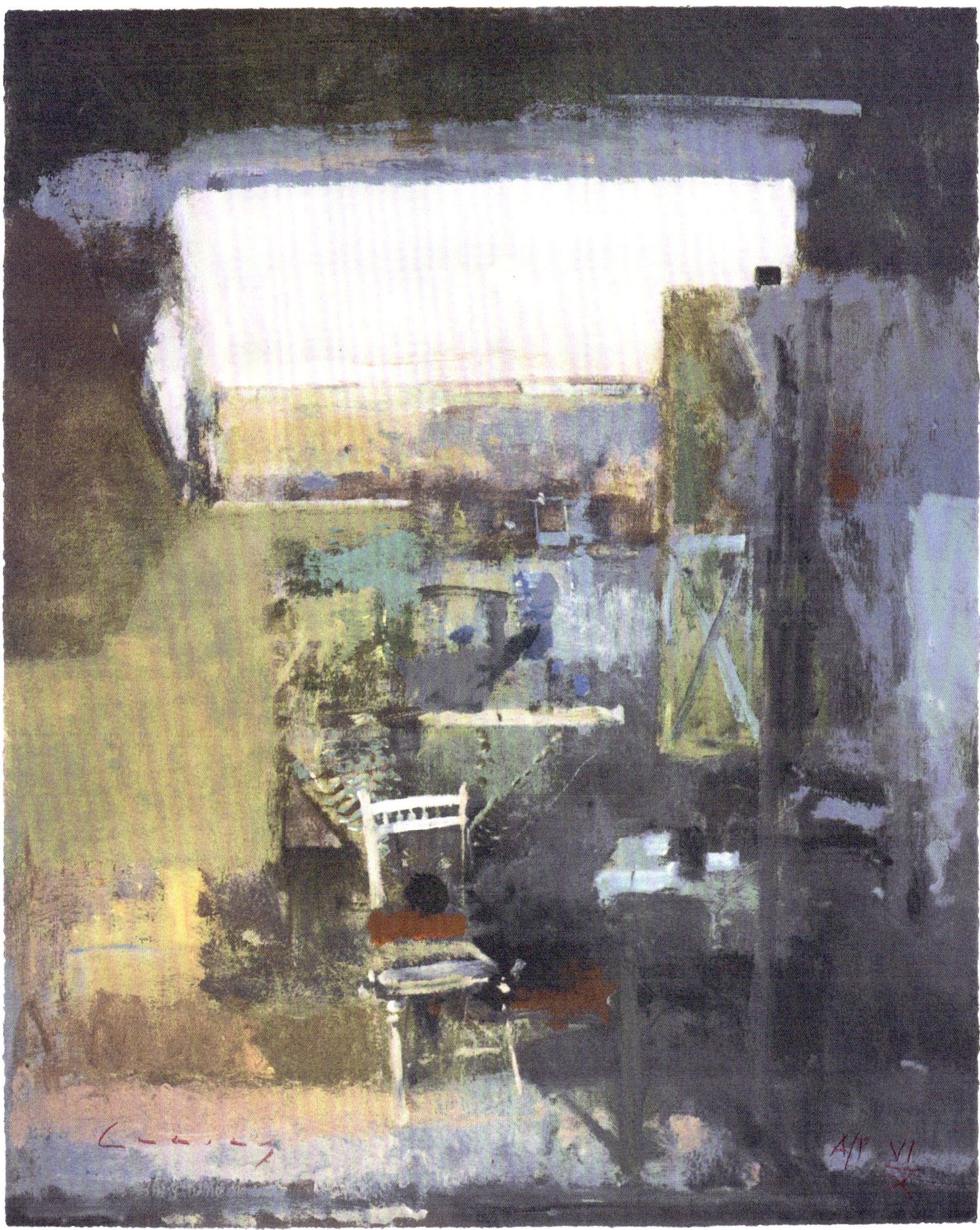
A/P VI

Gus Cummins RA (b. 1943)
Study: 'On Deck', 2012
Pencil, acrylic and gouache
49.9 x 66.4 cm
RCIN 212721

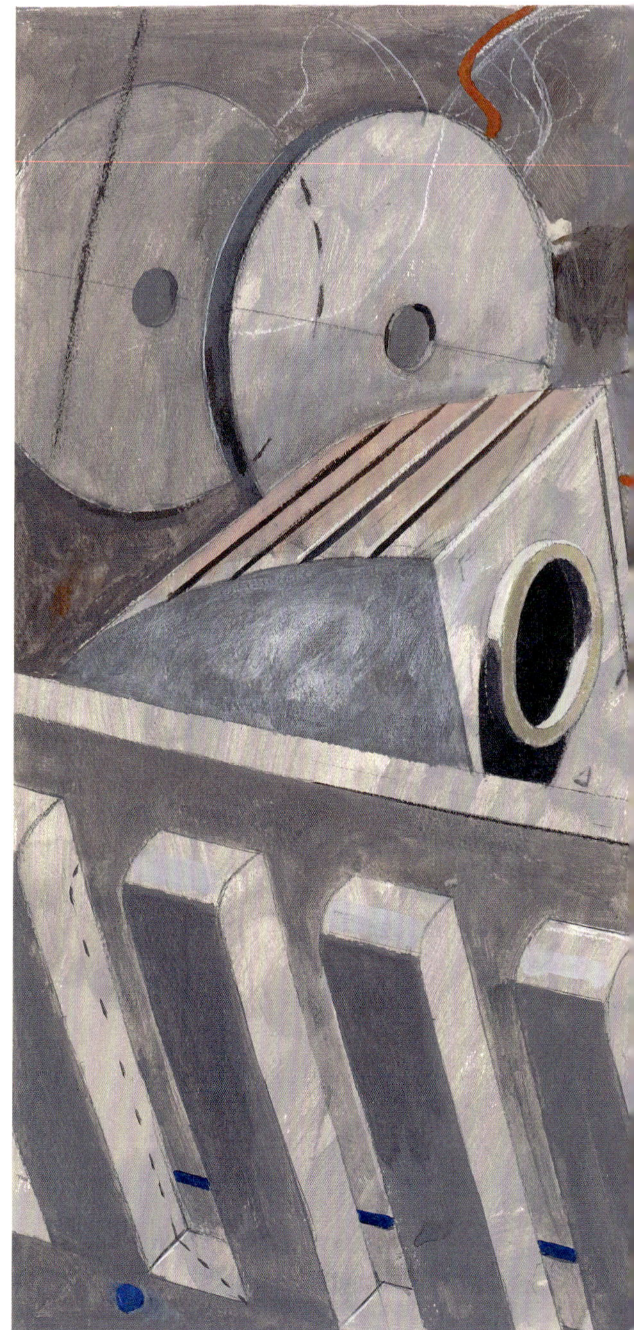

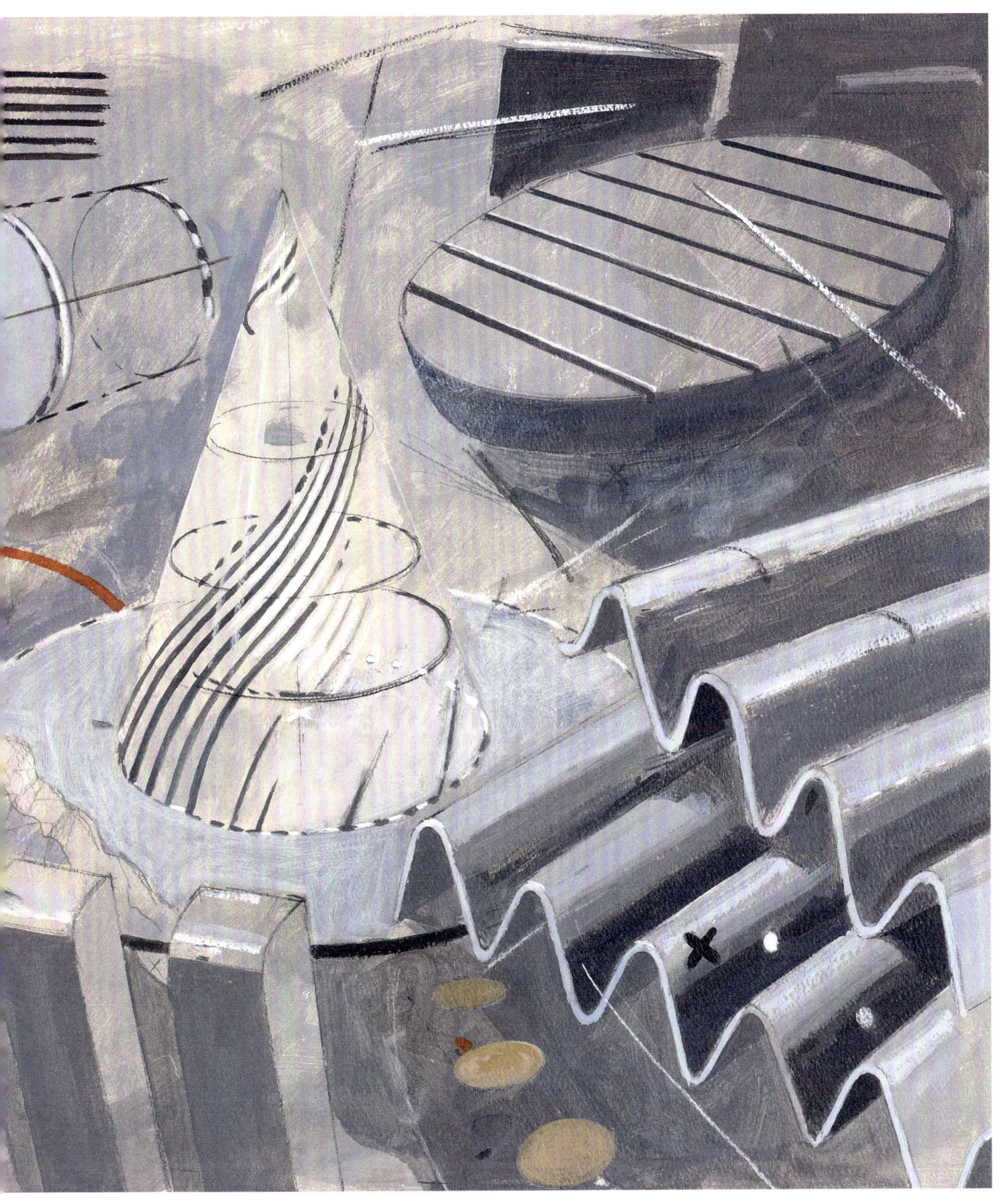

Professor Trevor Dannatt RA (b. 1920)

Her Britannic Majesty's Embassy, Riyadh, Kingdom of Saudi Arabia
The Chancery Building, 1985

Inkjet prints

29.7 x 21.0 cm and 29.7 x 42.0 cm (sheet)

23.5 x 15.5 cm and 23.5 x 37.4 cm (sight)

RCIN 212722.a–b

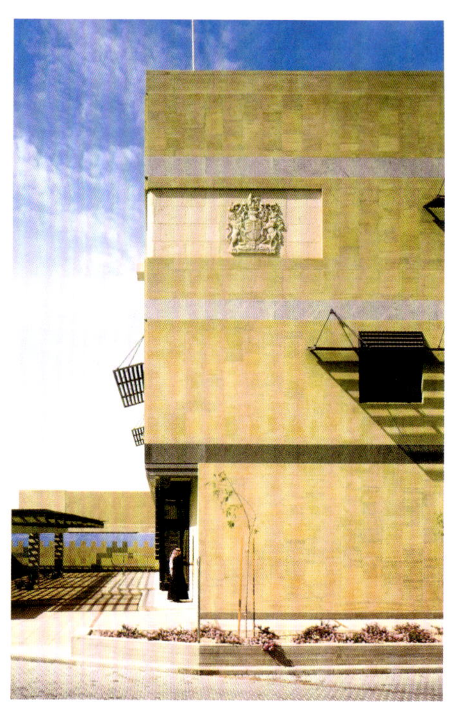

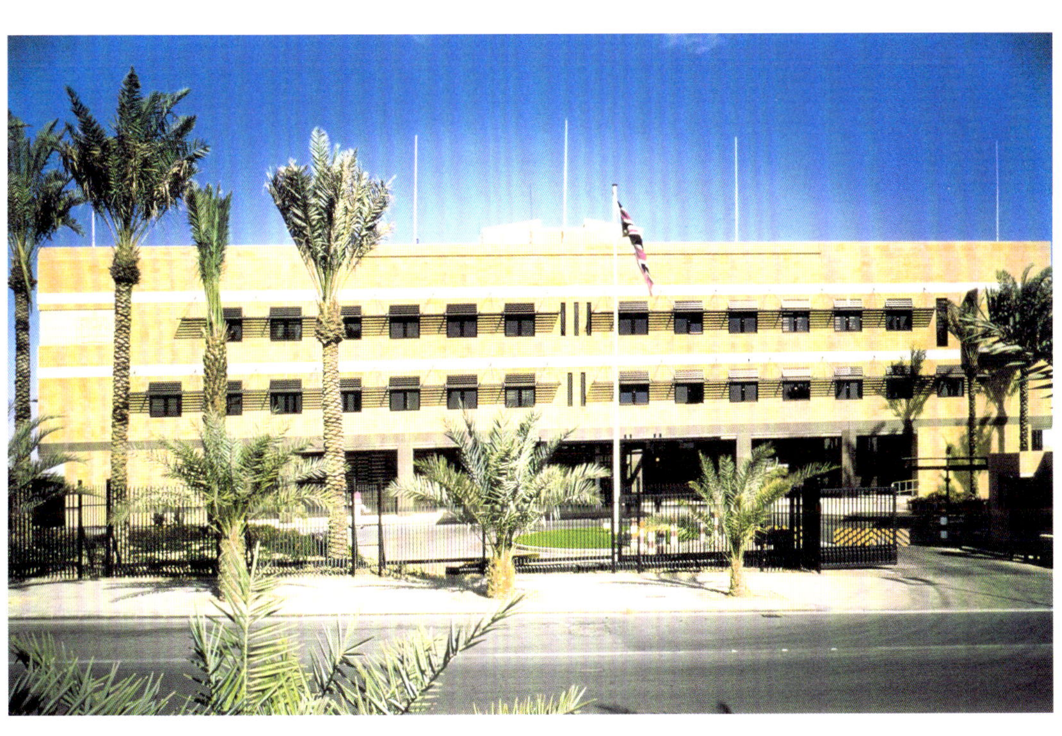

Richard Deacon CBE RA (b. 1949)

2.06.13, 2013

Pencil, pen and ink

24.1 x 32.0 cm

RCIN 212996

The 2nd of June was the date of the 60th anniversary of the Coronation. My mother went up to London for the Coronation in 1953. The rest of the family stayed behind, at my grandmother's. There was no television so we did not watch the pageant. However on her return my mother gave me a present of a stamp album – 'The Coronation Stamp Album' – probably also with some stamps and some hinges for mounting them. This ignited an interest in me in stamp collecting and, subsequently, in the larger questions of classification, naming and identification. These in turn ignited much of my interests and my curiosity about the world that fed into my becoming an artist. The drawing that I have offered has something of the squared pages you find in stamp albums about it, as well as being a kind of map or territory (although it is none of these things). Having the drawing dated to the 60th anniversary of the event that led, in some peculiar way, to my being who I am, seemed entirely appropriate to the idea of the Jubilee Gift.

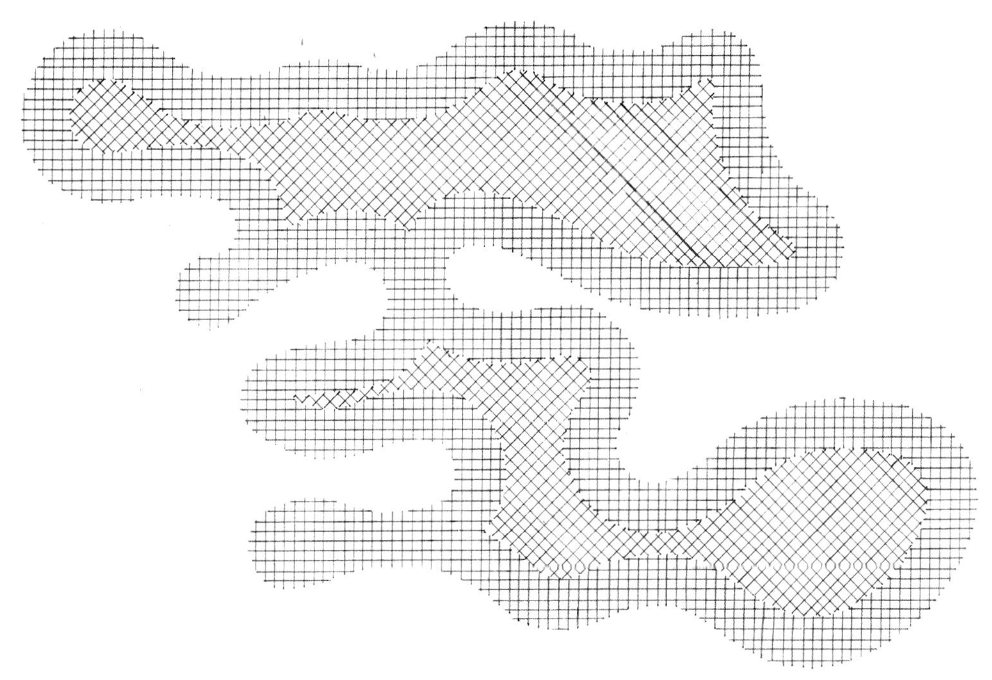

Spencer de Grey CBE RA (b. 1944)

The Sage Gateshead (Architects Foster + Partners), 2008

Inkjet print

44.3 x 53.1 cm

RCIN 212723

Photographer: George Gastin

The Sage Gateshead Architects Foster + Partners

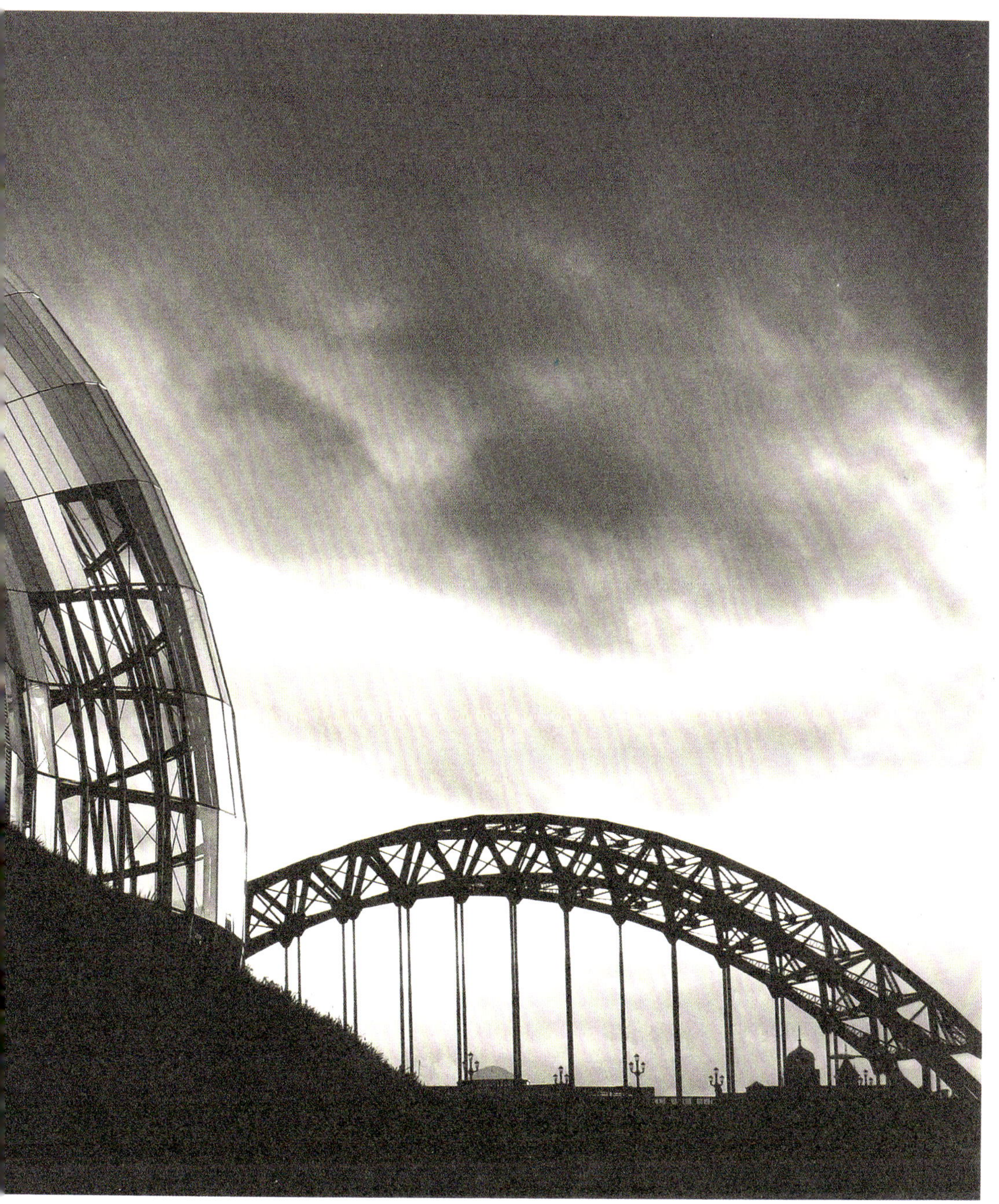

Spencer de Grey RA

Anne Desmet RA (b. 1964)
Olympic Shadows, 2012
Wood engraving
26.2 x 38.0 cm (sheet)
10.1 x 12.6 cm (image)
RCIN 212724

Between 2009 and 2012 I was working on a substantial body of wood engravings and collages relating to the changing landscape of London's Olympic site and collectively titled 'Olympic Metamorphoses'. My home in Hackney is close to the site and it felt as though the whole familiar cityscape on my doorstep was shifting seismically. Having long been interested in ideas of change and transformation linked to architectural evolution, degeneration and regeneration, this seemed a perfect subject for me and related well, thematically, to earlier bodies of work I have made on comparable subjects – from the restoration of the Piranesi-esque Victoria Baths in Manchester, to evolving images of Roman, medieval and contemporary Italy, to evocations of the historic/legendary Tower of Babel.

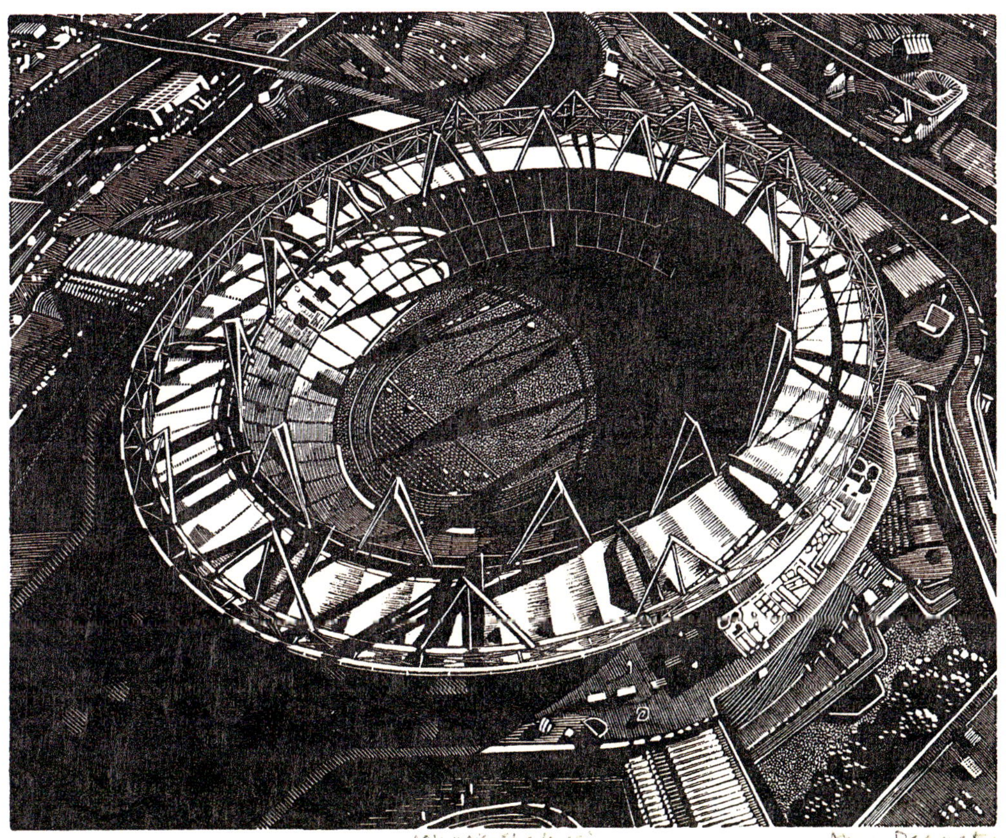

A/P 'Olympic Shadows' Anne Desmet

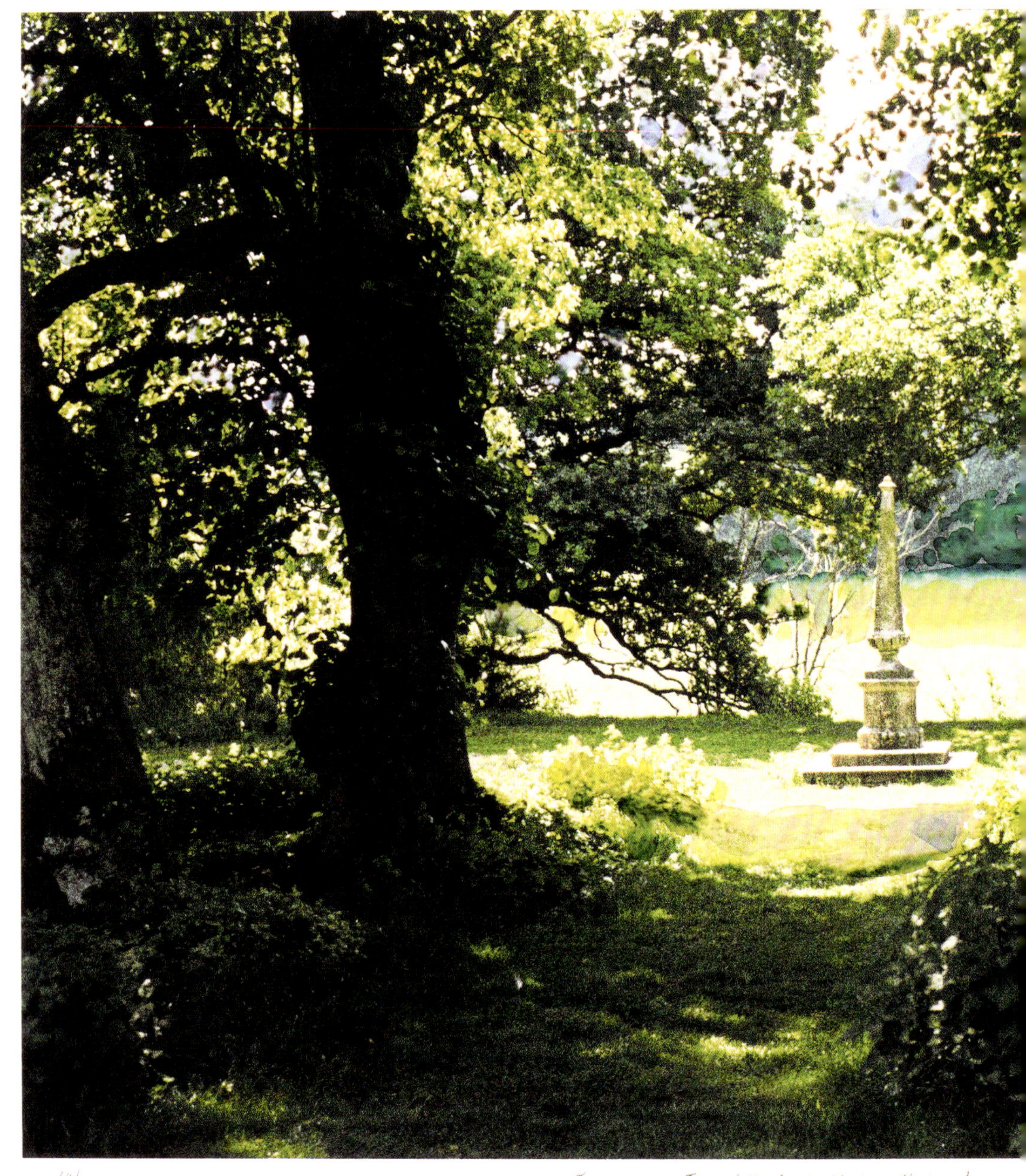

14/20 Transitions: Five (The Sun's Chalice, Hinton Ampner

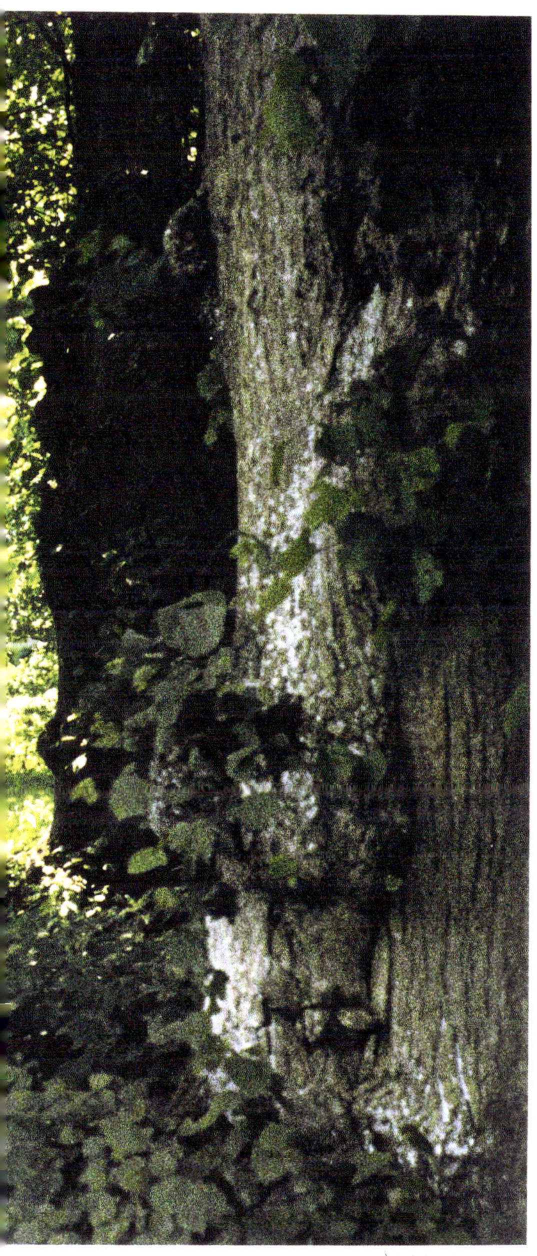

'I spent a long time selecting this particular image, and it is very serene and peaceful. I thought the Queen might find it contemplative. I don't know how she survives all the pressures she is under. She has a gruelling life.'

Dr Jennifer Dickson RA (b. 1936)
Transitions: Five (The Sun's Chalice, Hinton Ampner), 2008
Inkjet print with watercolour
49.7 x 62.5 cm
RCIN 212725

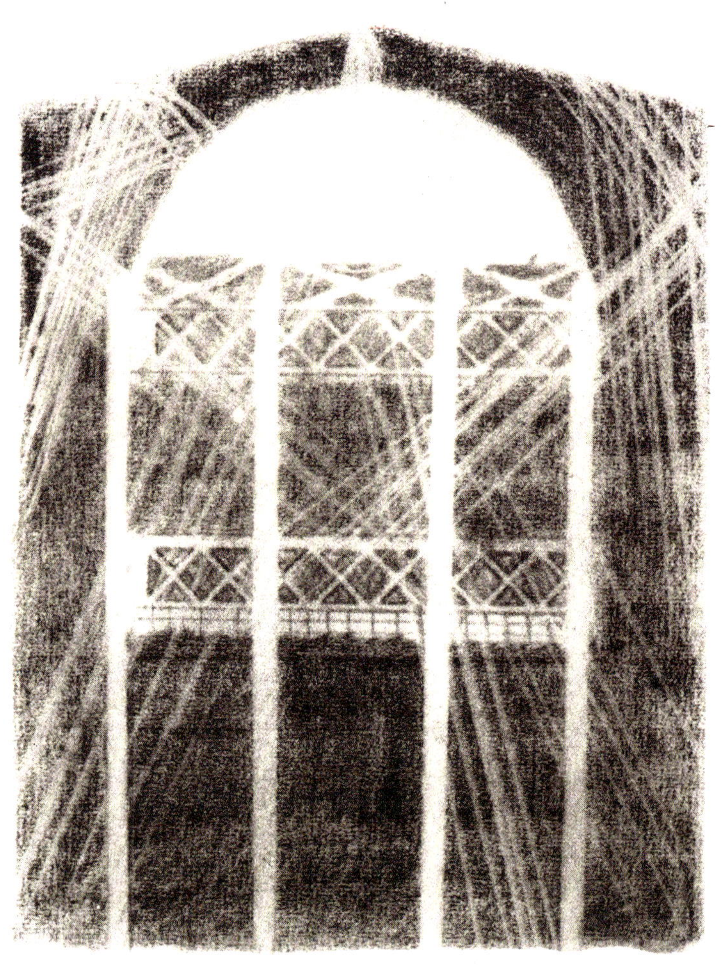

Sir Philip Dowson CBE PPRA (b. 1924)
'Light Study' (Clare College Library), 1997
Photo-etching
30.5 x 25.1 cm (sheet)
21.0 x 17.9 cm (plate)
RCIN 213002

Kenneth Draper RA (b. 1944)

Vertical Space, 1991

Pastel

40.7 x 35.4 cm

RCIN 212726

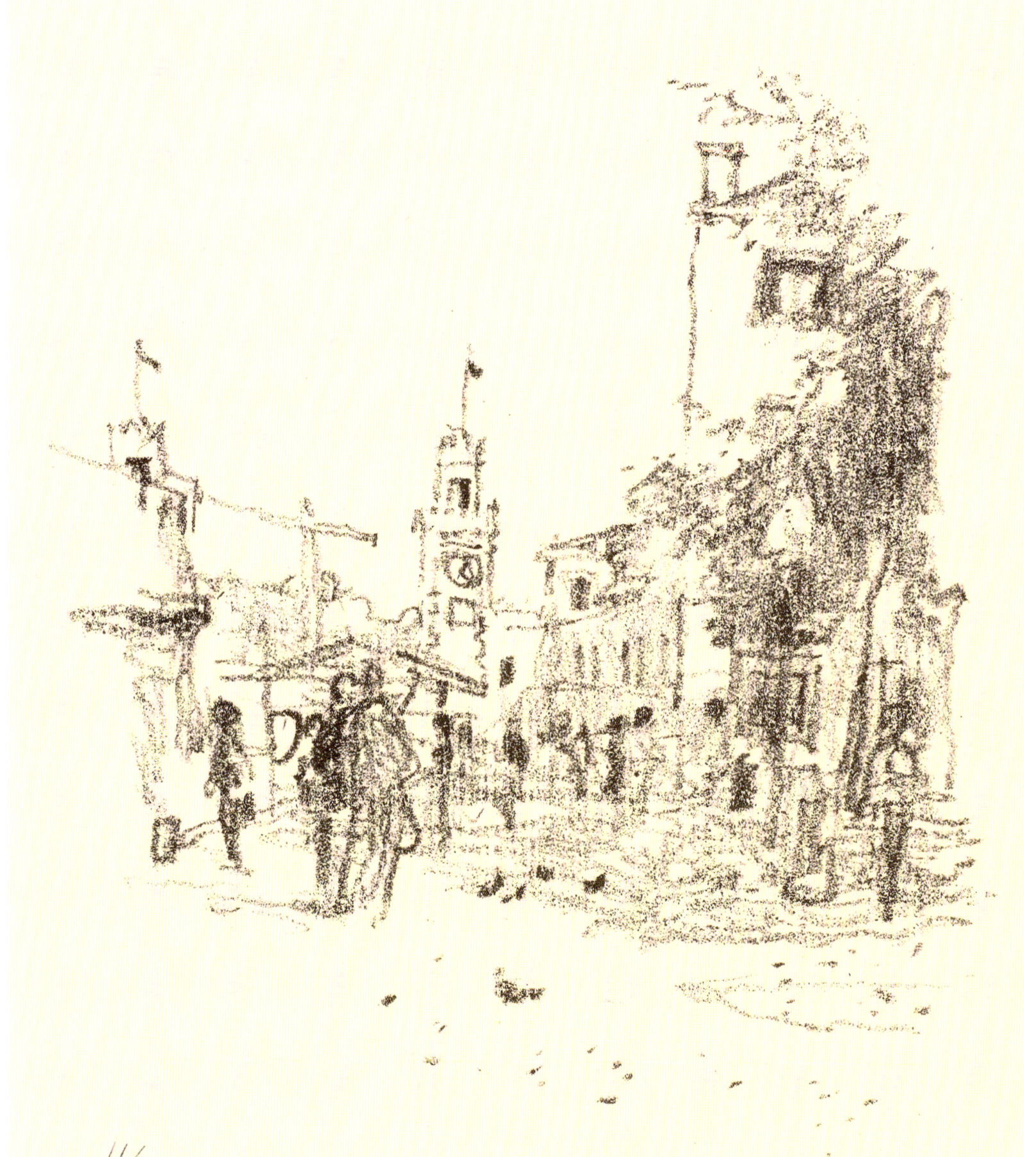
11/30

Bernard Dunstan RA PPRWA (b. 1920)

Venice, *c.*2005

Lithograph

31.8 x 21.6 cm

RCIN 212727

Jennifer Durrant RA (b. 1942)

From a Series, 'Last Conversations', 2003–8

Acrylic and collage

19.0 x 32.0 cm (max)

RCIN 212728

Professor Tracey Emin CBE RA (b. 1963)

HRH Royal Britania, 2012

Monoprint

29.6 x 21.0 cm

RCIN 212729

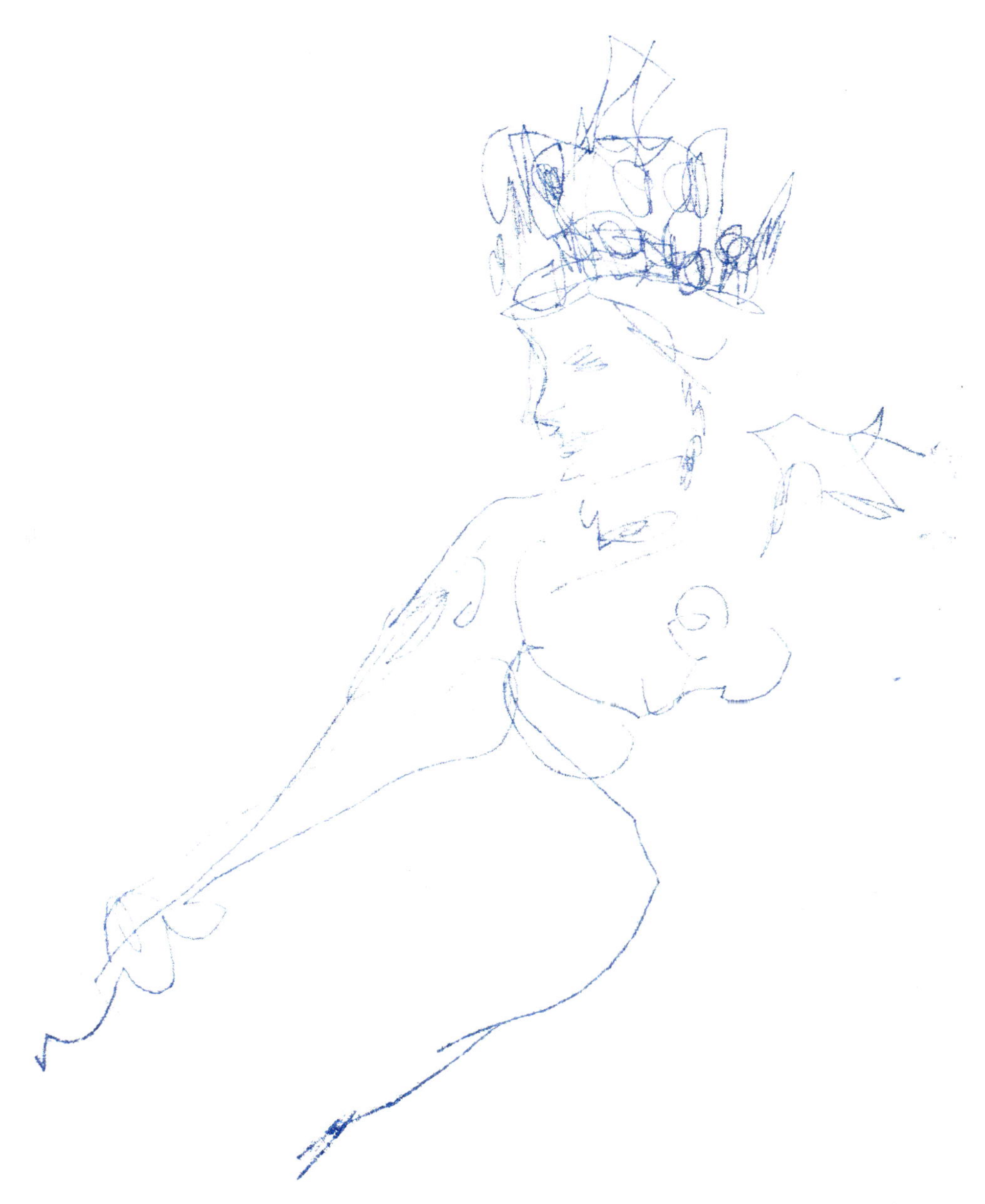

Anthony Eyton RA (b. 1923)

Uluru (Ayer's Rock), 2008

Screenprint

44.6 x 45.8 cm

RCIN 212730

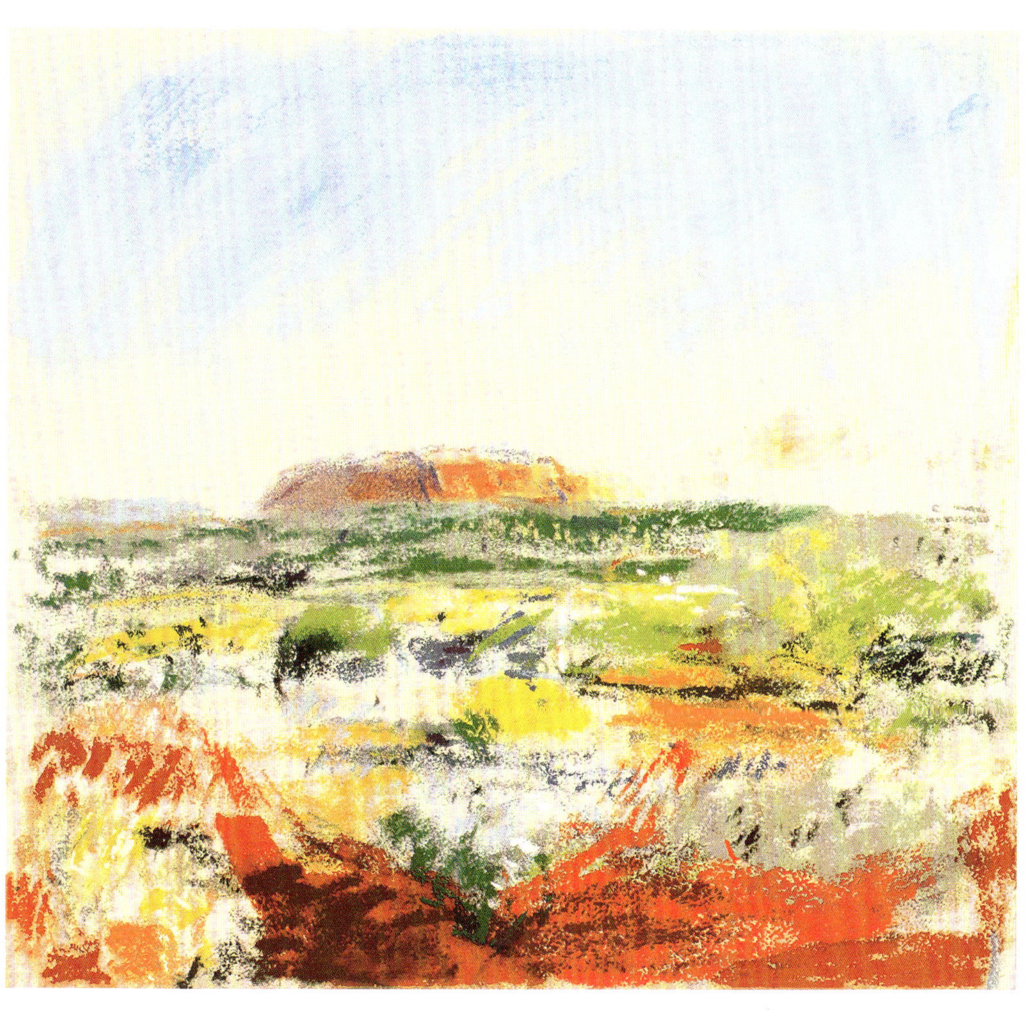

Professor Stephen Farthing RA (b. 1950)

Study for the 5th Miracle Painting, 2012

Pencil, pen and ink, watercolour, gouache and acrylic

35.7 x 50.7 cm

RCIN 212731

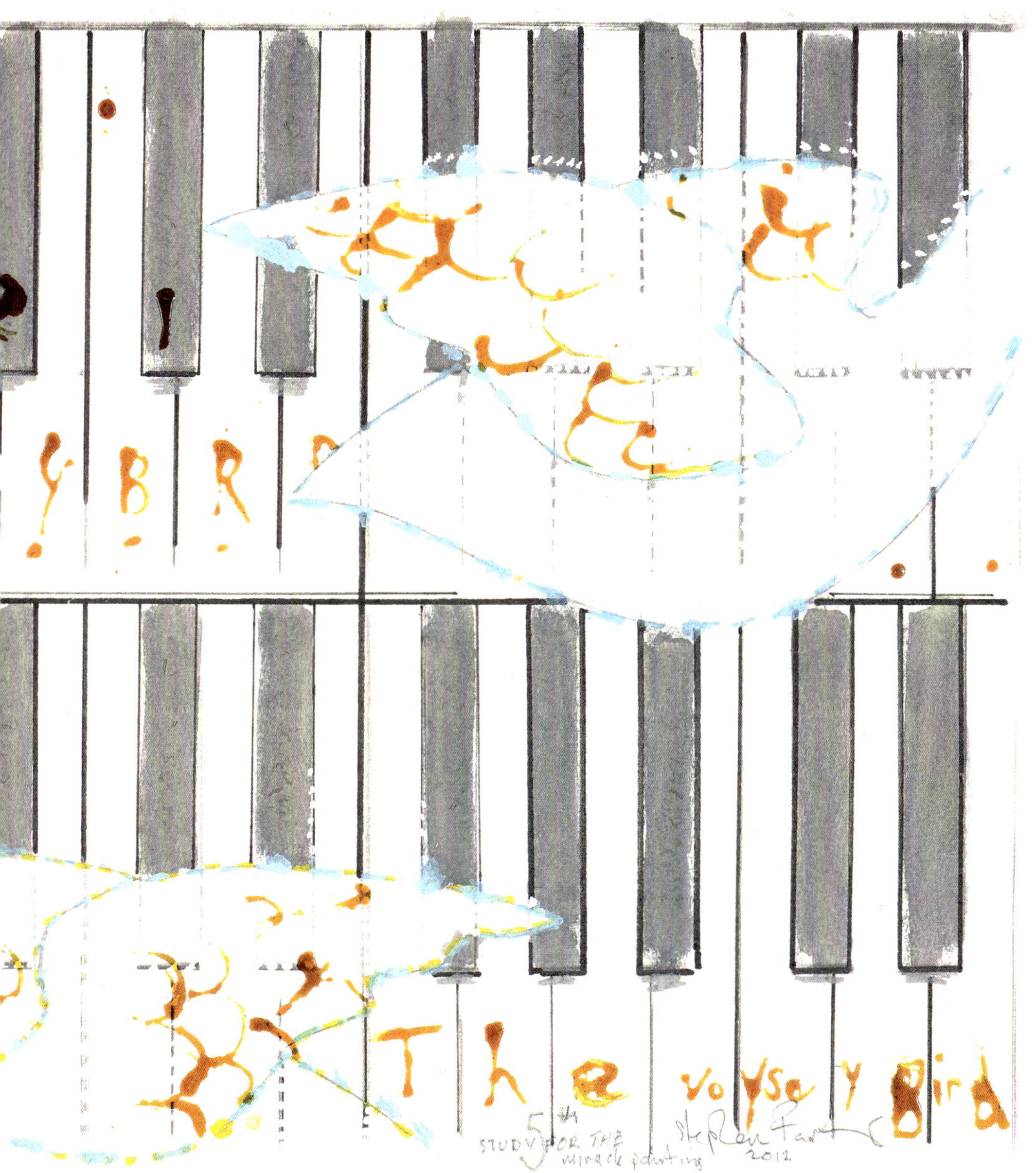
5th STUDY FOR THE miracle painting
2012

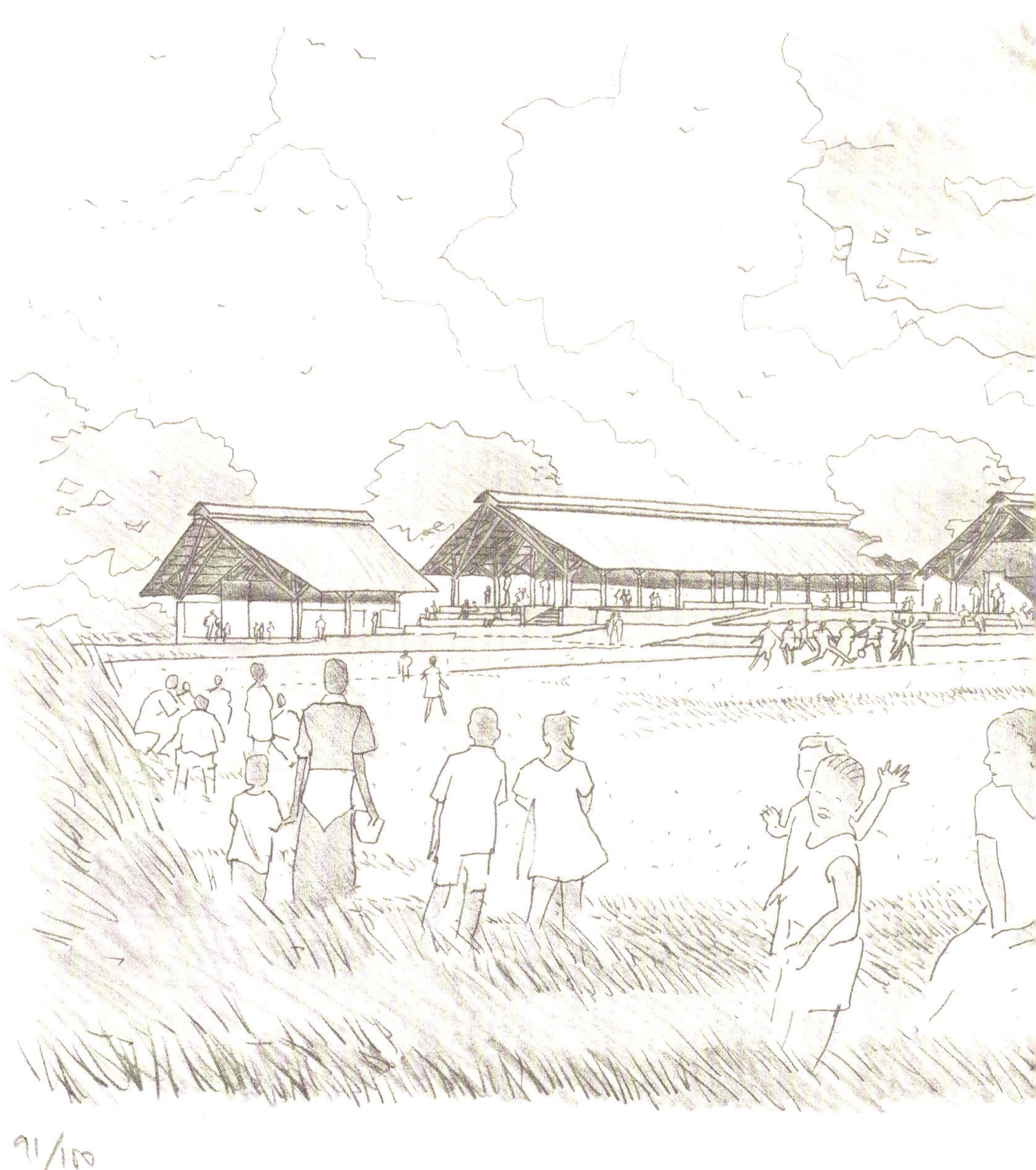

91/100

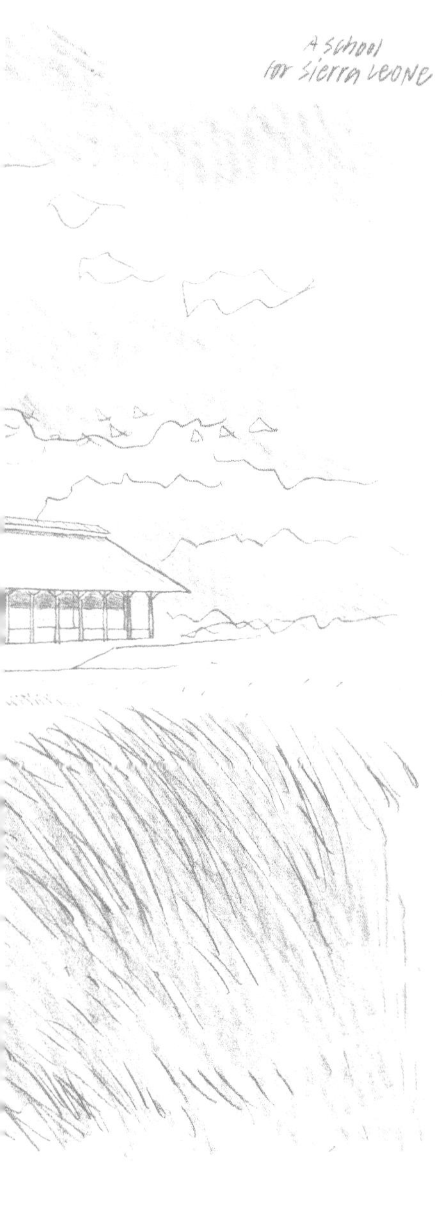

Lord Foster of Thames Bank OM RA (b. 1935)

A School for Sierra Leone, 2009

Lithograph

32.5 x 43.5 cm

RCIN 212732

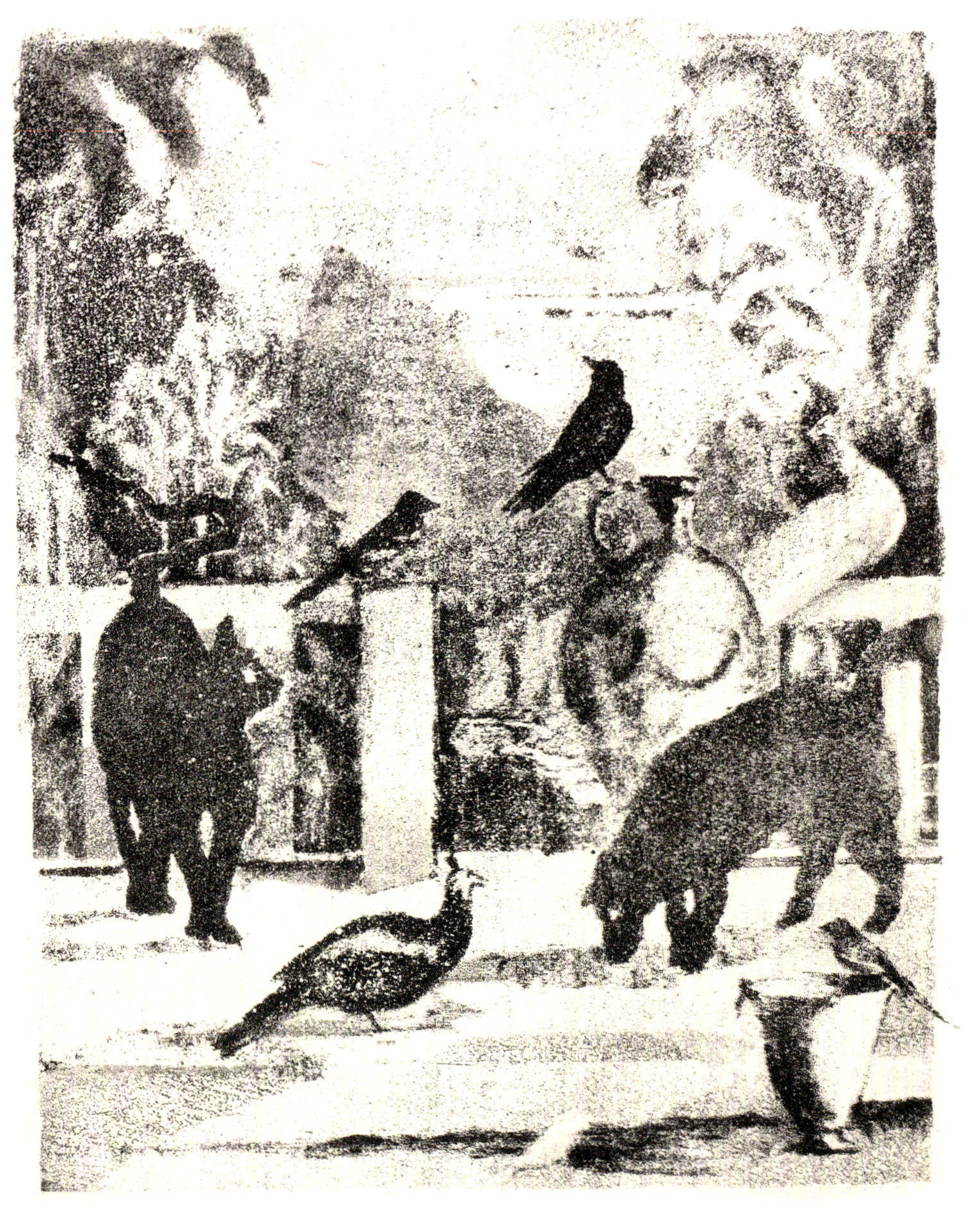

Peter Freeth RA (b. 1938)

Shop Talk on Parnassus (Le Chat de M. Manet Rencontre le Chien de M. Seurat), 2012

Aquatint

50.3 x 42.7 cm (sheet)

34.5 x 28.1 cm (plate)

RCIN 212733

Antony Gormley OBE RA (b. 1950)
Terra Nova For The Queen, 2009
Carbon and casein on paper
19.1 x 28.0 cm
RCIN 212734

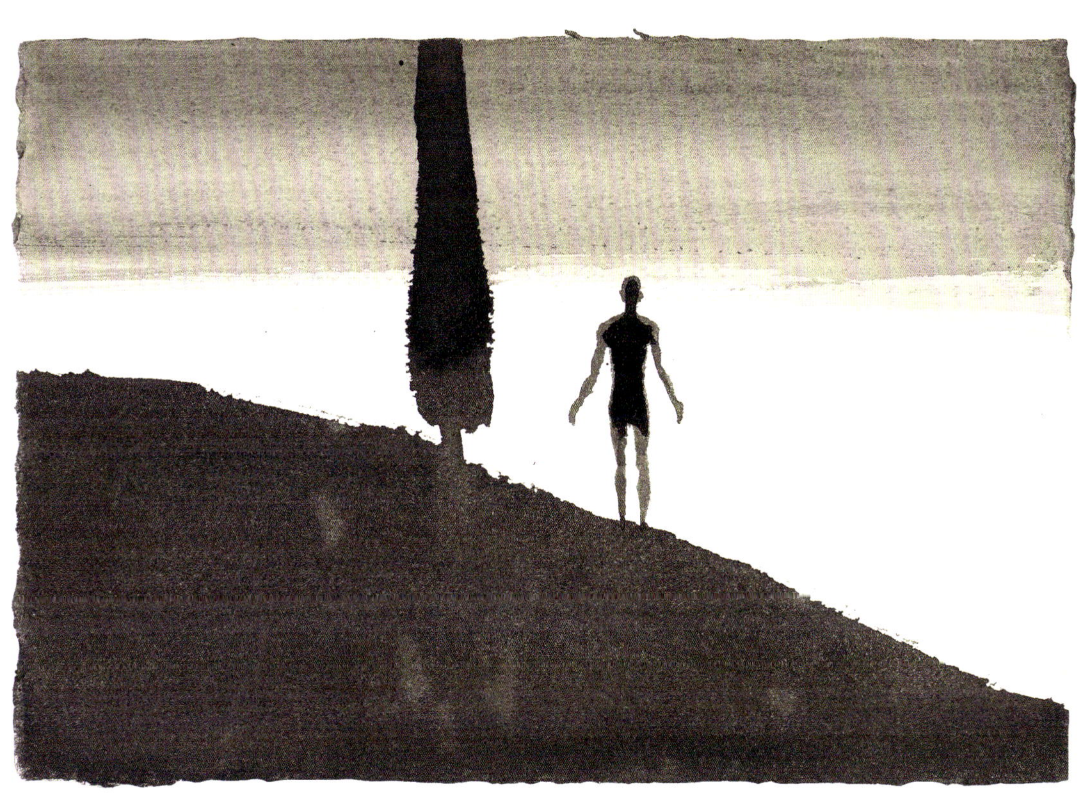

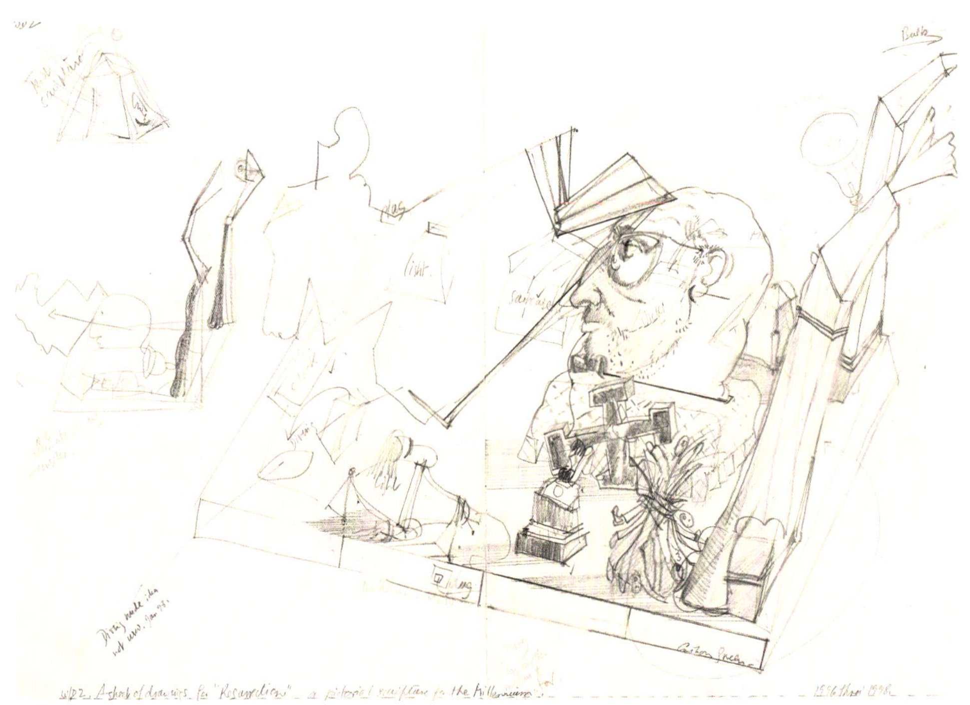

Anthony Green RA (b. 1939)

3 sheets of drawings for 'Resurrection' – A Pictorial Sculpture for the Millennium, 1996–8

Pencil

each 41.4 x 58.8 cm

RCIN 212735–7

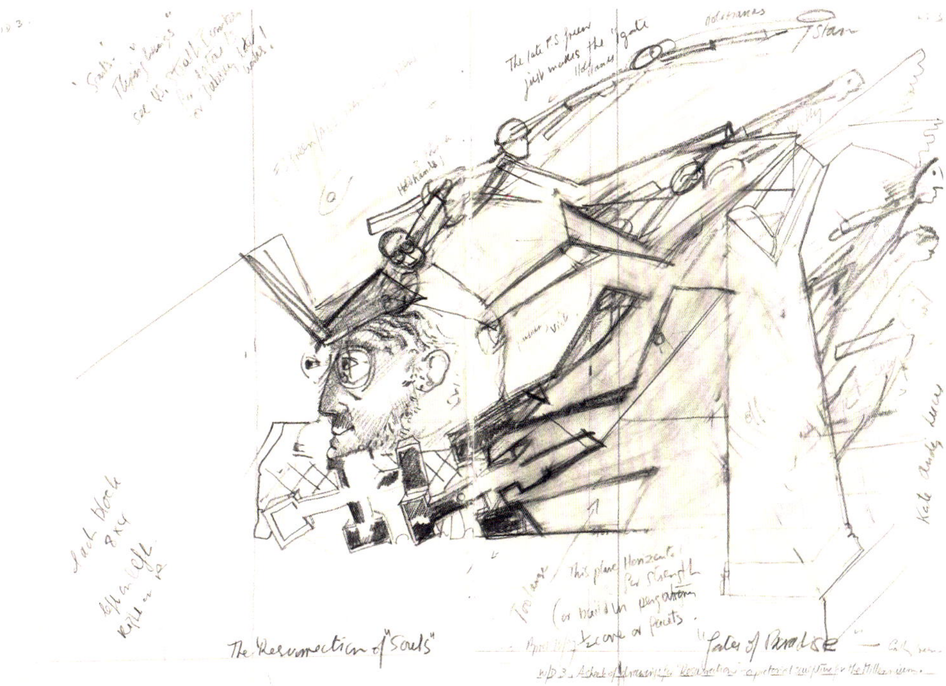

Base

WD4. A sheet of drawings for "Resurrection" - a pictorial sculpture for the Millennium.

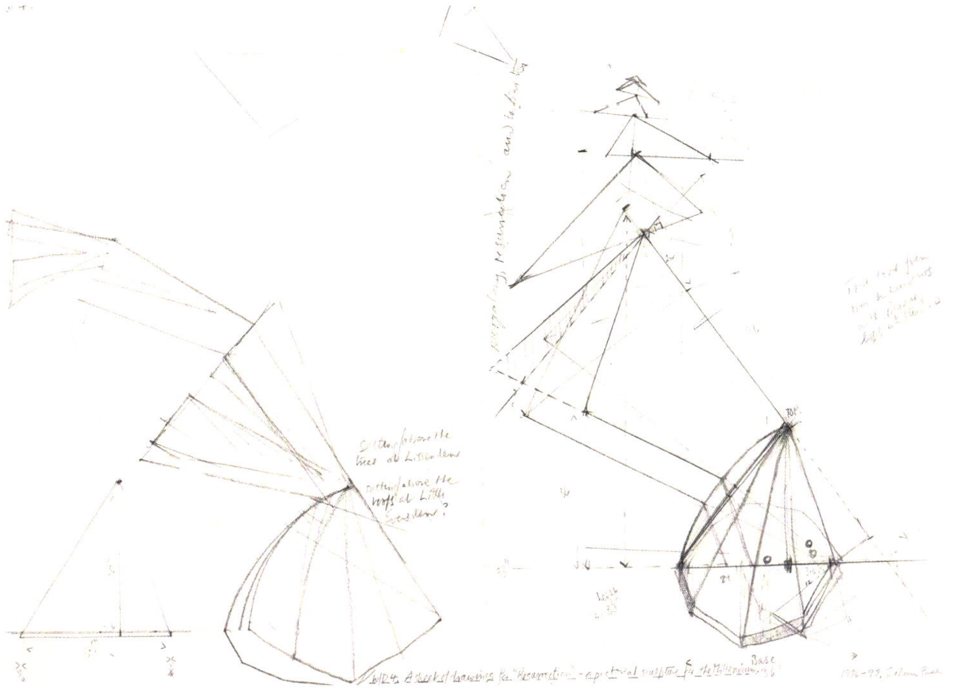

WD 3.

'Souls' "Flying Wings" see US Stealth Bombers for details or Dalesky etc wakes!

F.S. green / AES green

each block 8 x 4

The 'Resurrection of "Souls"'

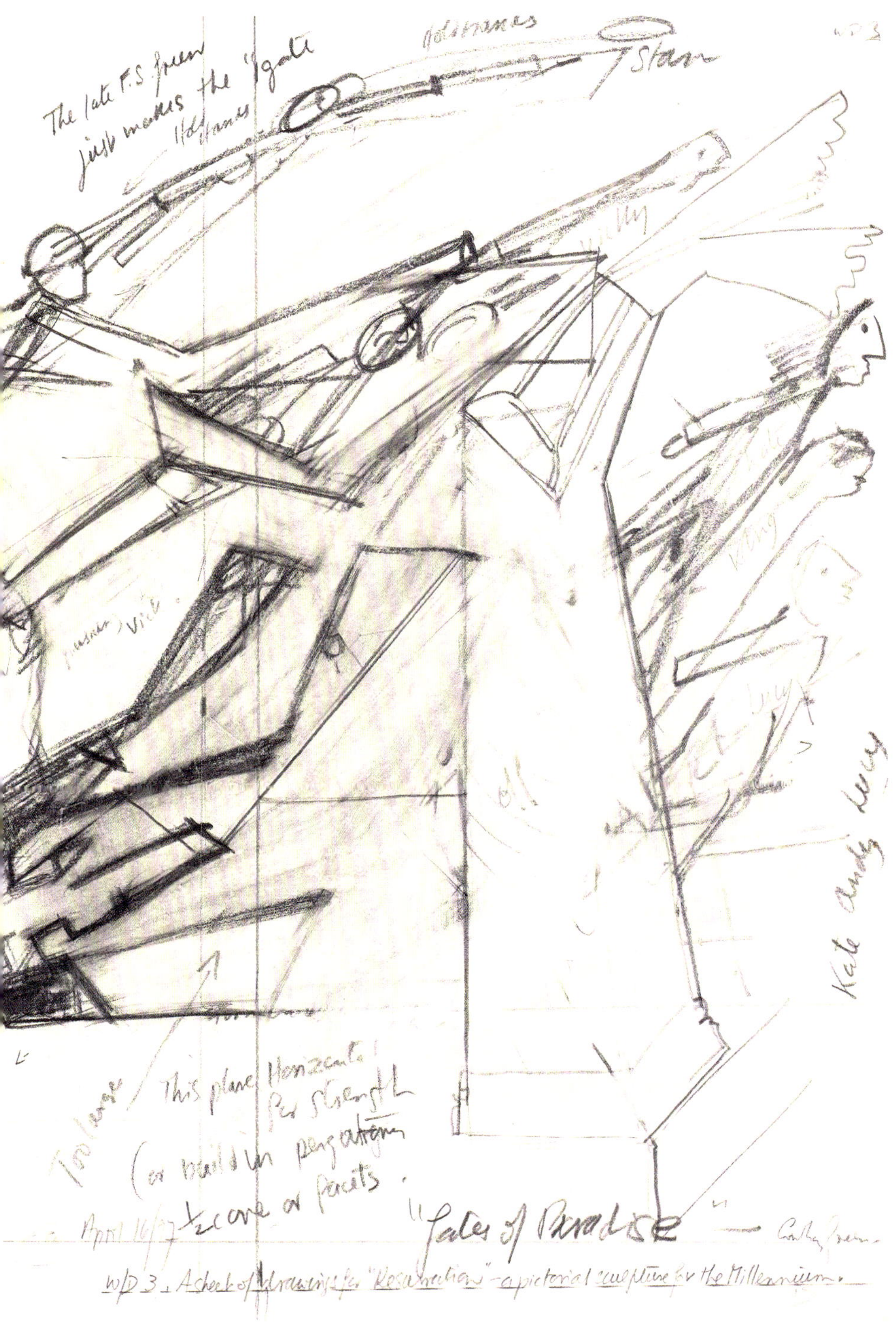
The late F.S. Green
just makes the 'gate
Stan
This plane Horizontal
For Strength
Kate Andy Lucy
"Gates of Paradise"
W/D 3 . A sheet of drawings for "Resurrection" – a pictorial sculpture for the Millennium.

Sir Nicholas Grimshaw CBE PPRA (b. 1939)
Structural Memories II, 2008
Soft-ground etching with aquatint
38.6 x 38.0 cm (sheet)
7.6 x 7.6 cm (each plate)
RCIN 212738

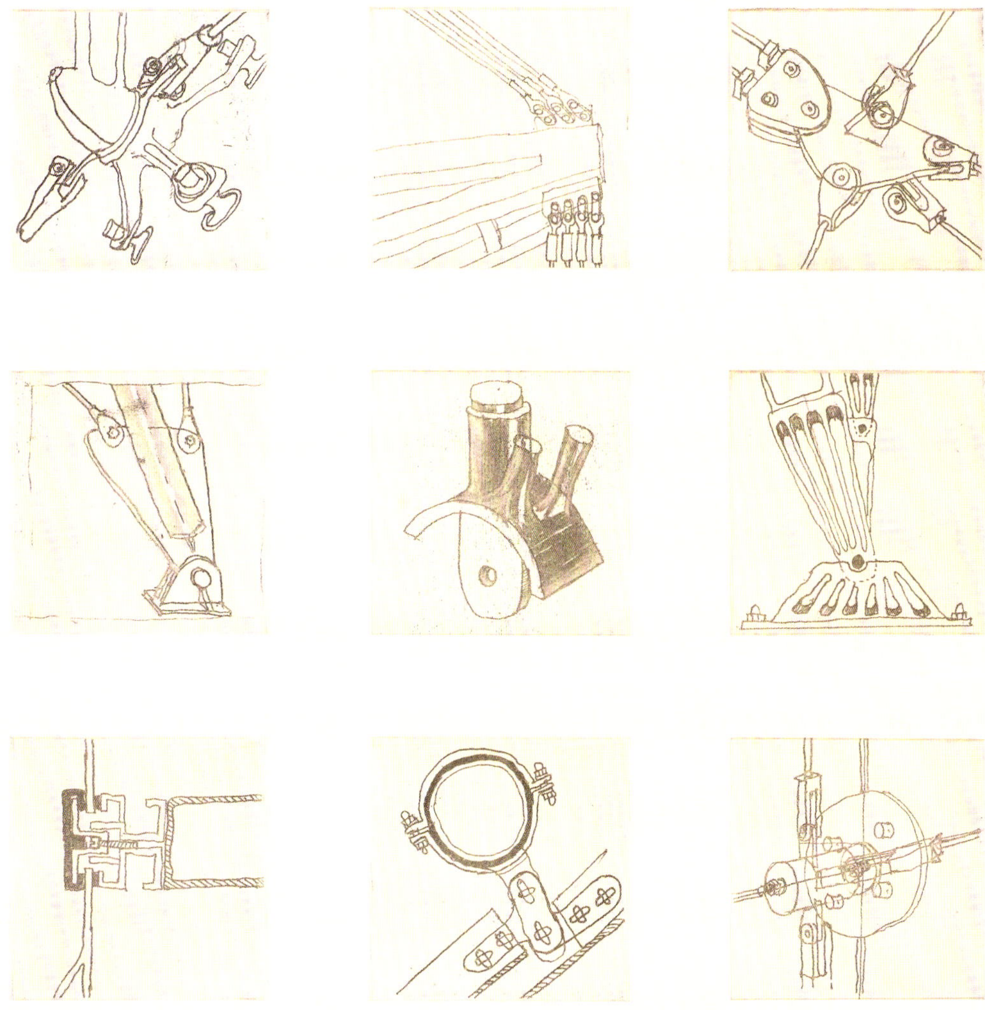
Structural Memories II
Nick Grimshaw 15/4/08

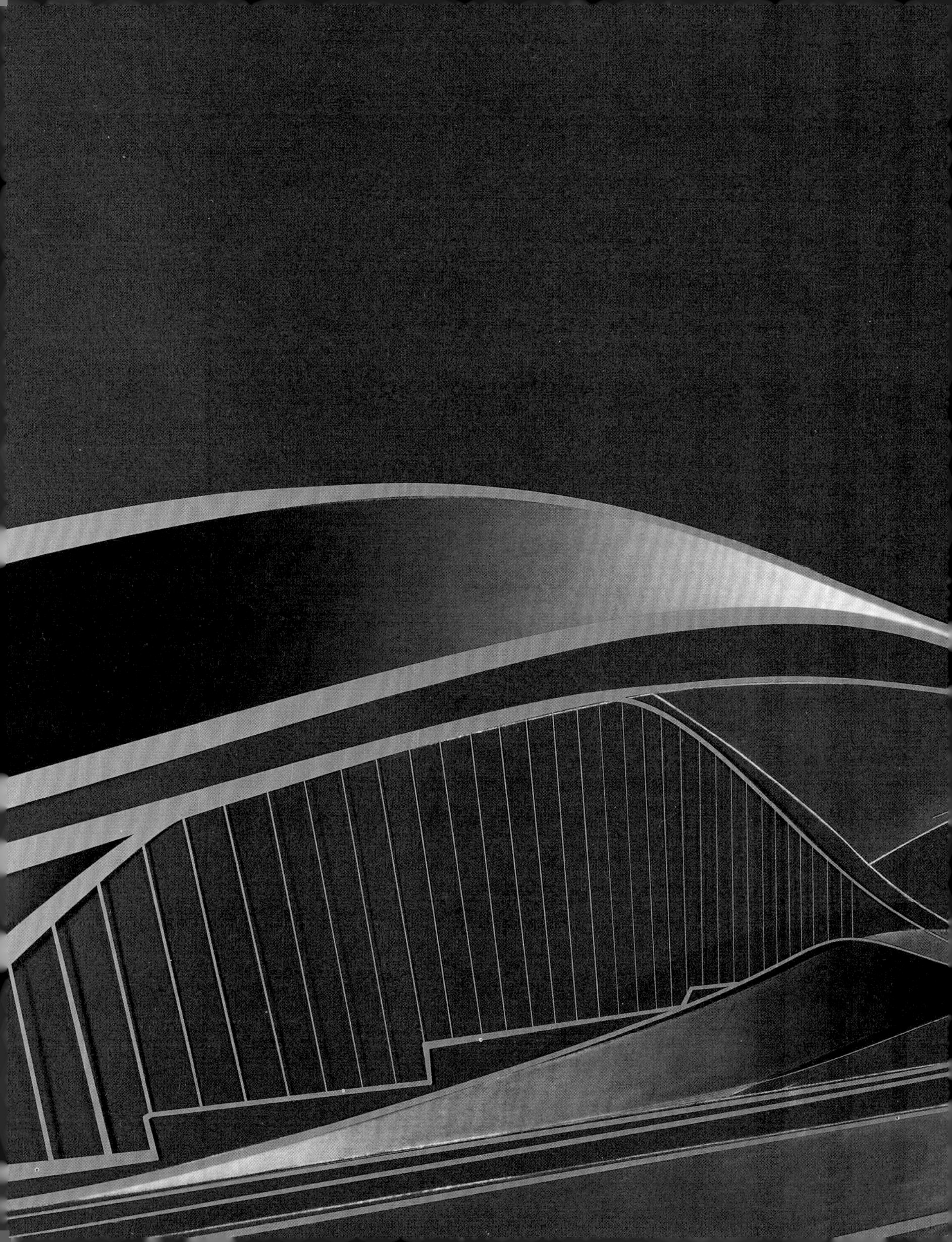

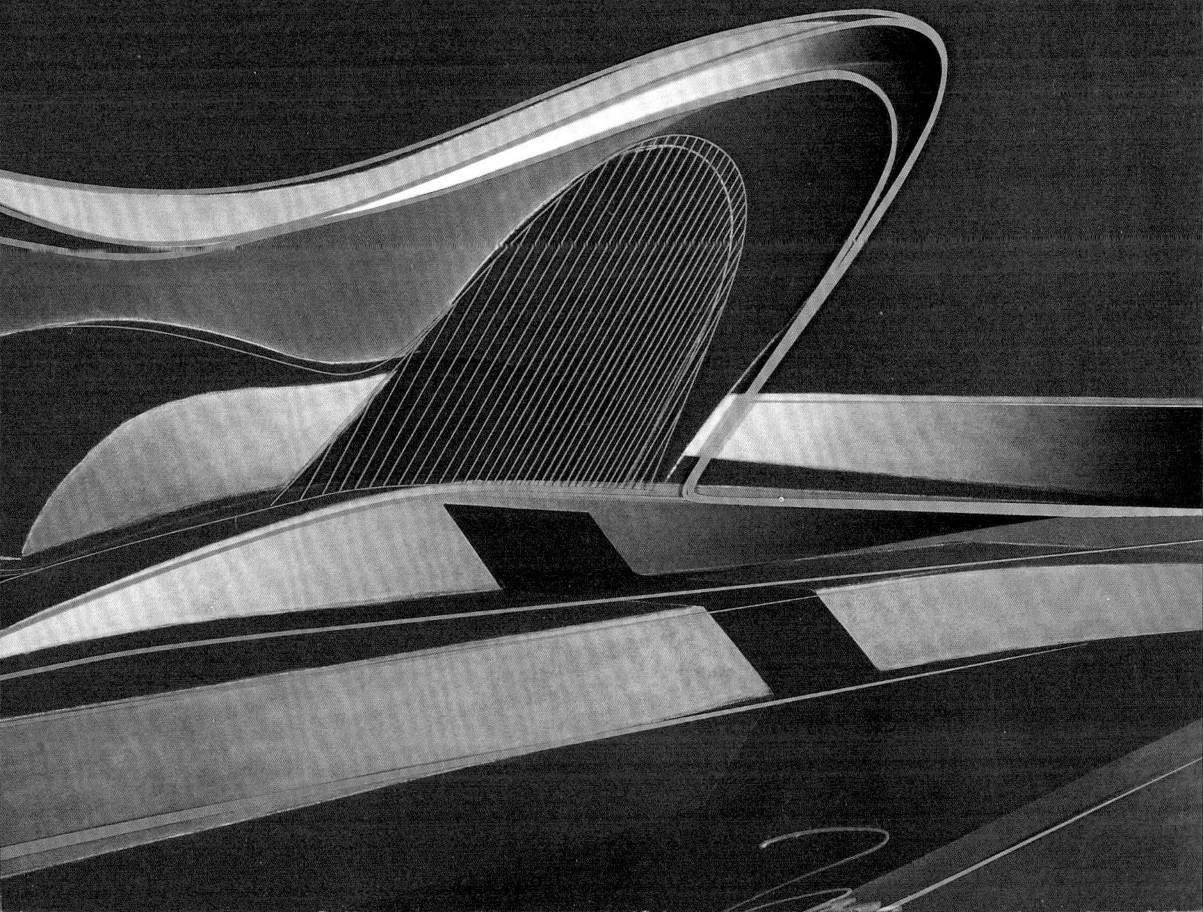

Dame Zaha Hadid DBE RA (b. 1950)
London Aquatics Centre, 2012
Mixed media on paper and acetate
41.4 x 57.9 cm
RCIN 212739

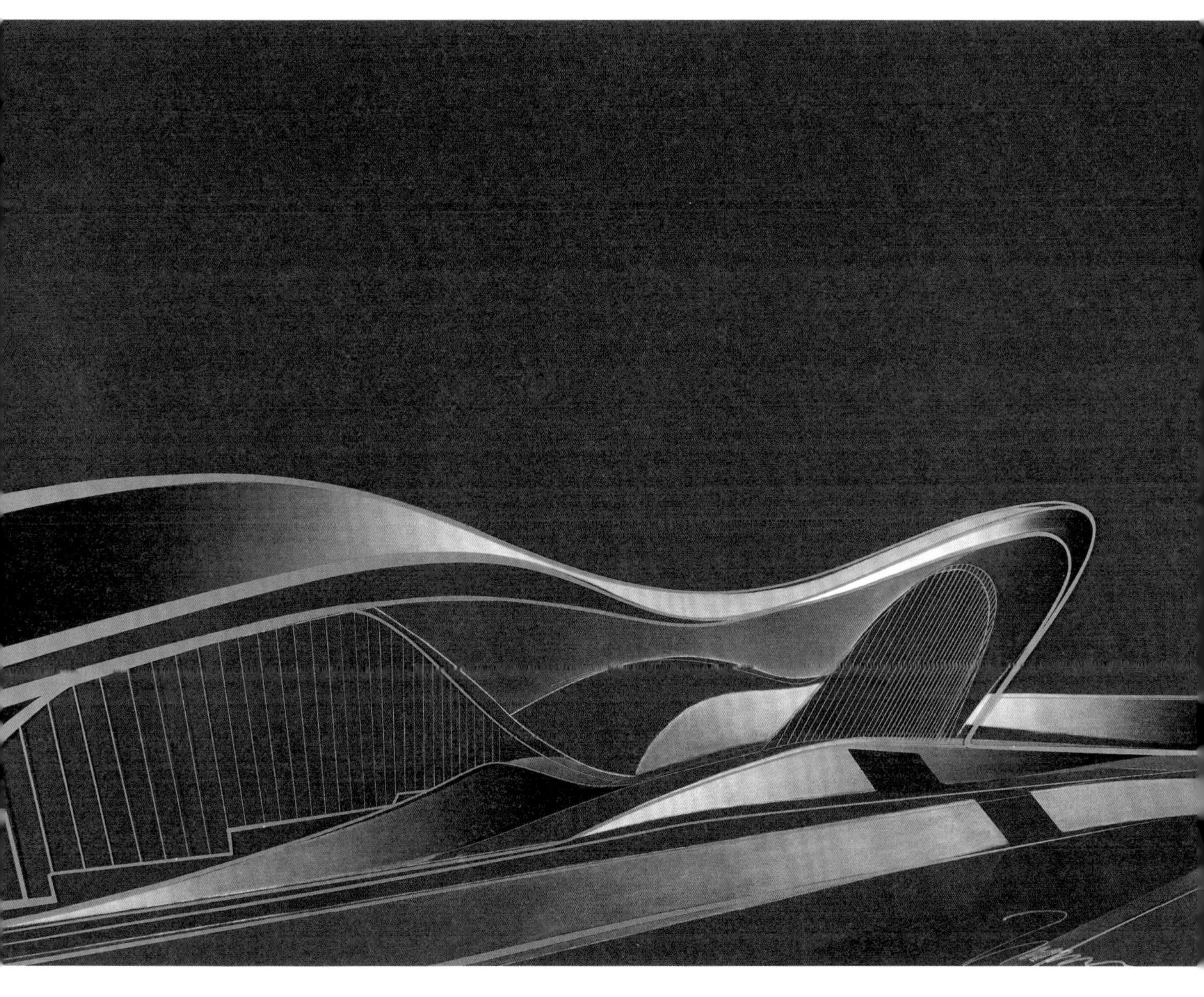

Nigel Hall RA (b. 1943)
Drawing 1591, 2012
Gouache and charcoal
42.0 x 61.3 cm
RCIN 212740

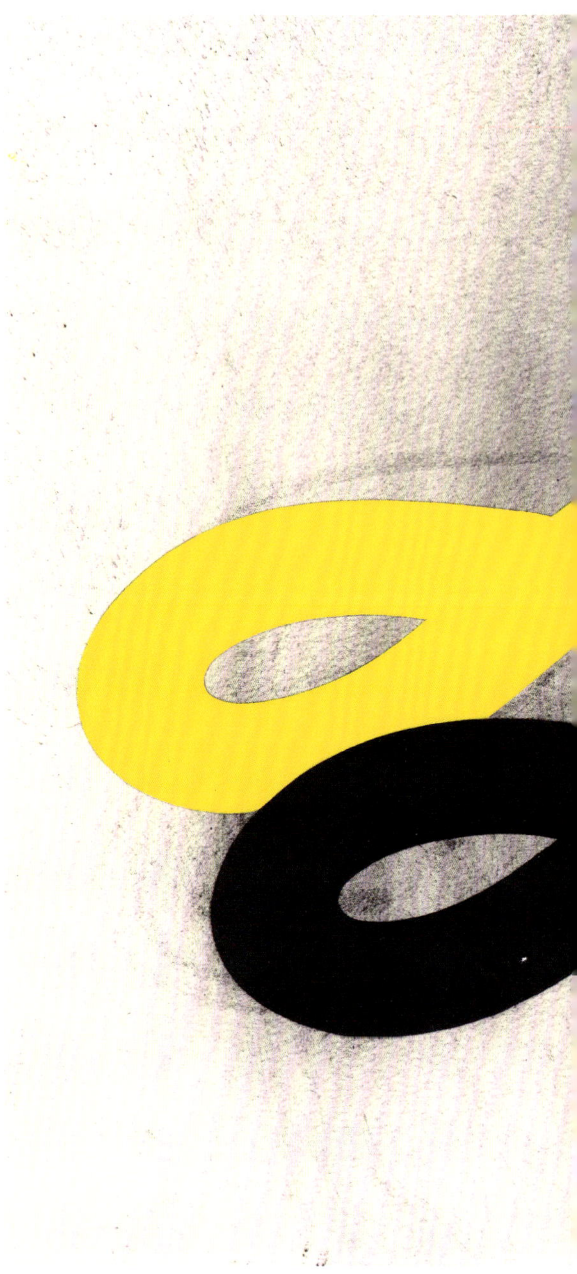

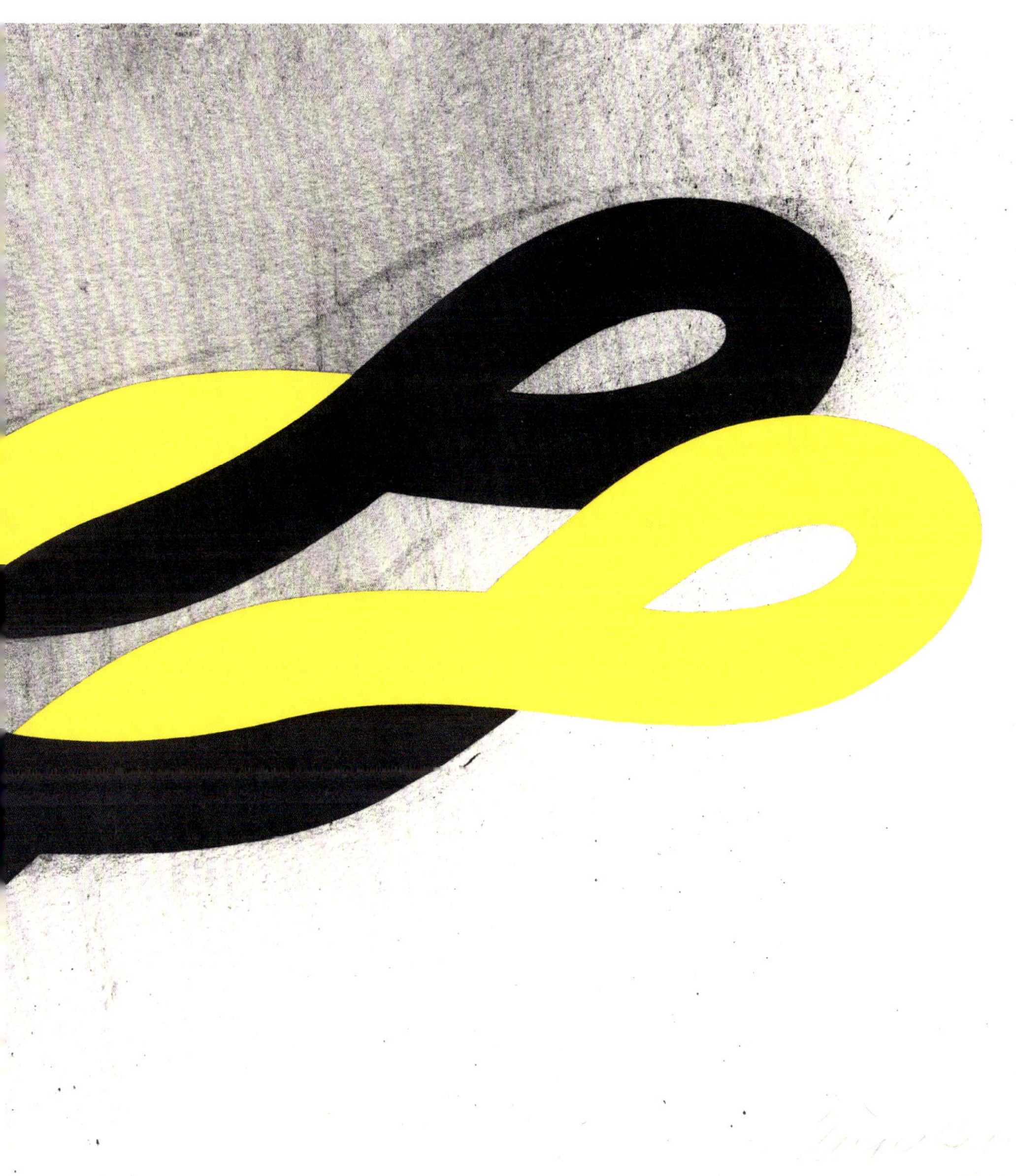

David Hockney OM CH RA (b. 1937)
2012 Queen Elizabeth II Diamond Jubilee, 2012
Inkjet printed iPad drawing
50.8 x 35.6 cm (sheet)
35.5 x 26.7 cm (image)
RCIN 212741

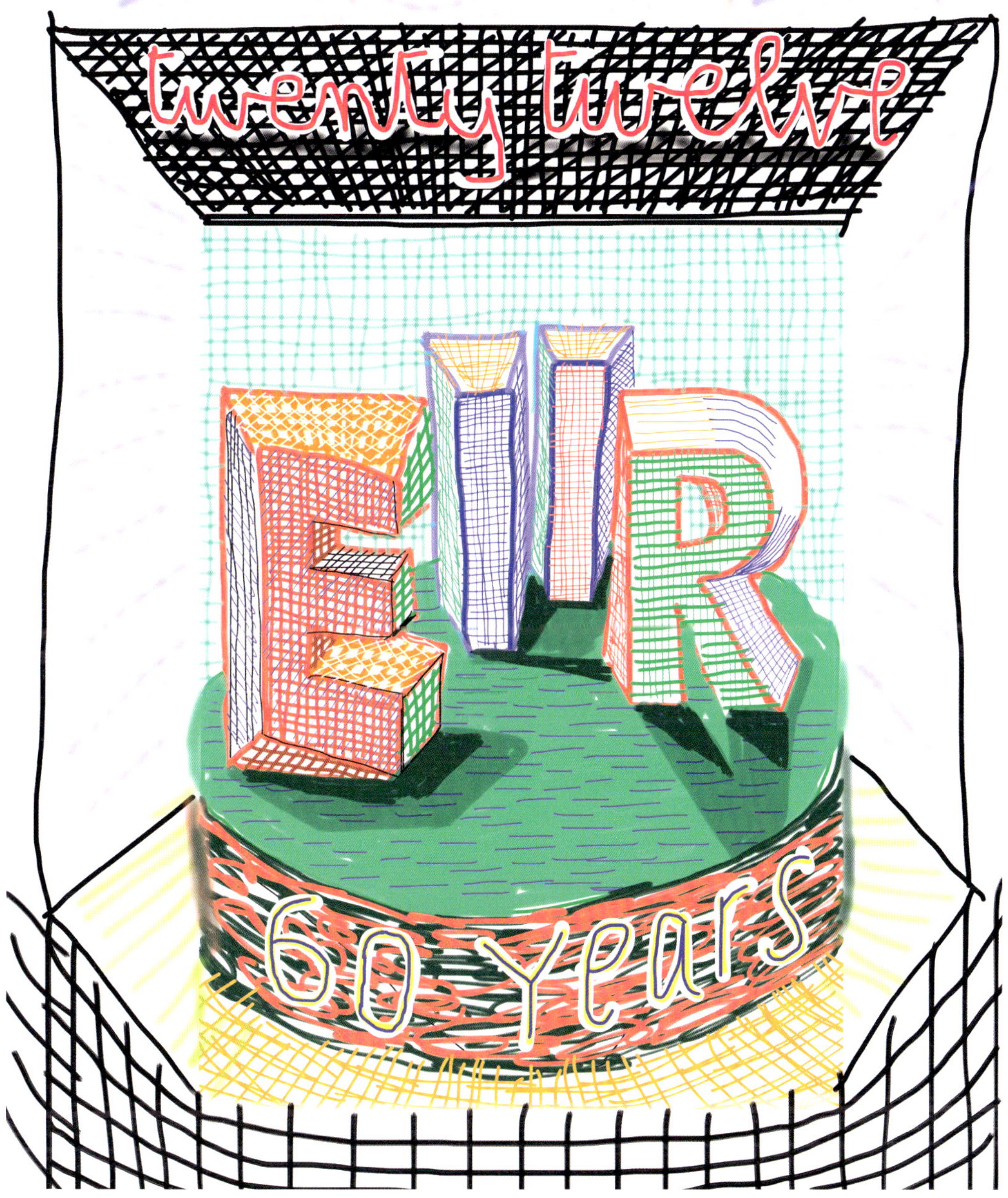
2012
twenty twelve
EIIR
60 years

Sir Michael Hopkins CBE RA (b. 1935)
Buckingham Palace Ticket Office, 1995
Inkjet print
46.9 x 64.8 cm
Photographer: Tim Soar
RCIN 212742

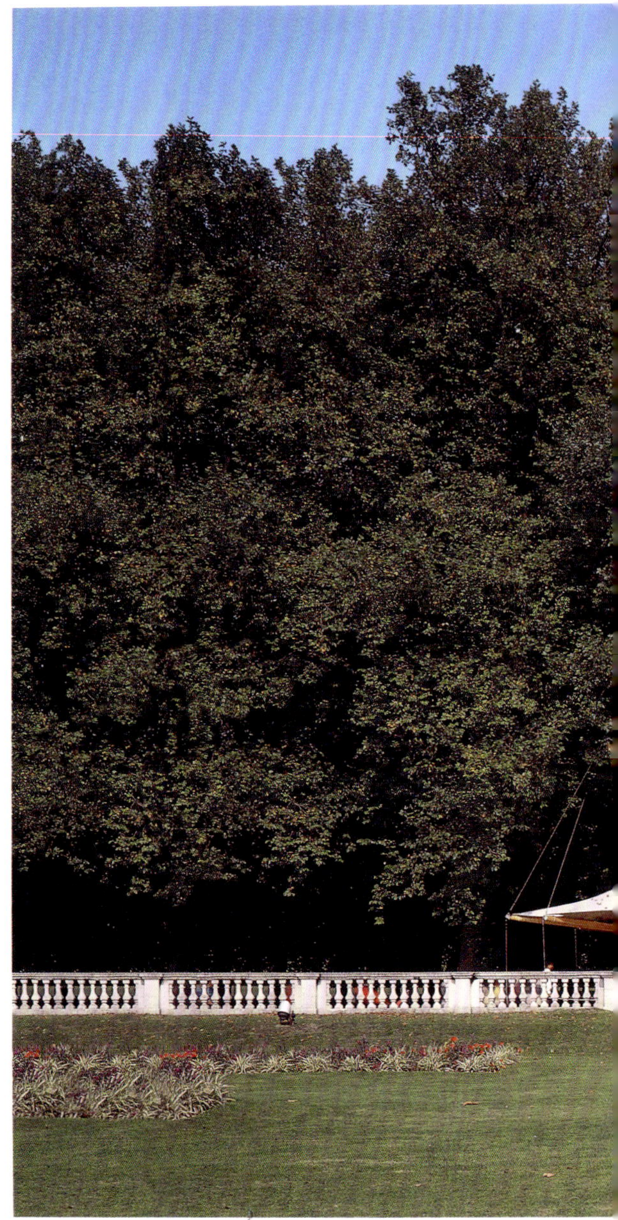

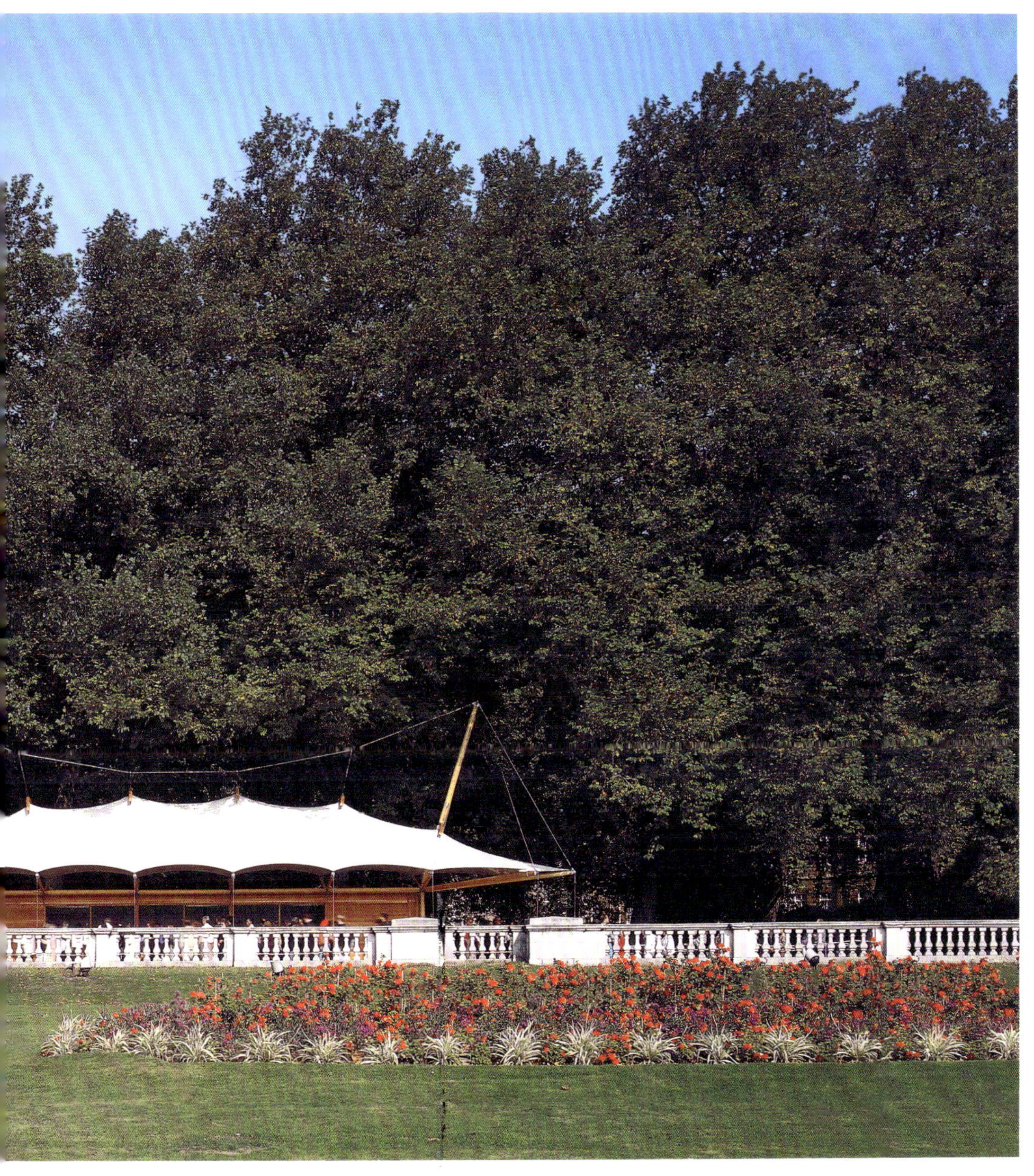

Michael Hopkins '95

Ken Howard OBE RA (b. 1932)

Florentine Farmhouse, 1959

Pencil, watercolour and gouache

38.2 x 53.9 cm

RCIN 212743

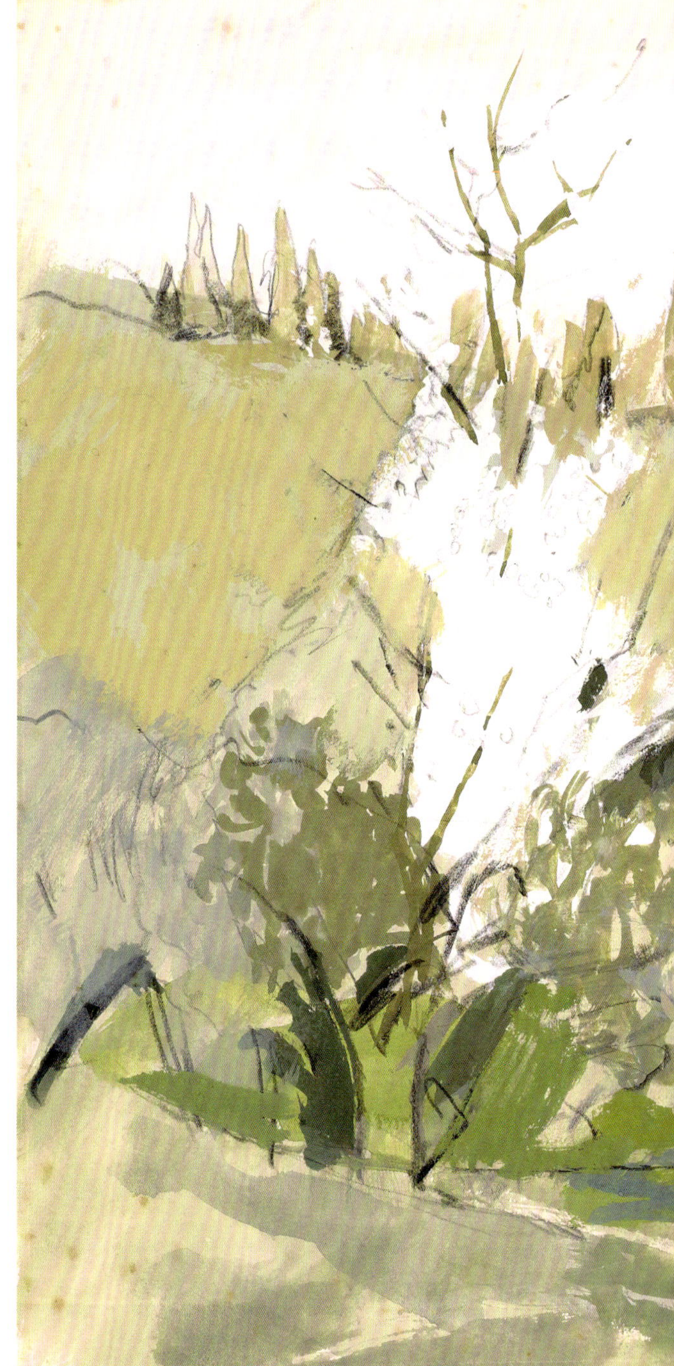

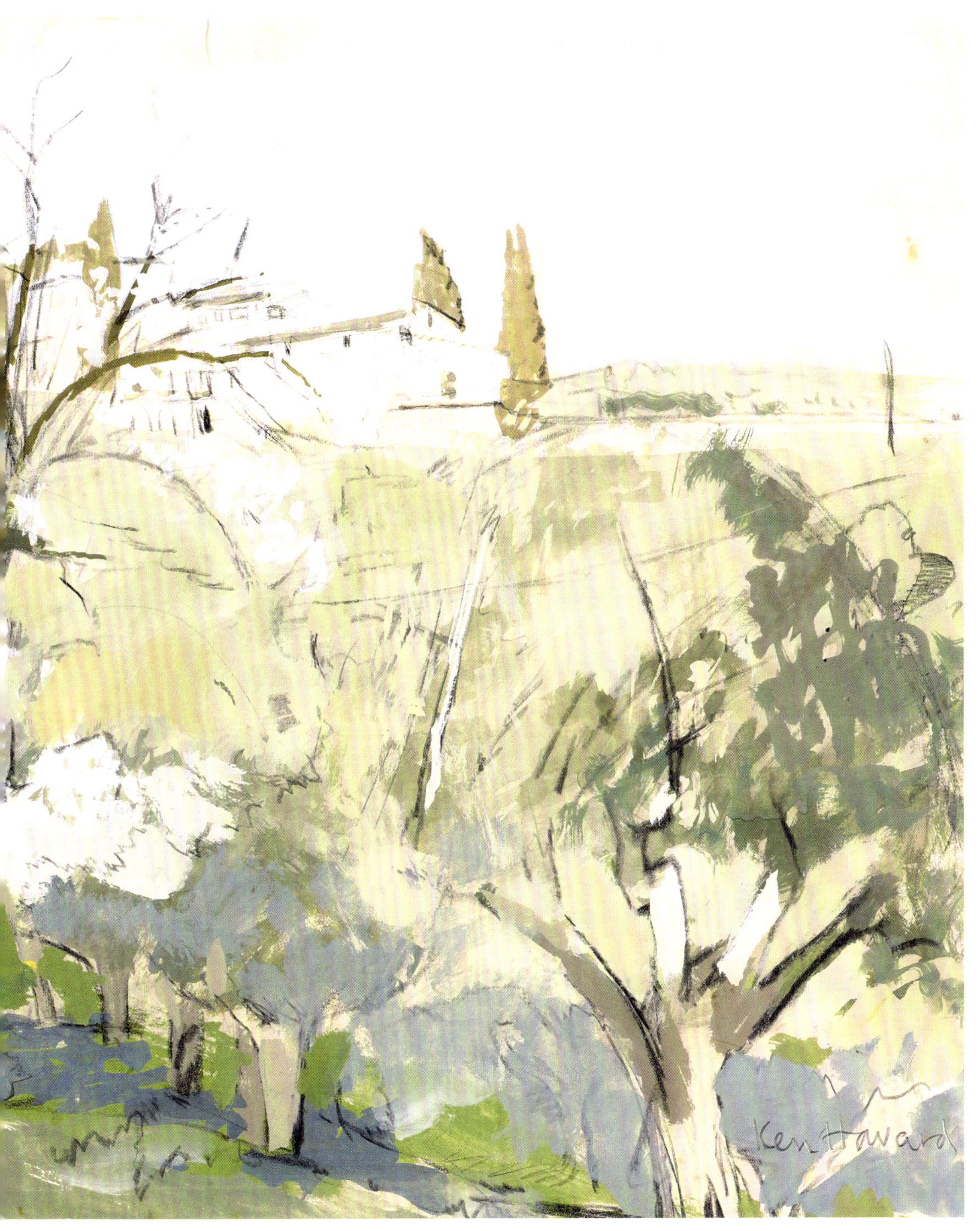
Ken Howard

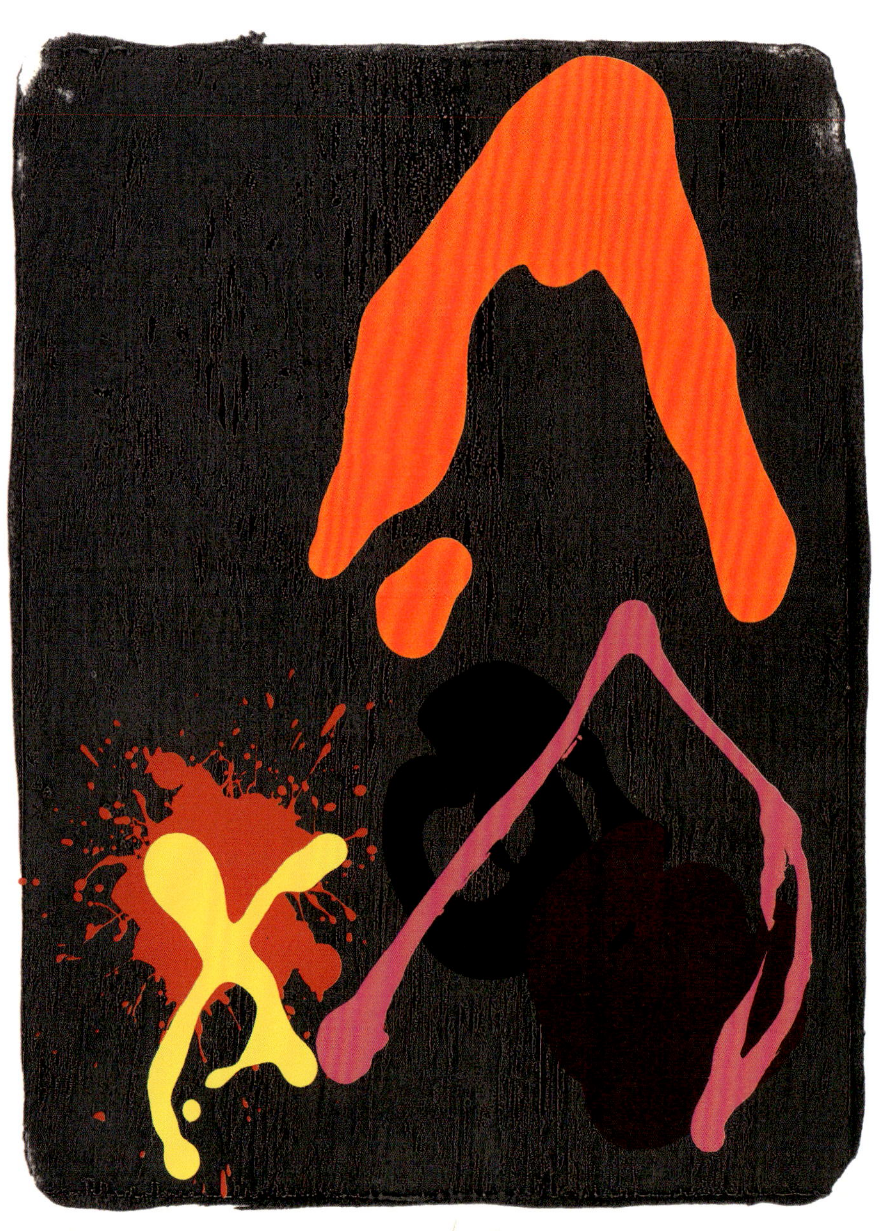

John Hoyland RA (1934–2011)
Spirit Side, 1997
Screenprint with woodblock
58.4 x 47.3 cm
RCIN 212744

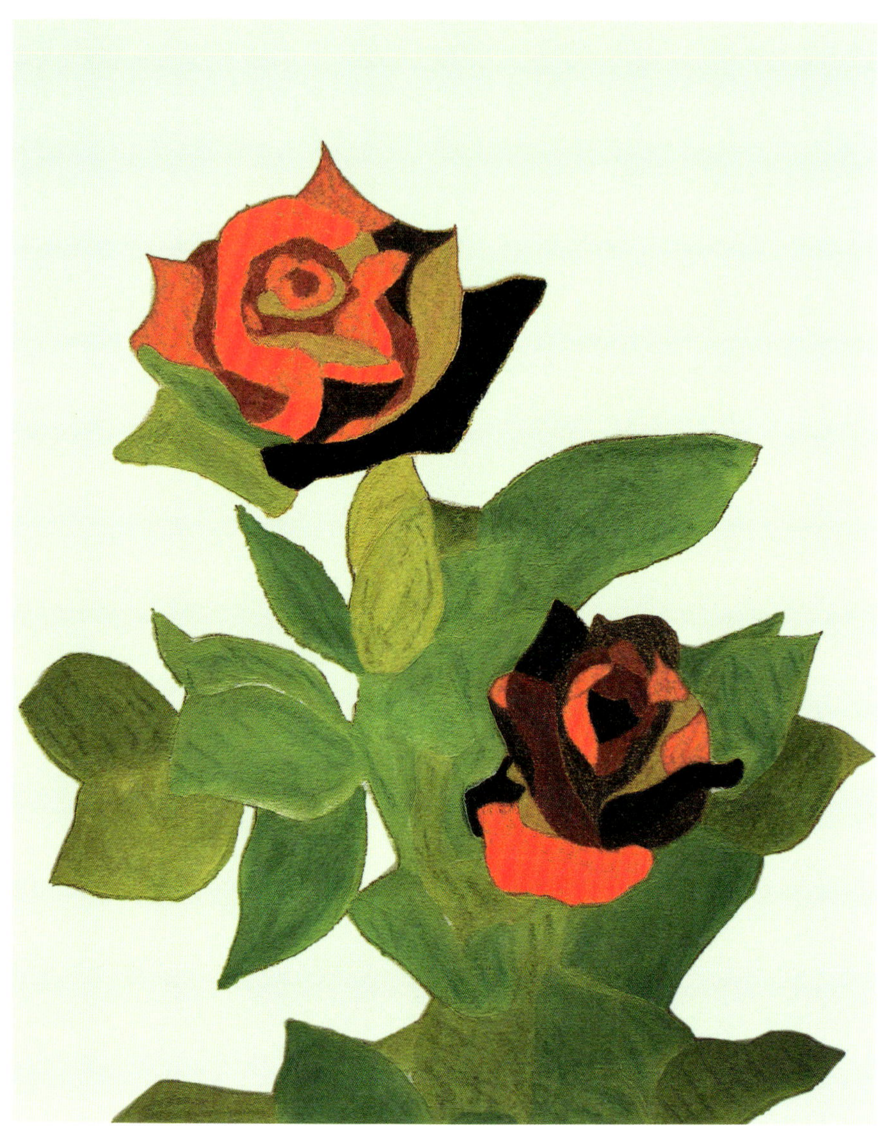

Gary Hume RA (b. 1962)
Duel, 2010
Giclée print
46.2 x 39.0 cm
RCIN 212994

'The image was commissioned by Sir Elton John, for the edition of the *Independent* on World Aids Day, 1 December 2010. It appeared on the front cover of the paper. I chose a rose because it's a beautiful thing that blooms and then dies. I bought some coloured pencils called Skin Colours of the World. I used them as a palette for the work in gesso and chalk.'

Professor Paul Huxley RA (b. 1938)

XIX.47, 2012

Acrylic over pencil and pen

65.9 x 46.9 cm

RCIN 212745

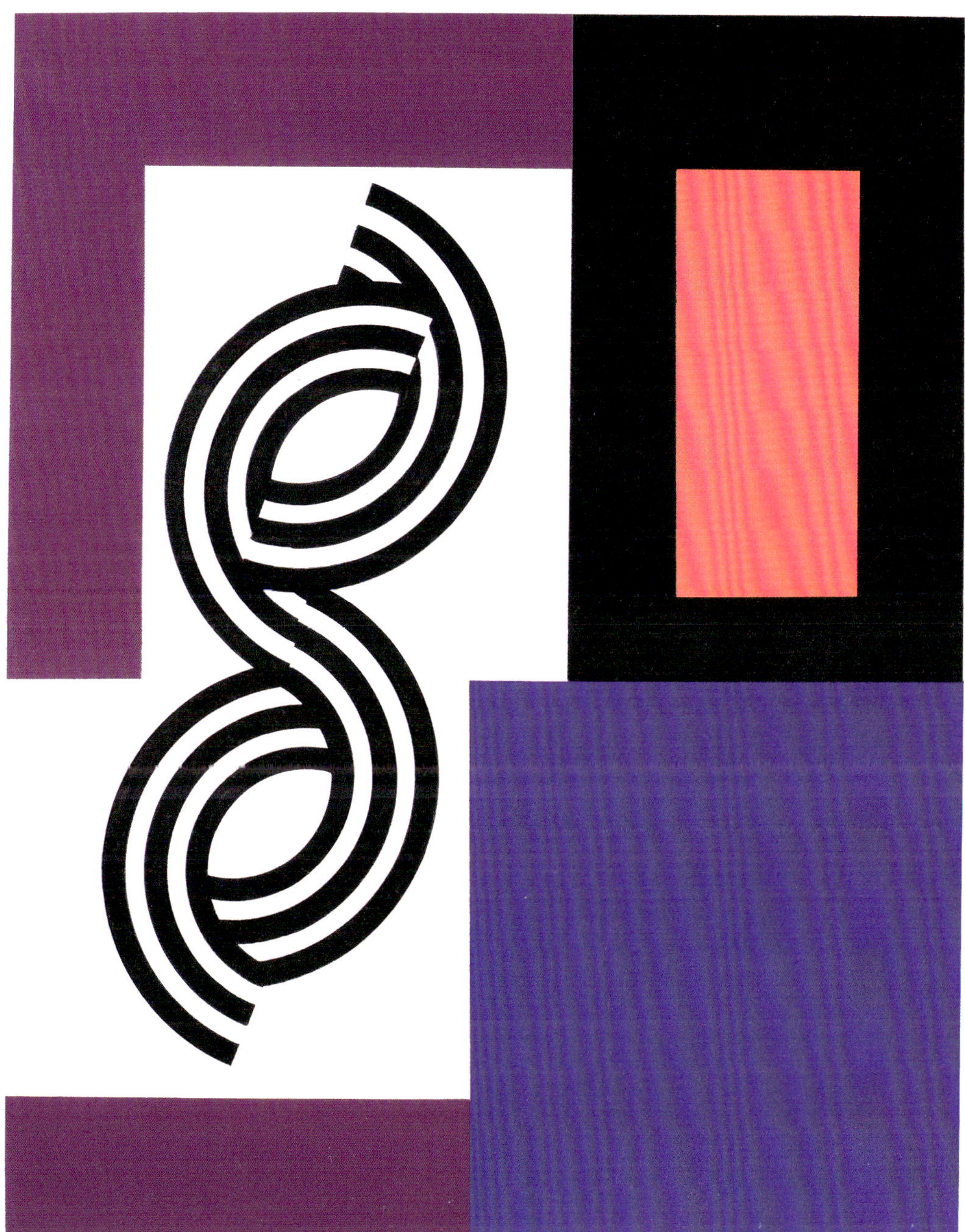

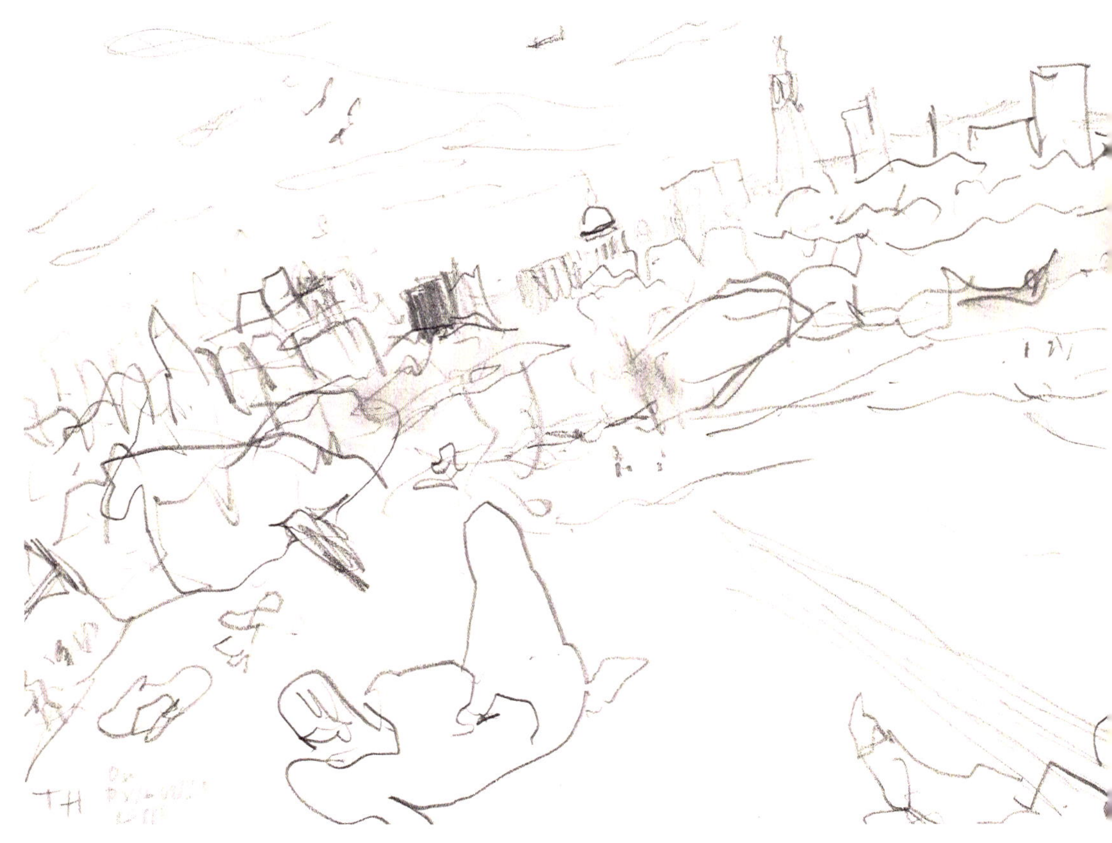

Timothy Hyman RA (b. 1946)

On Primrose Hill, 2010

Pencil

14.7 x 42.0 cm

RCIN 212746

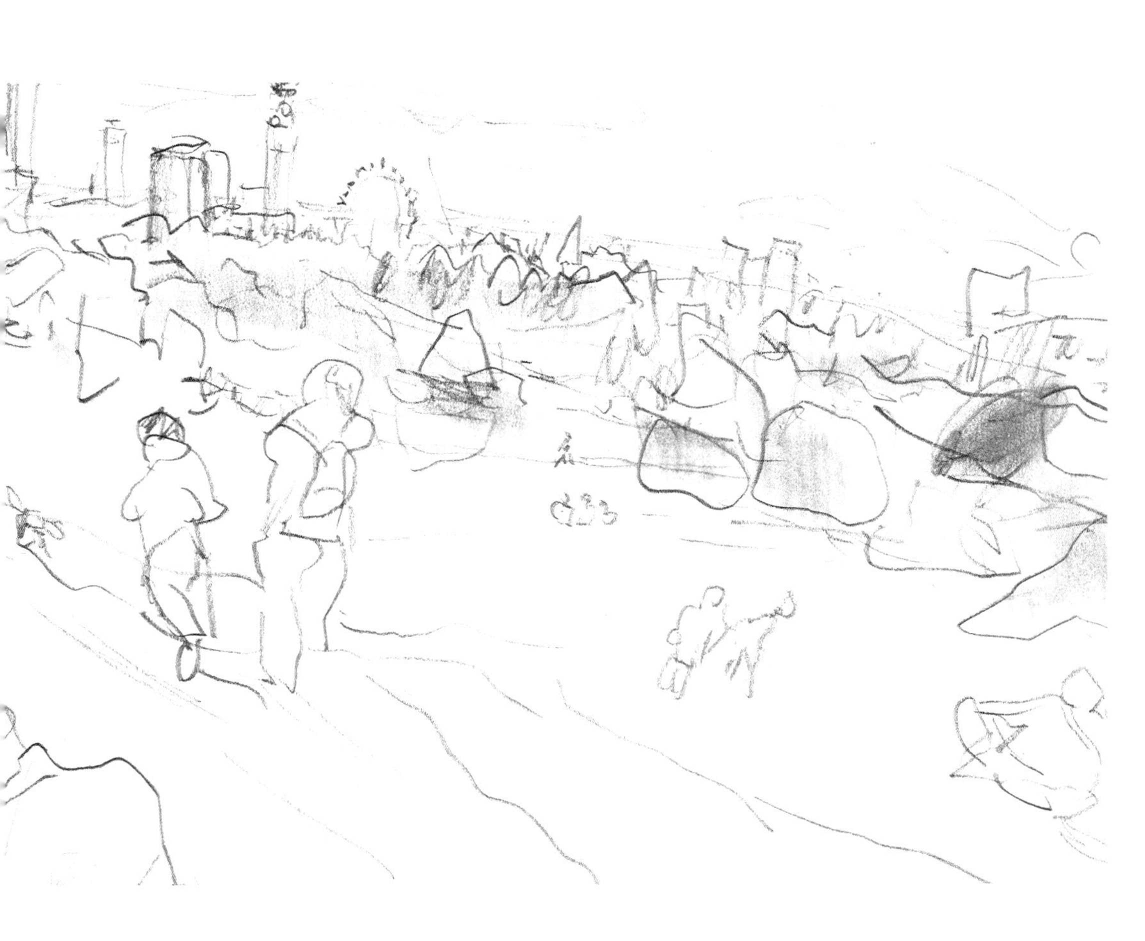

Albert Irvin OBE RA (b. 1922)

Borough I, 2004

Screenprint

52.0 x 43.5 cm

RCIN 212747

Printed at Advanced Graphics, London

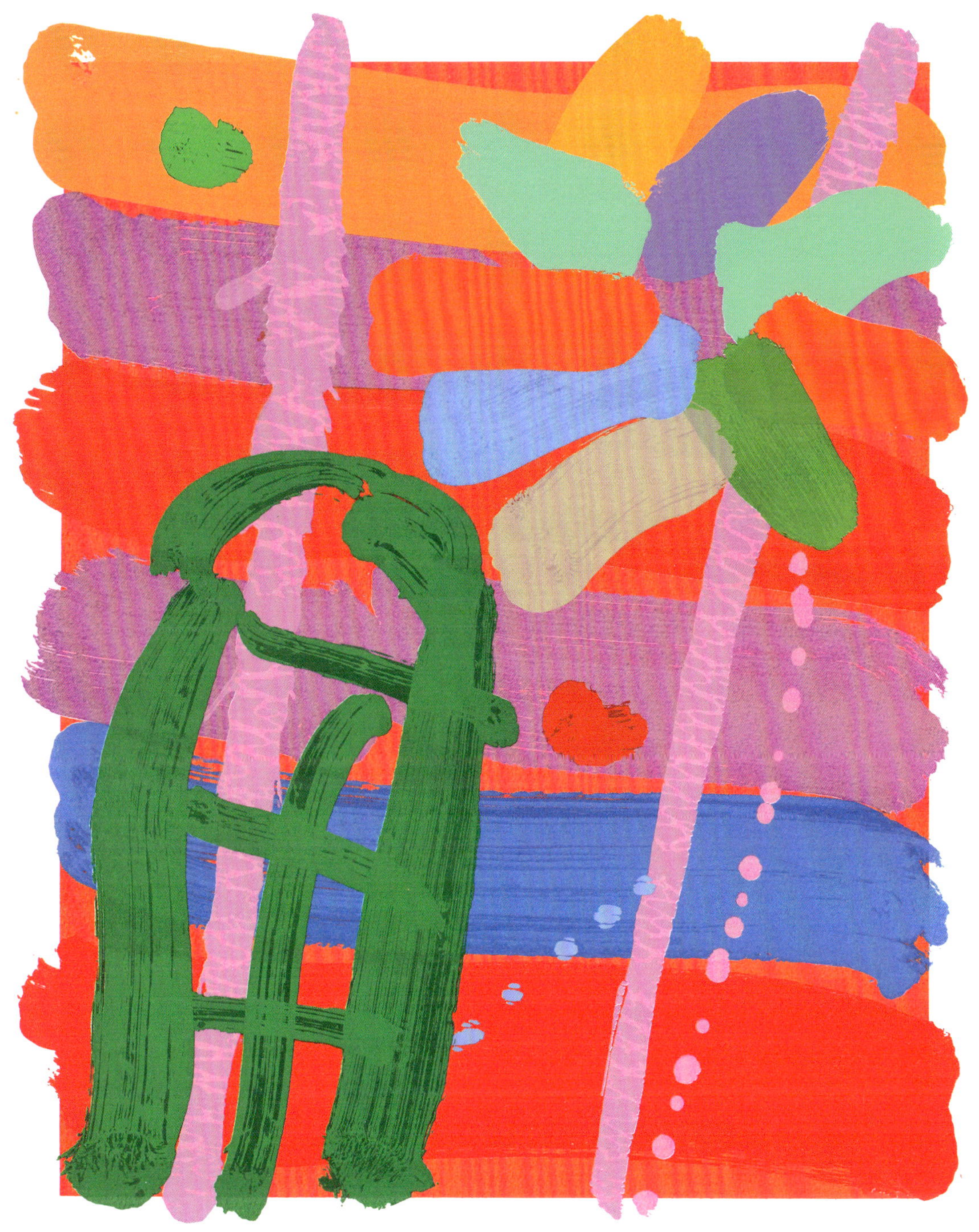

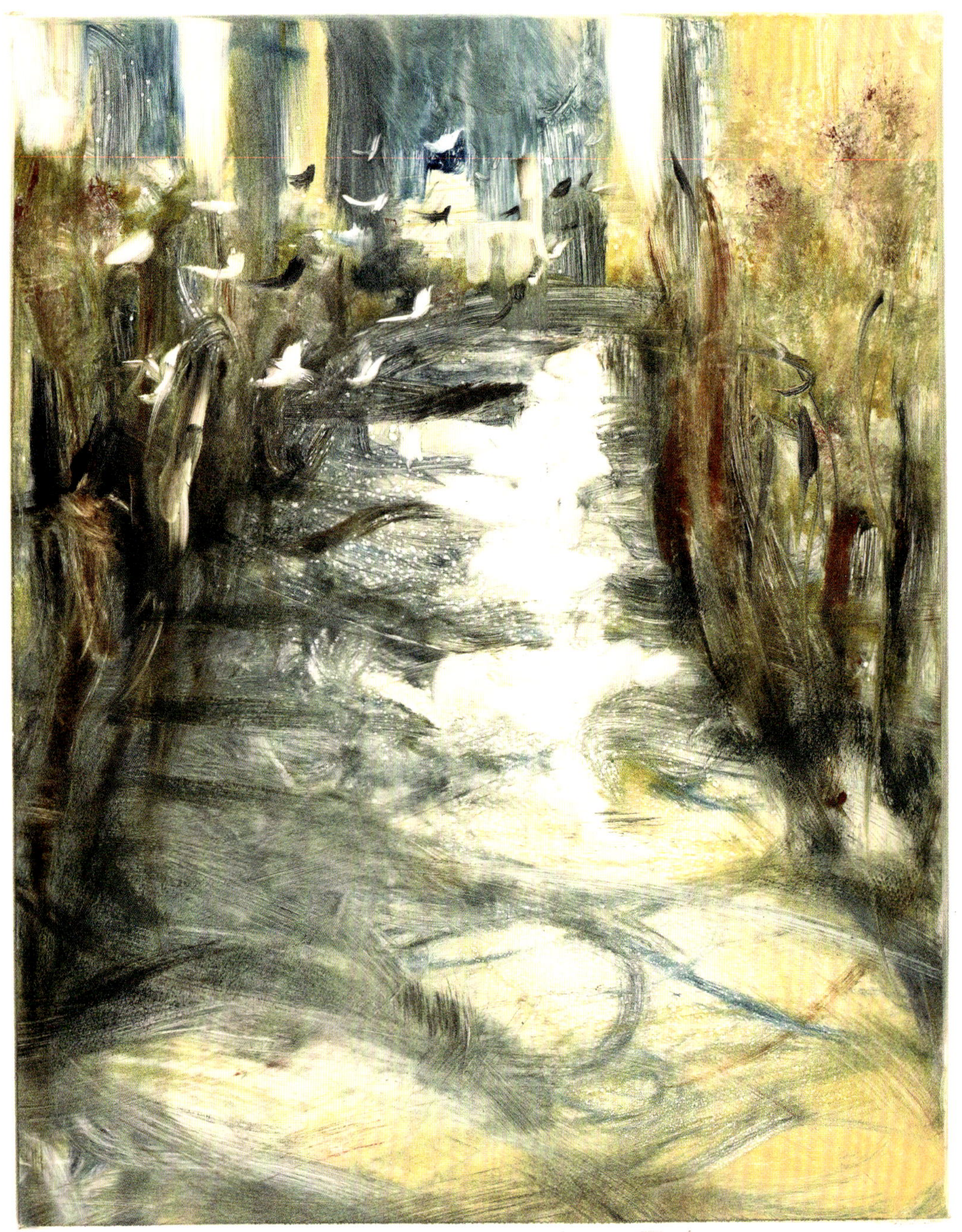

Opposite page:

Bill Jacklin RA (b. 1943)

Road with Birds IV, 2012

Monotype

68.1 x 55.7 cm

RCIN 212748

Overleaf:

Tess Jaray RA (b. 1937)

Terrace, 1991

Etching and aquatint, printed in green

38.2 x 56.7 cm (sheet)

21.8 x 40.7 cm (plate)

RCIN 212749

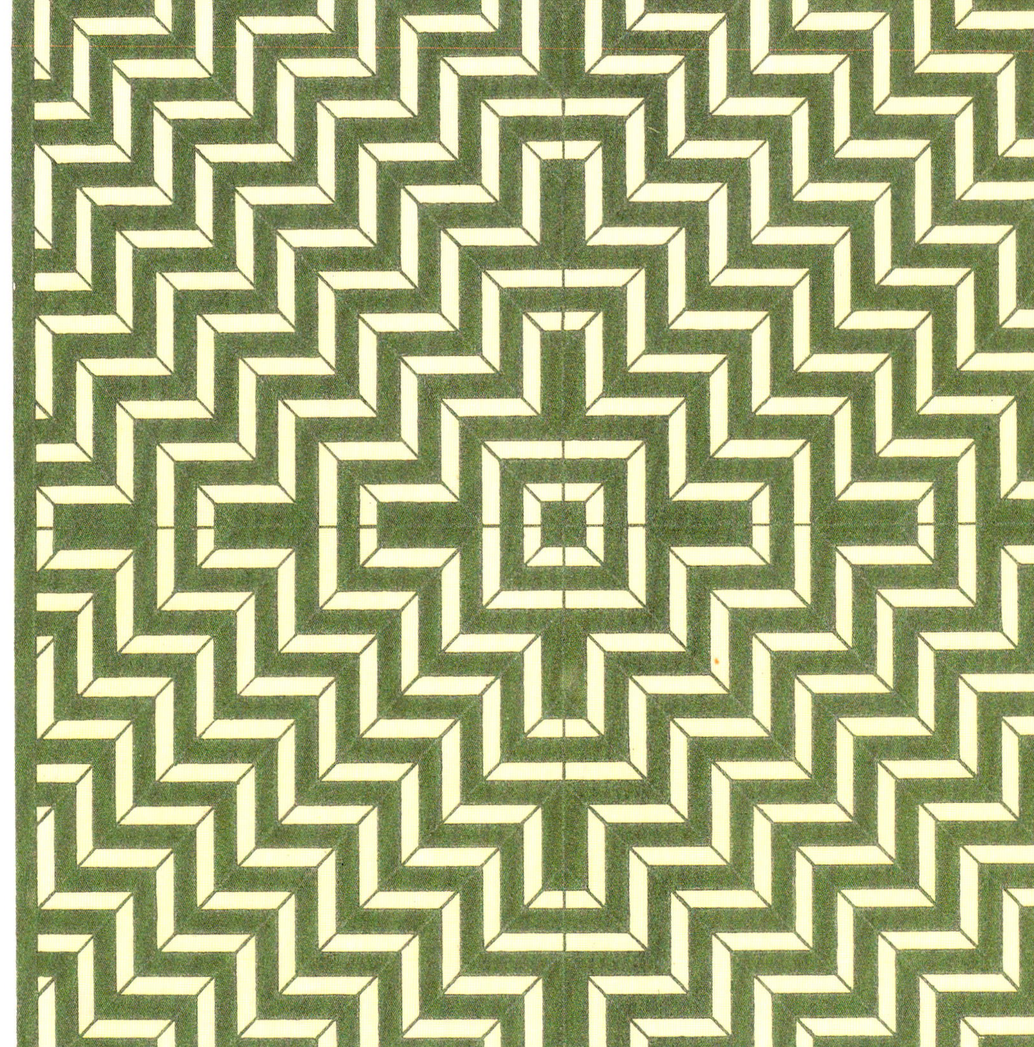

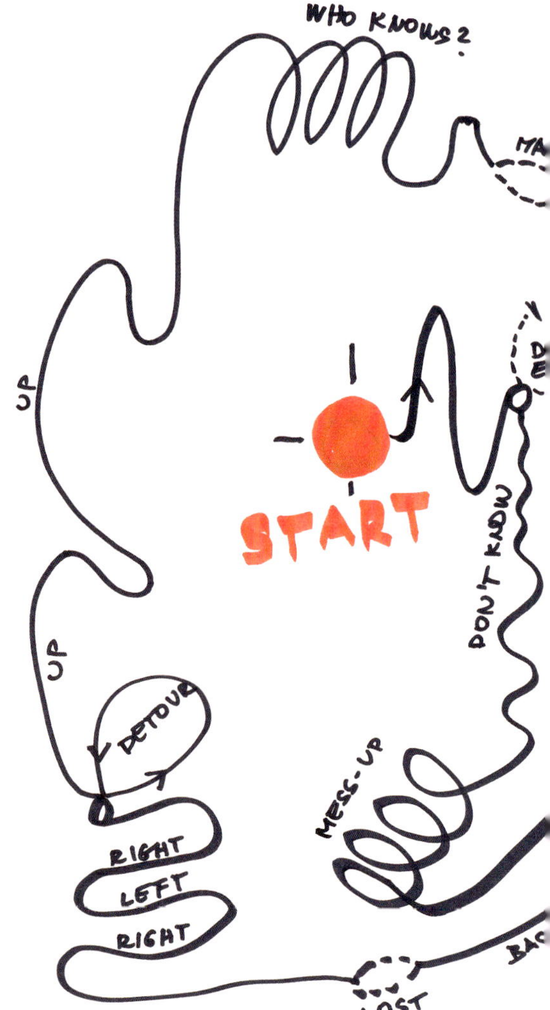

Eva Jiřičná CBE RA (b. 1939)
How we do it, 2012
Marker pen
45.0 x 64.0 cm
RCIN 212750

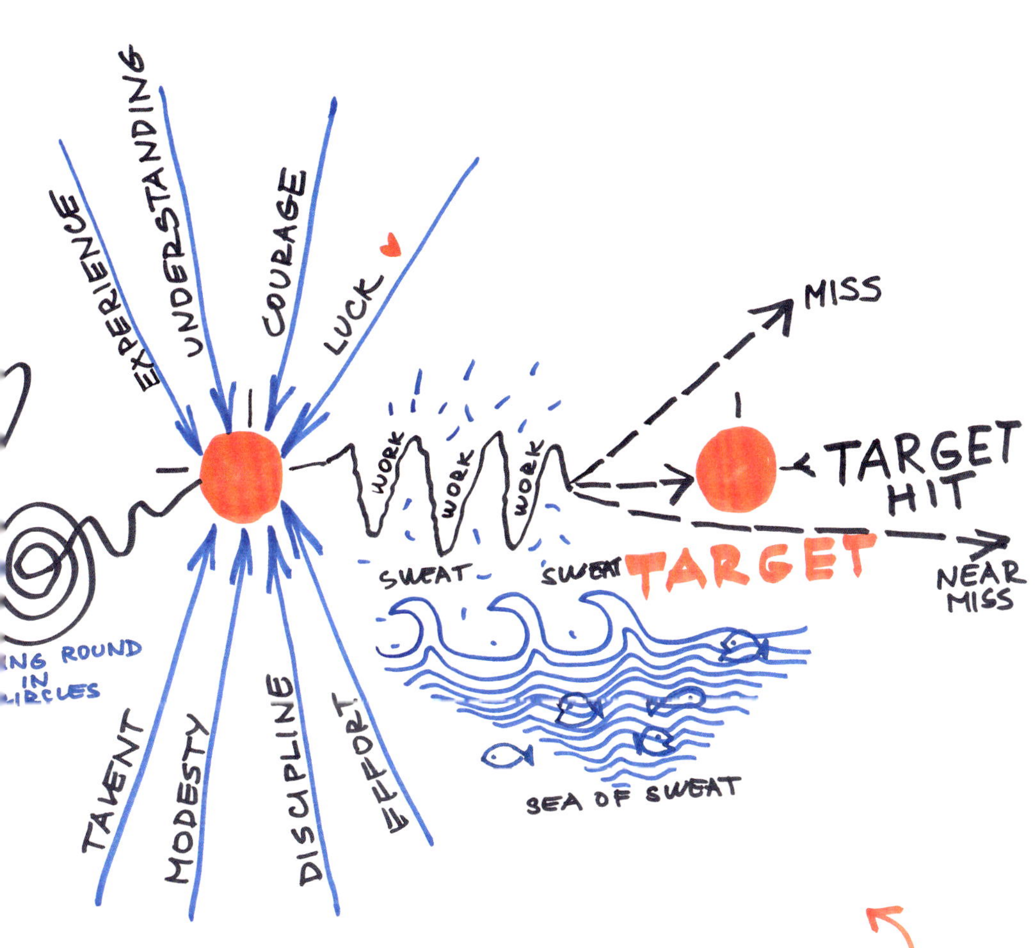

HOW WE DO IT

With admiration
30/7/12

Allen Jones RA (b. 1937)

Kiri te Kanawa as 'Butterfly' for 'Understanding Opera'/Thames TV, 1982

Pencil, pen and ink and coloured pencils

28.3 x 39.0 cm

RCIN 212751

Overleaf:

Anish Kapoor CBE RA (b. 1954)

Untitled, 2011

Gouache

33.0 x 51.0 cm

RCIN 212752

[illegible] Butterfly [illegible] baby

- looking out

- [illegible]

[illegible]

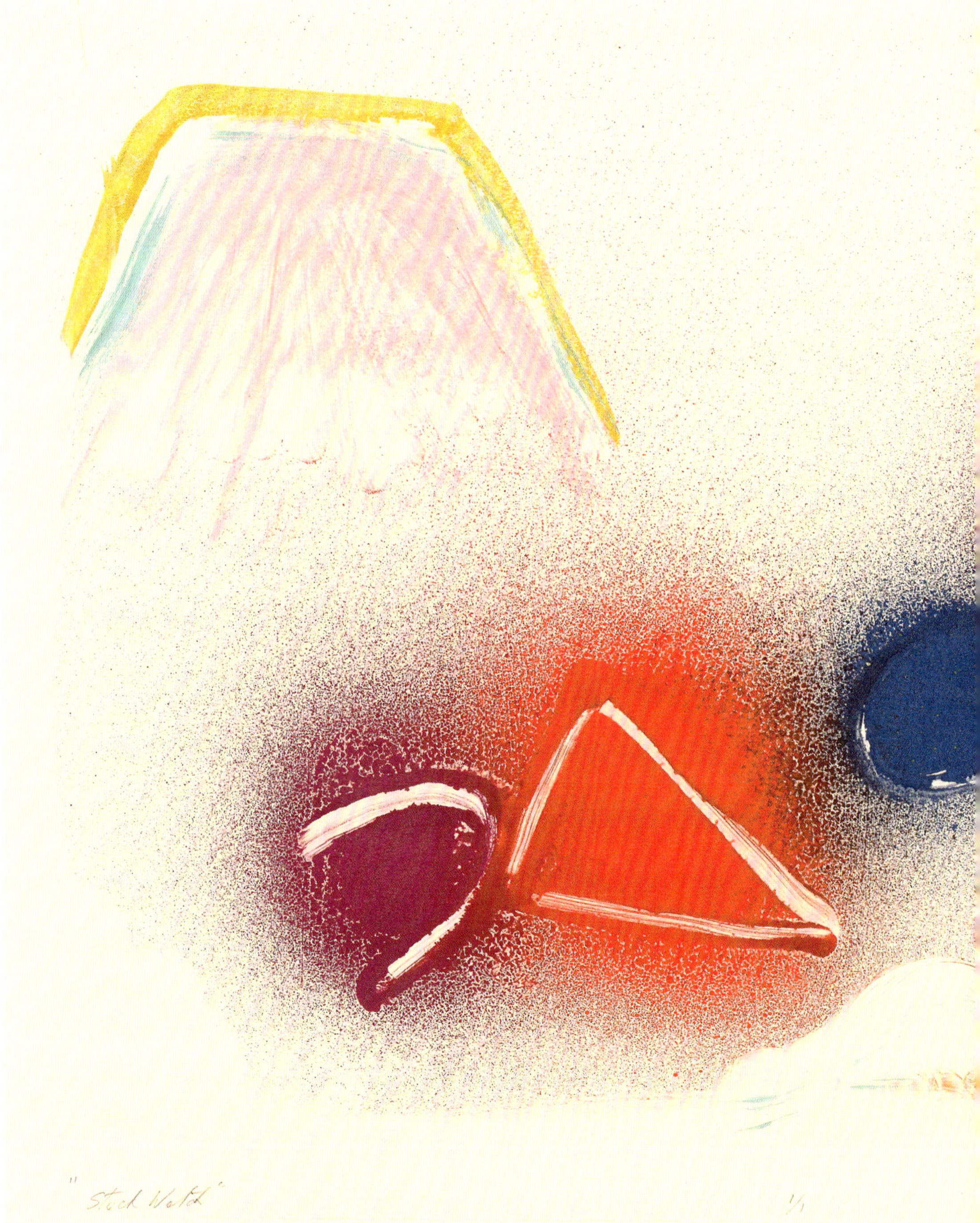
"Stock Watch"
1/1

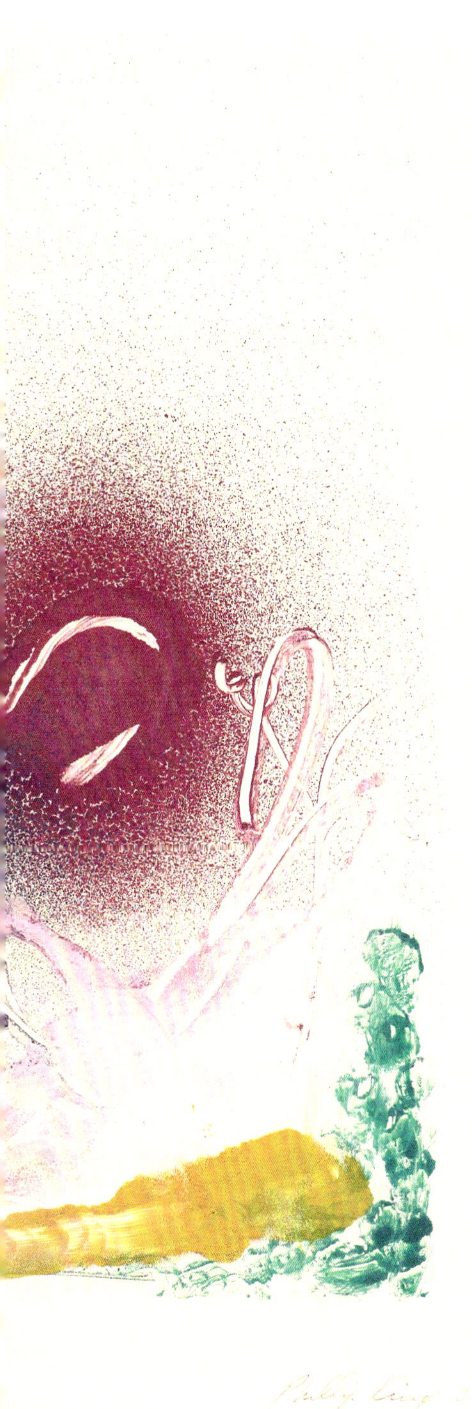

Professor Phillip King CBE PPRA (b. 1934)

Stack Watch, 2011

Monotype

41.7 x 51.7 cm

RCIN 212753

'The symbol of the Isle of Man has been with me since earliest days as a Manxman. I have used the Triskelion as an inspiration for two major sculptures, including one that greets air passengers as they arrive on the island. Since Her Majesty is The Lord of Man I could think of no more suitable work of mine to present as a Royal Academician.'

Professor Bryan Kneale RA (b. 1930)
The legs of Man, 2003
Inkjet print
48.2 x 42.2 cm
RCIN 212754

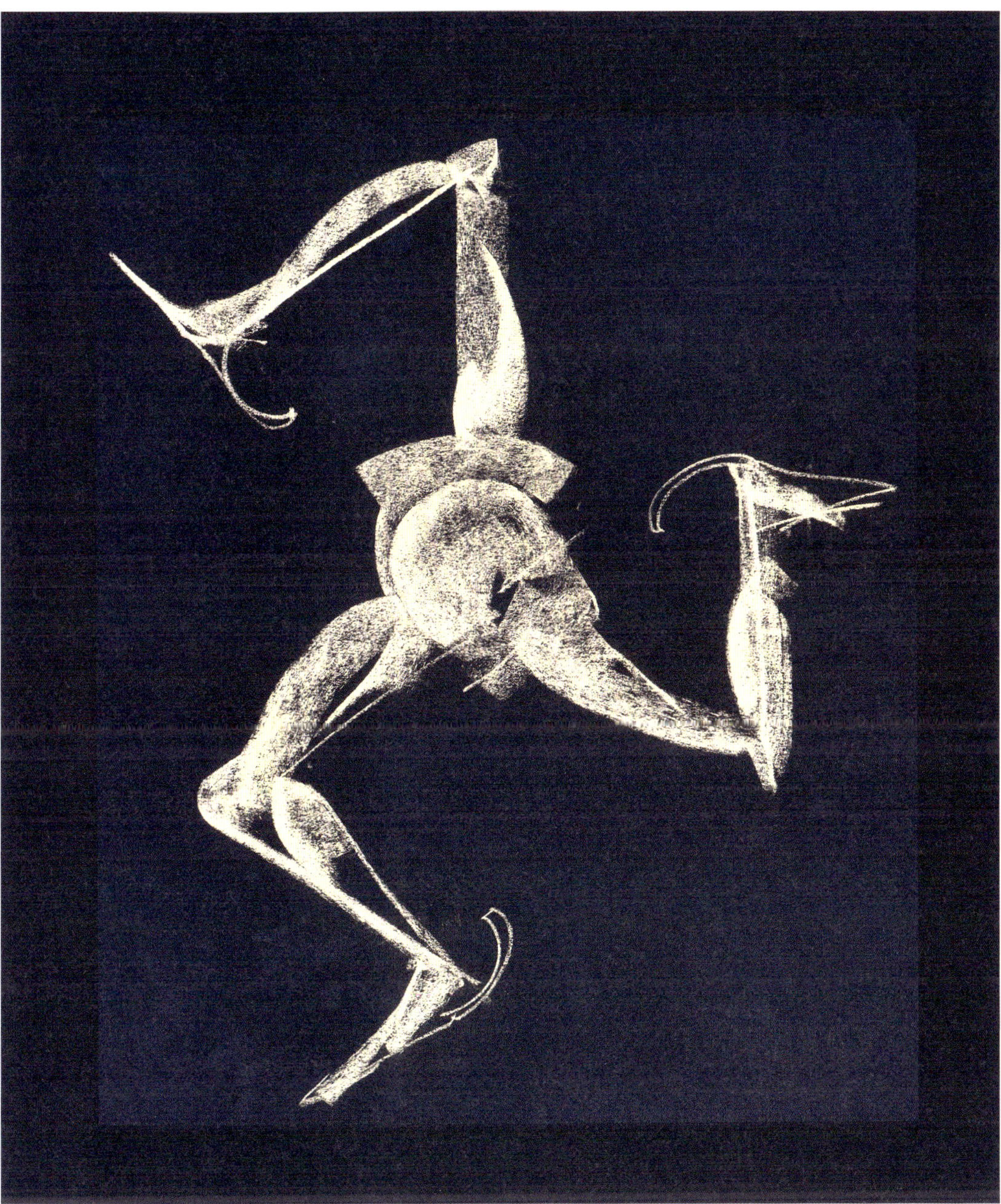

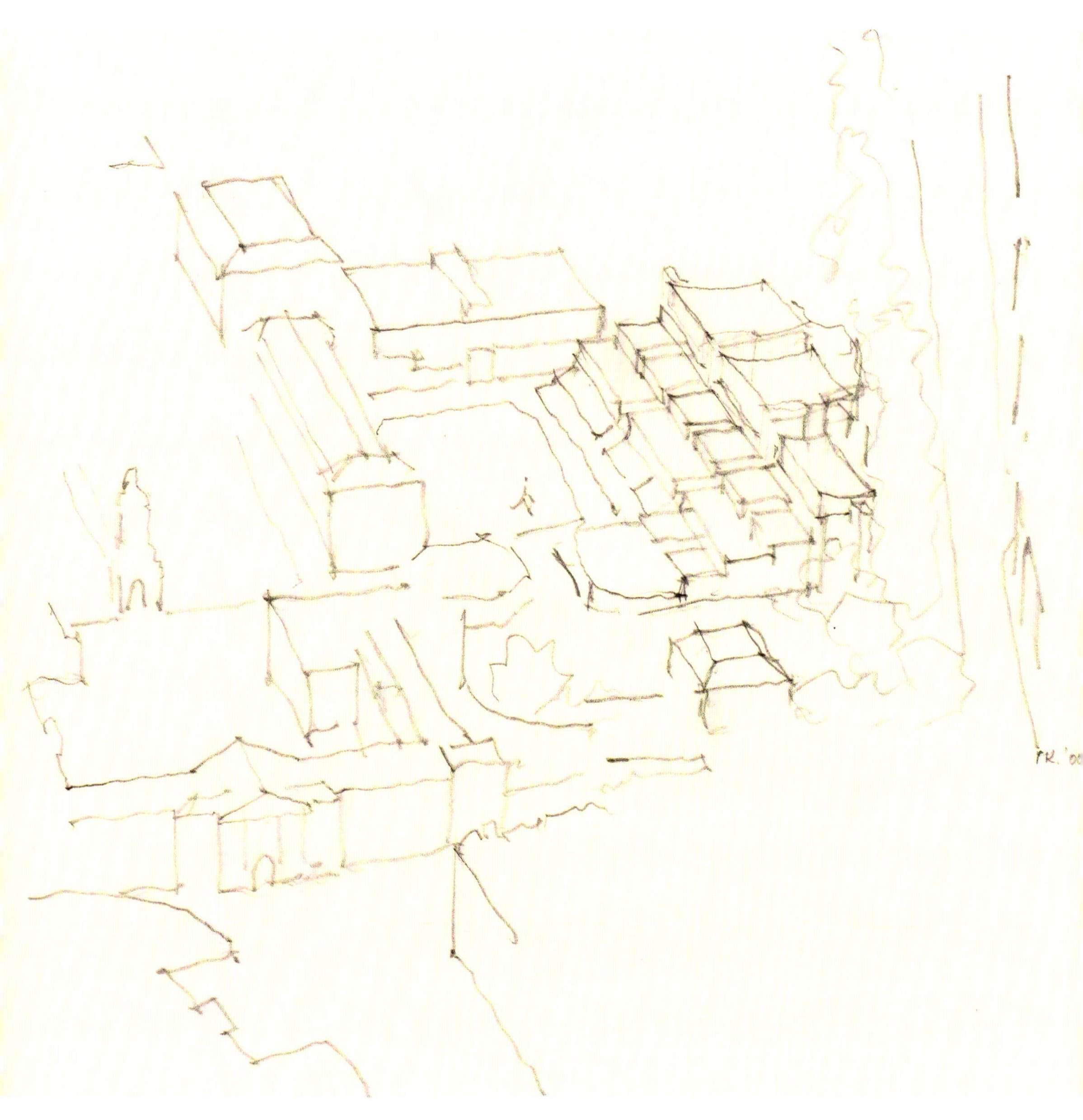

Paul Koralek CBE RA (b. 1933)
Sketch for Extension to Arts Building, Trinity College Dublin, 2000
Pencil on tracing paper
20.9 x 26.4 cm
RCIN 212755

Sonia Lawson RA (b. 1934)

Twin Forms, 2003

Screenprint

62.5 x 44.9 cm

RCIN 212756

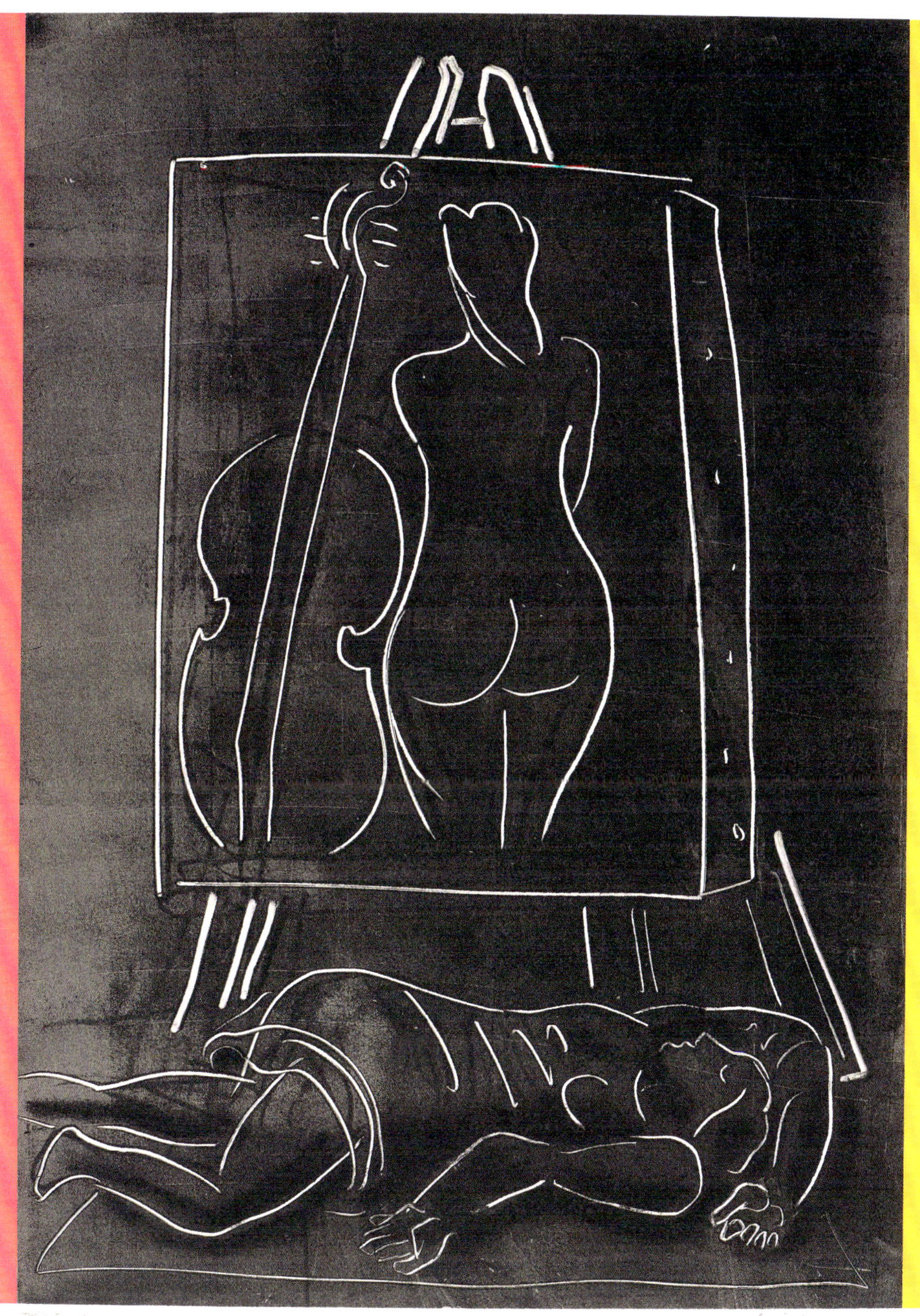

Sonia Lawson

Christopher Le Brun PRA (b. 1951)

The Complete Journey, 2011

Watercolour

50.2 x 59.1 cm

RCIN 212757

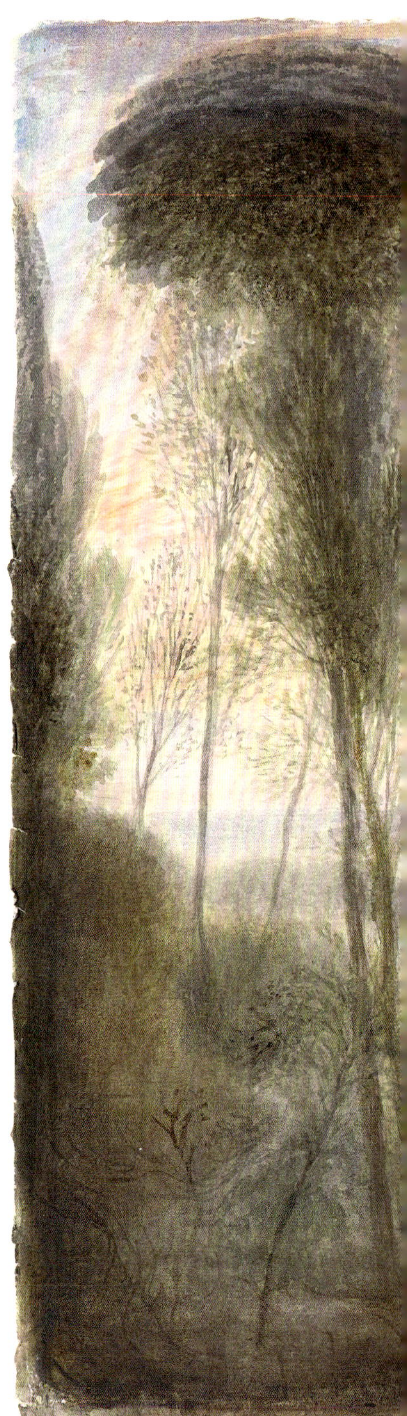

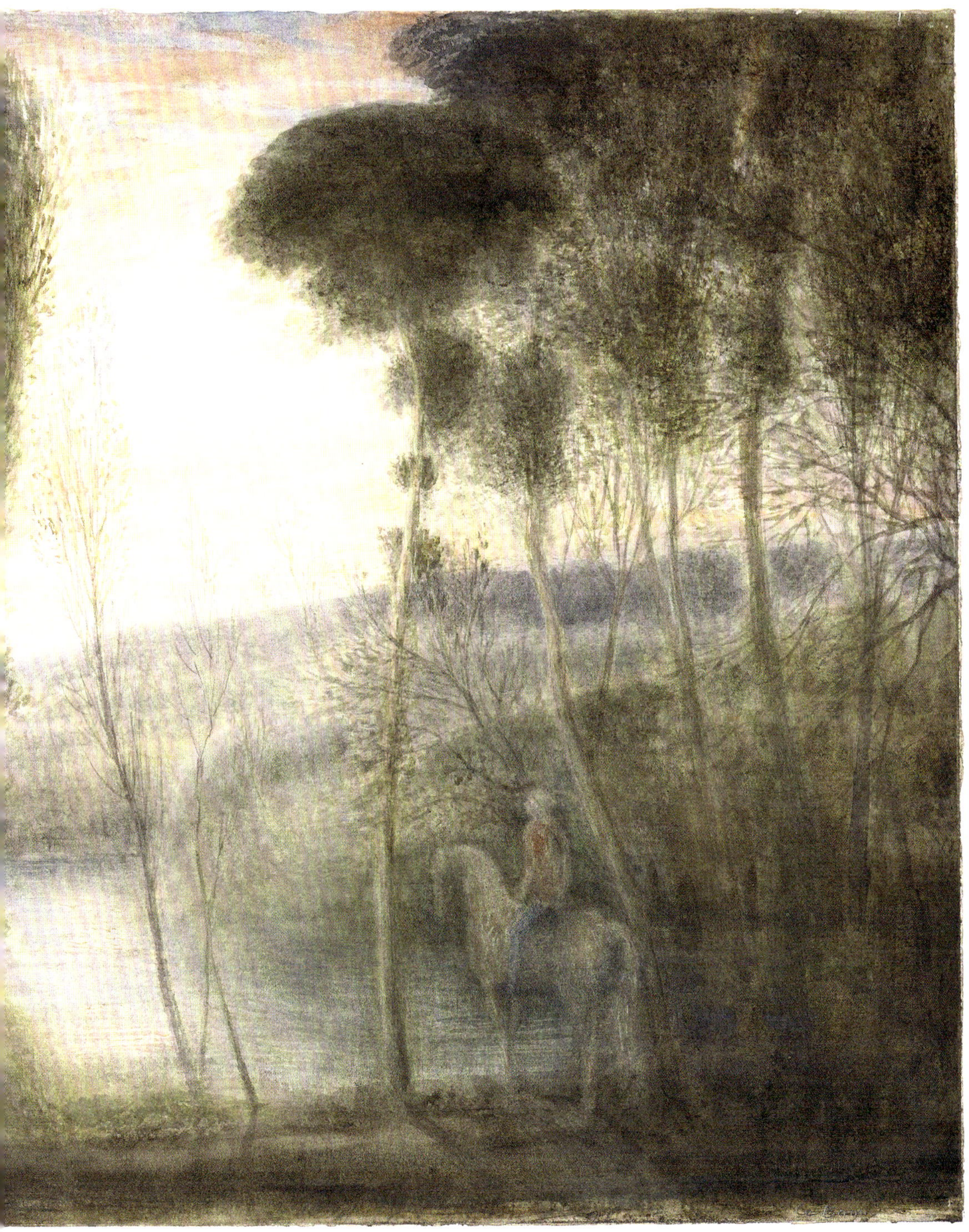

Richard Long CBE RA (b. 1945)
A Day's Walk across Dartmoor, 2001
A Riverside Walk up the Avon, 2008
Screenprint
49.9 x 38.3 cm
RCIN 212758

A DAY'S WALK ACROSS DARTMOOR
FOLLOWING THE DRIFT OF THE CLOUDS

A RIVERSIDE WALK UP THE AVON
FOLLOWING A RISING TIDE
FROM THE MOUTH AT LOW TIDE
TO THE TIDE HEAD AT HIGH TIDE

Sir Richard MacCormac CBE PPRIBA RA (b. 1938)
View 1. From the Garden. Burrell's Field for Trinity College, Cambridge, 1996
Inkjet print
55.1 x 57.0 cm
RCIN 212759

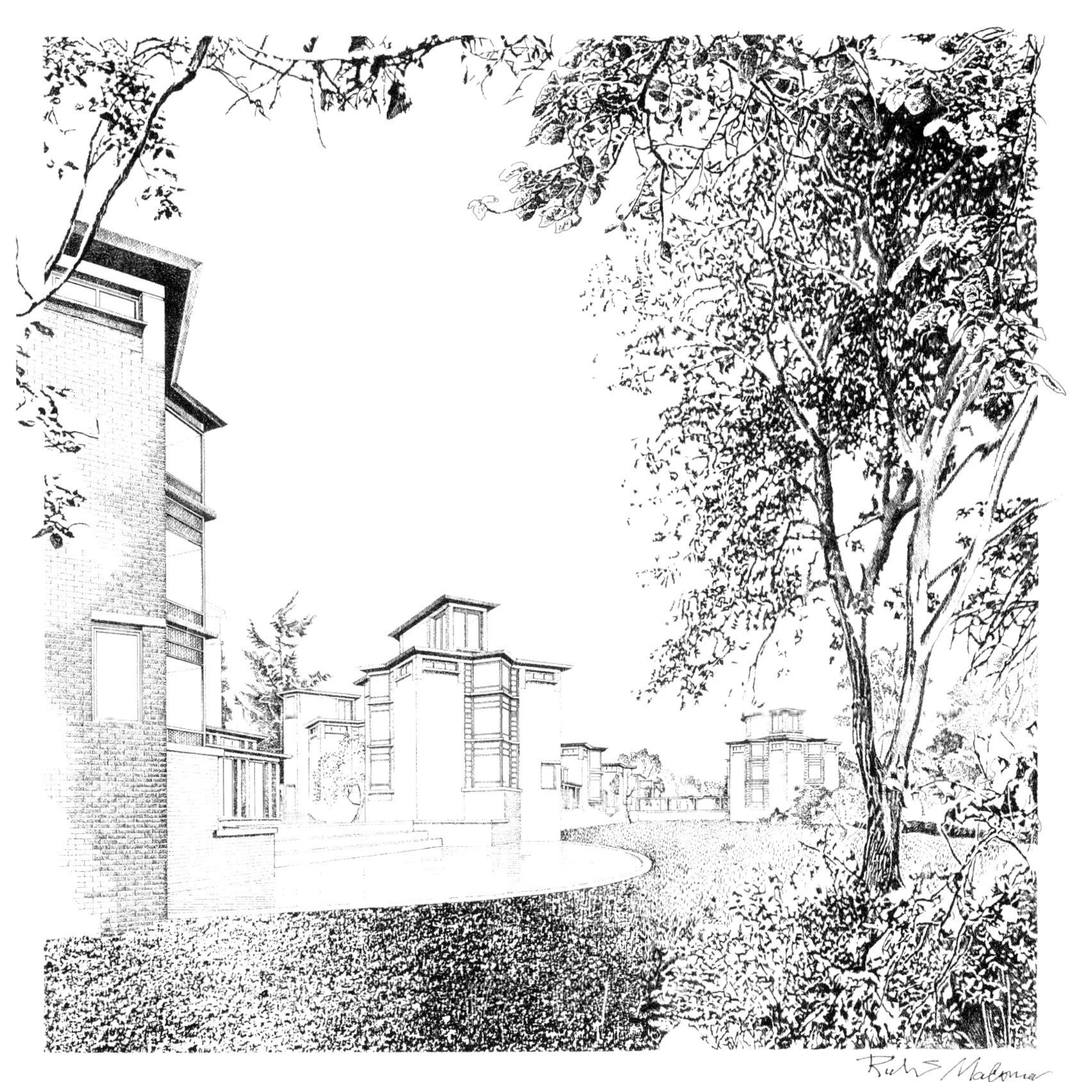

VIEW 1. FROM THE GARDEN

Professor David Mach RA (b. 1956)

Saints and Sinners, 2000

Pencil, pen and ink and collage

39.3 x 32.0 cm

RCIN 212760

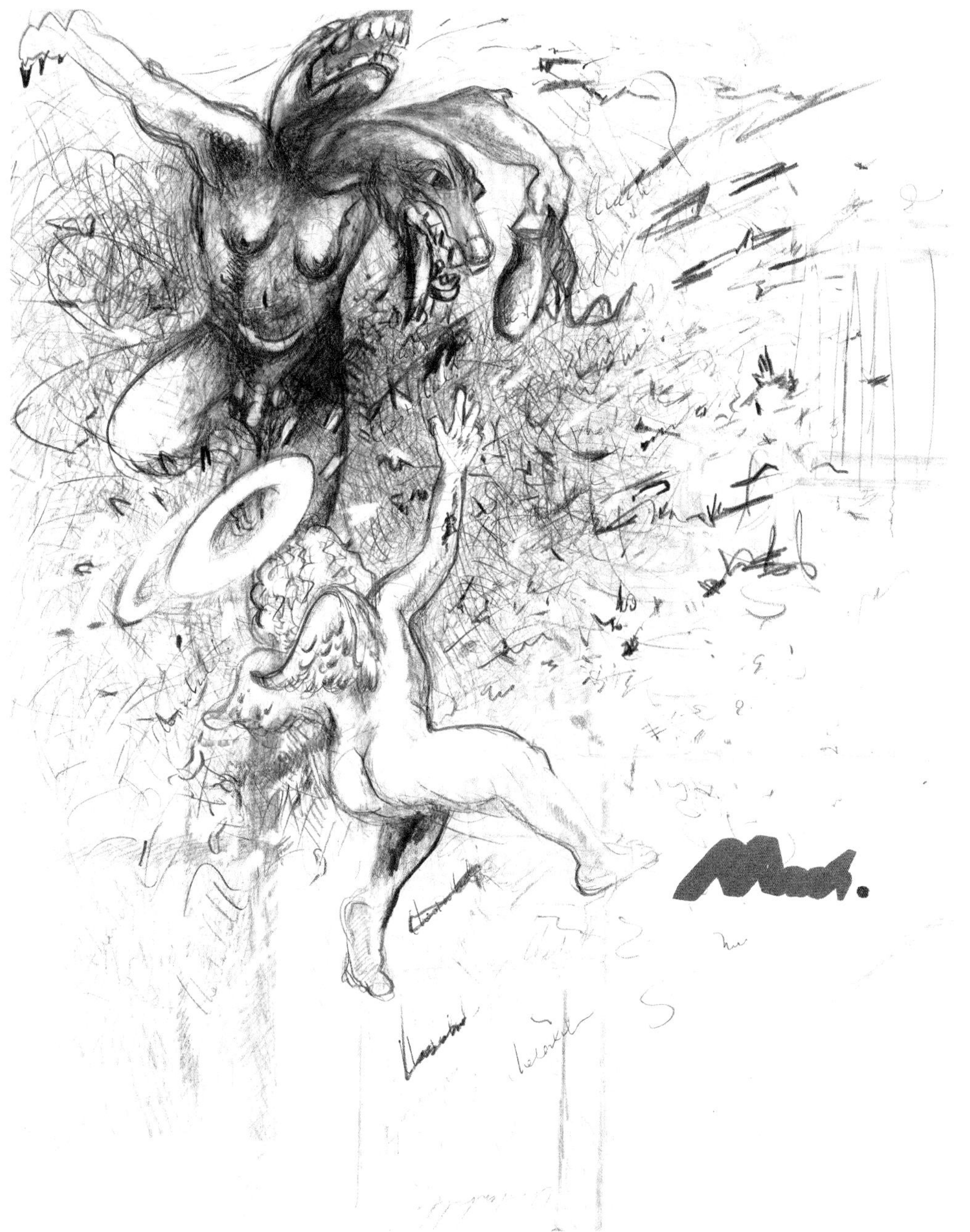

John Maine RA (b. 1942)

Westminster Abbey Sacrarium, 2012

Pencil and conté crayon

49.8 x 35.5 cm

RCIN 212761

The Cosmati pavement has been the place of coronation of Kings and Queens since the thirteenth century and it was here that Her Majesty was crowned in 1953. At that time the pavement was protected by a carpet, but now it has been conserved and it is open for all to see. My drawing recreates the sculptural character of this part of the Abbey, rather than describing every topographical detail.

I have been a member of the Westminster Abbey Fabric Commission since 1997. As a member of the group advising on the conservation of the Cosmati pavement, I have had the opportunity to study it intimately, and this inspired my exhibition 'After Cosmati' at the Royal Academy in November 2011. I produced many sketches of the pavement, one of which showed the Sacrarium from the Muniments room high above. *Westminster Abbey Sacrarium 2012* is a more fully realised drawing which I made in my studio especially for the presentation portfolio.

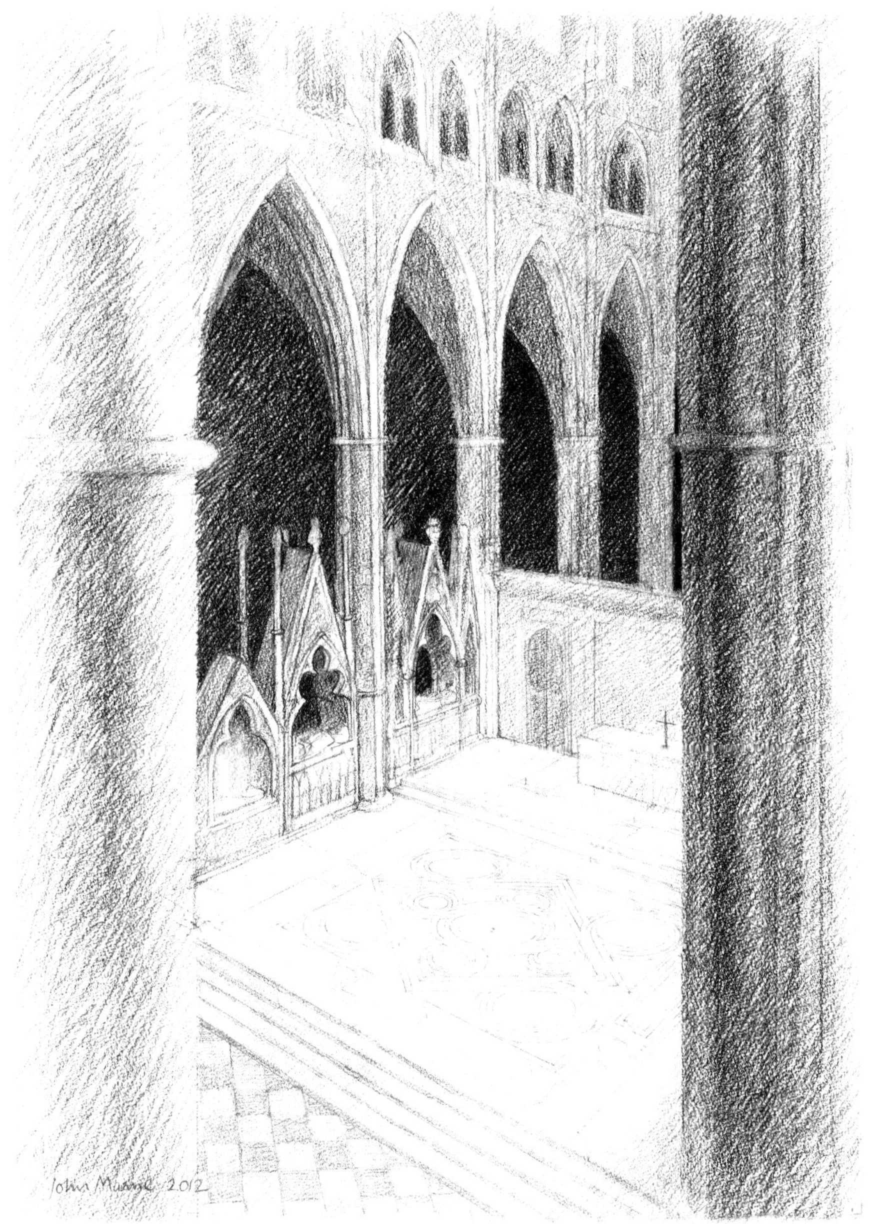

Leonard Manasseh OBE RA PPRWA (b. 1916)

Daylight, 2012

Pencil, pen and ink, watercolour
and correcting fluid

29.2 x 23.9 cm

RCIN 212762

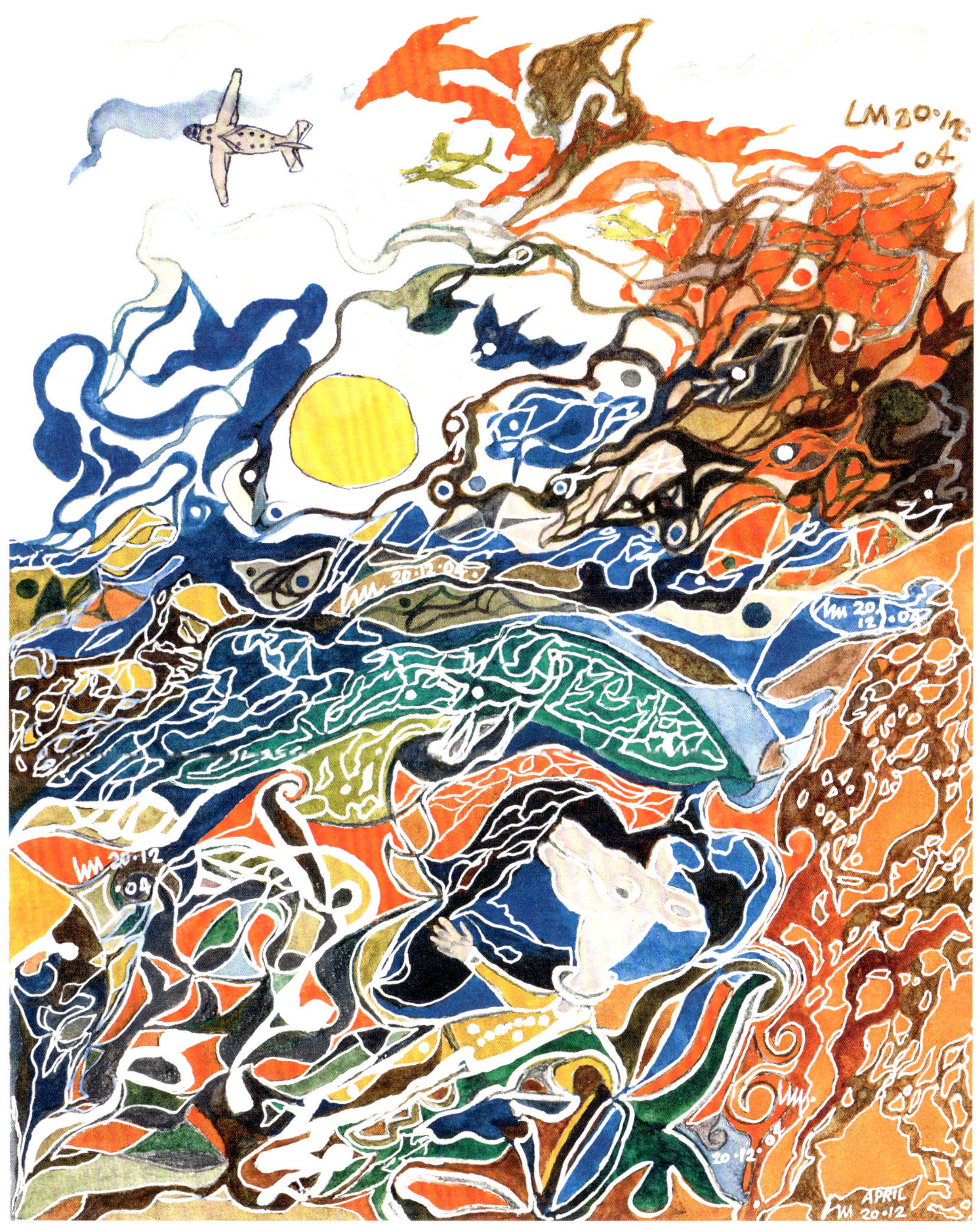
LM 20·12·04
APRIL 20·12

Michael Manser CBE RA PPRIBA (b. 1929)

The Queen's Suite, Heathrow Airport, 1988 (printed in 2012)

Inkjet print

50.7 x 68.7 cm

RCIN 212763

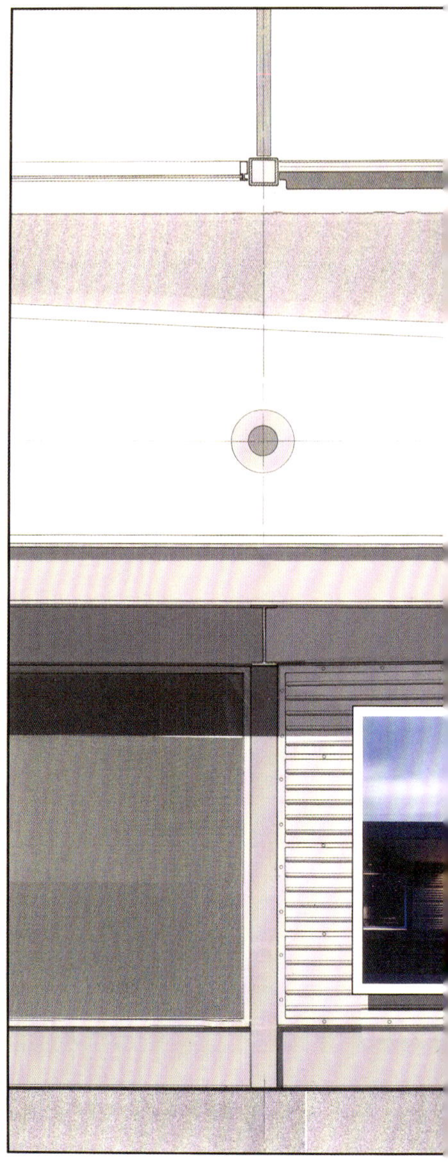

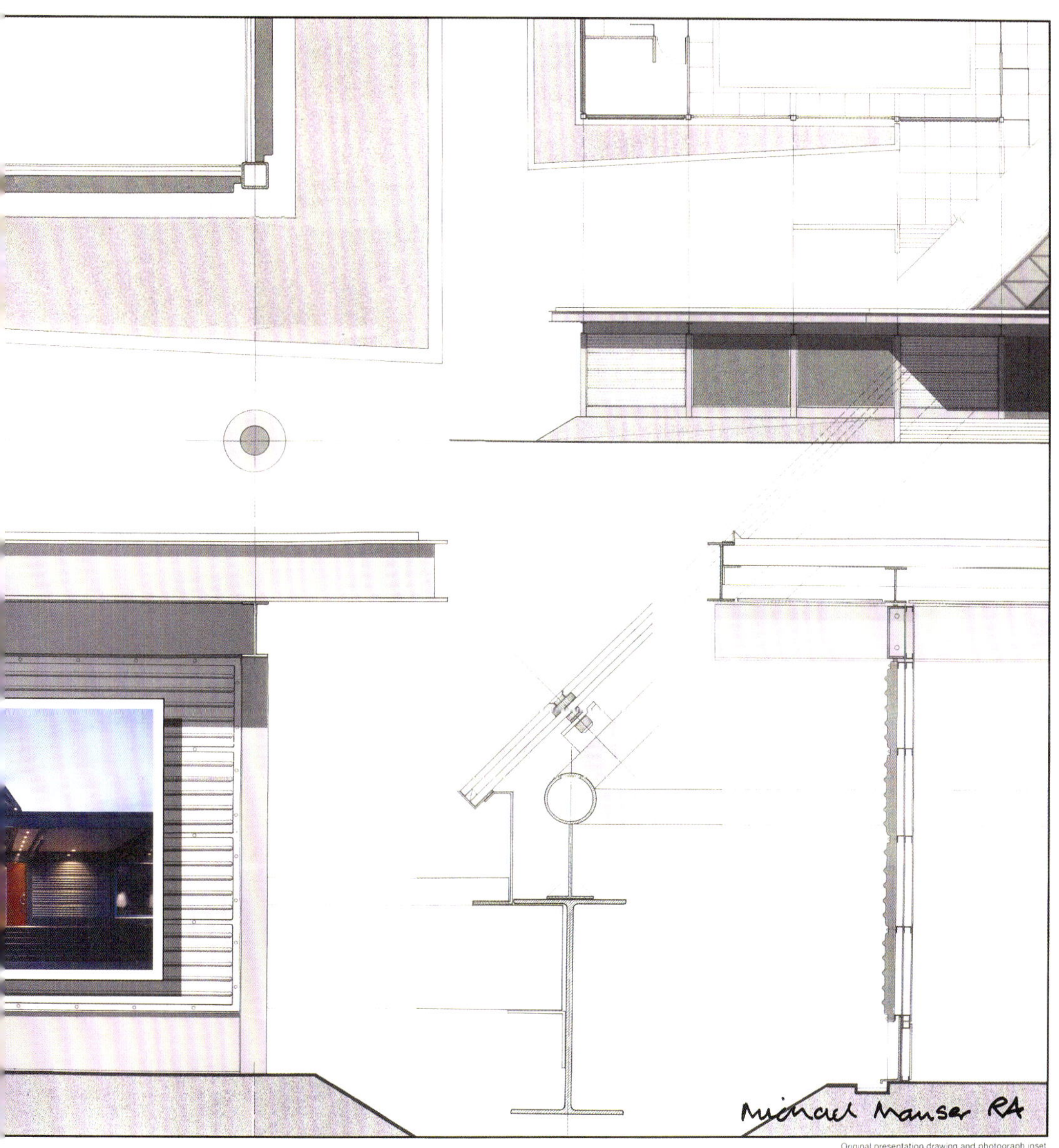

Original presentation drawing and photograph inset

38 by Michael Manser CBE RA DipArch PPRIBA.

Dr Leonard McComb RA (b. 1930)

Camellias, 2012

Etching

48.1 x 55.1 cm (sheet)

35.7 x 42.4 cm (plate)

RCIN 212764

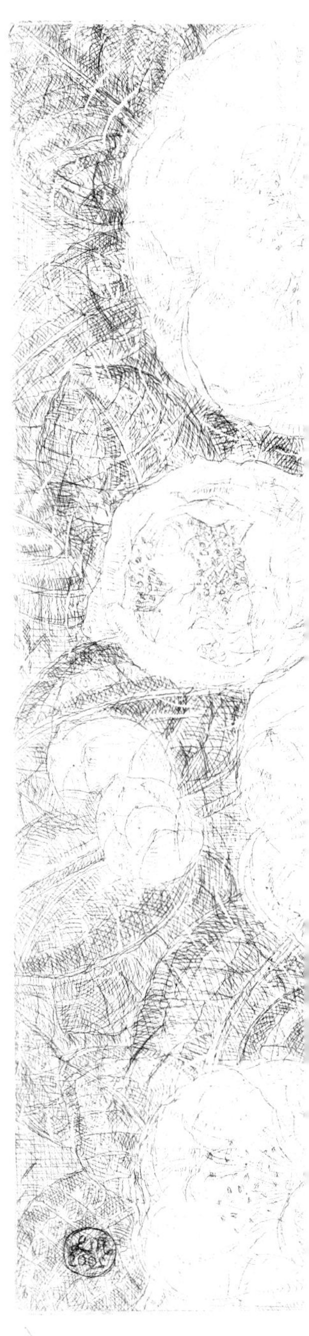

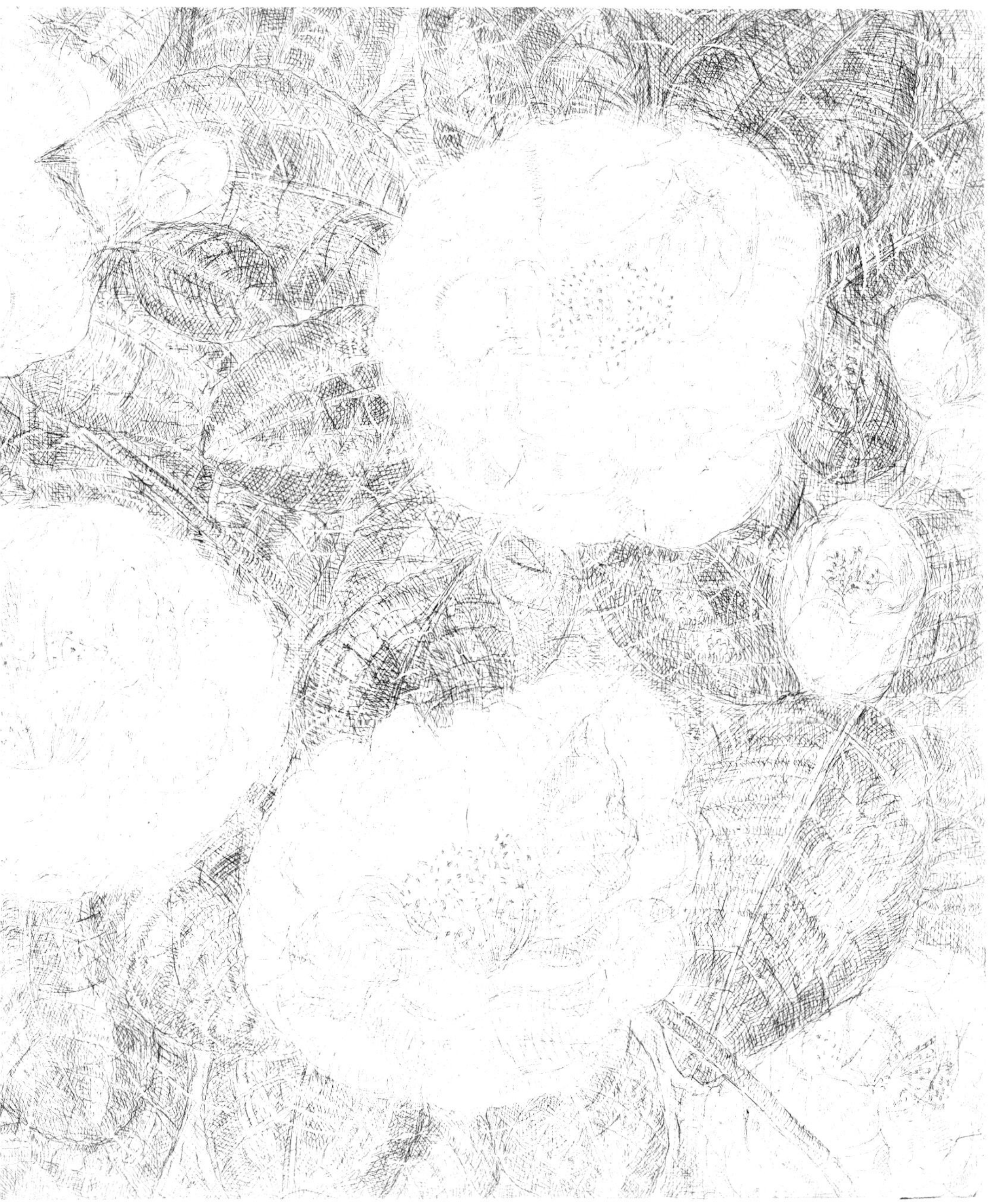

Professor Ian McKeever RA (b. 1946)
Assembly Watercolour, 2006
Pencil and watercolour
32.0 x 24.0 cm
RCIN 212765

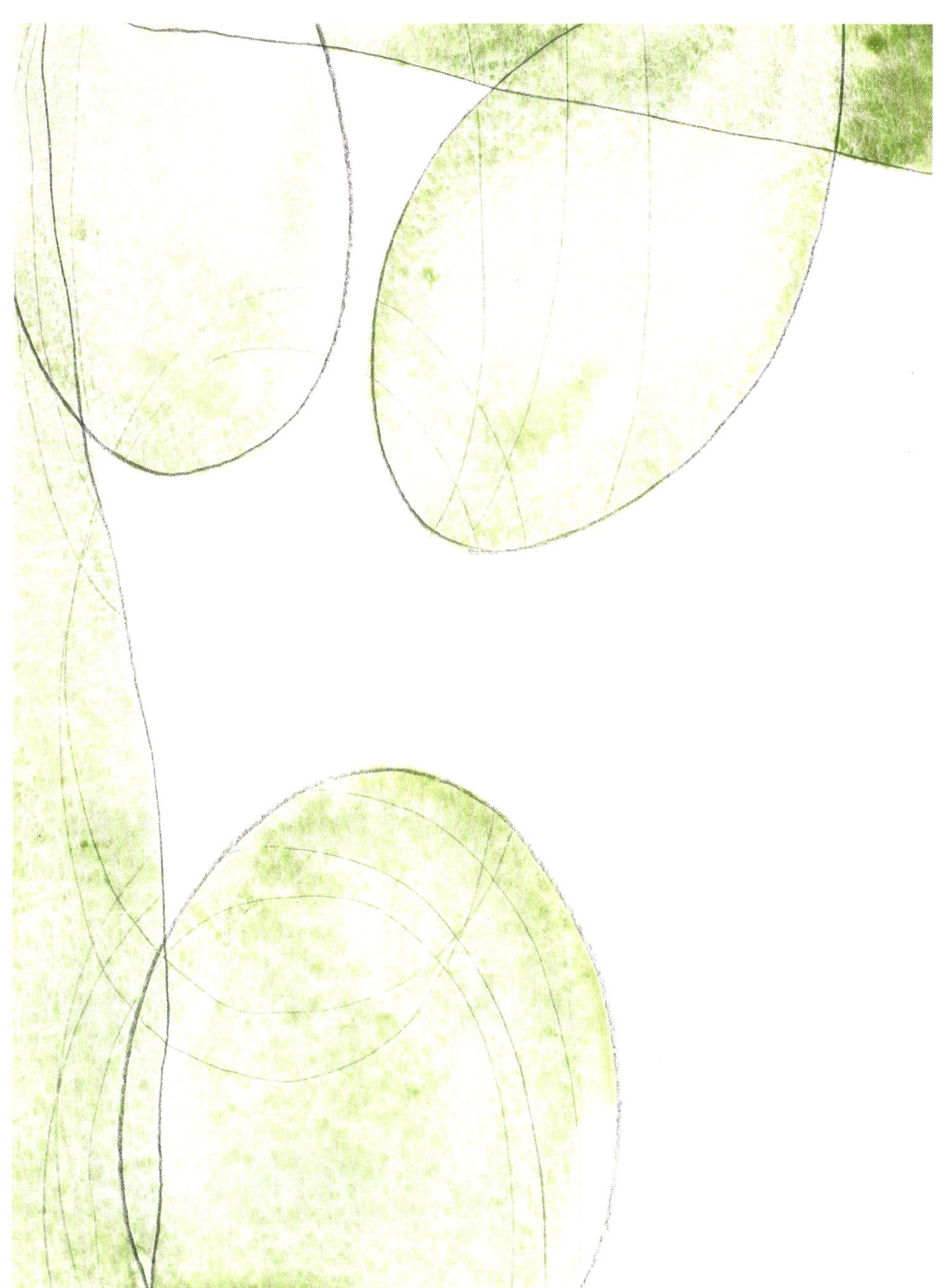

Lisa Milroy RA (b. 1959)

Dress, 2012

Ink and wash on paper and silk

38.7 x 27.1 cm

RCIN 212766

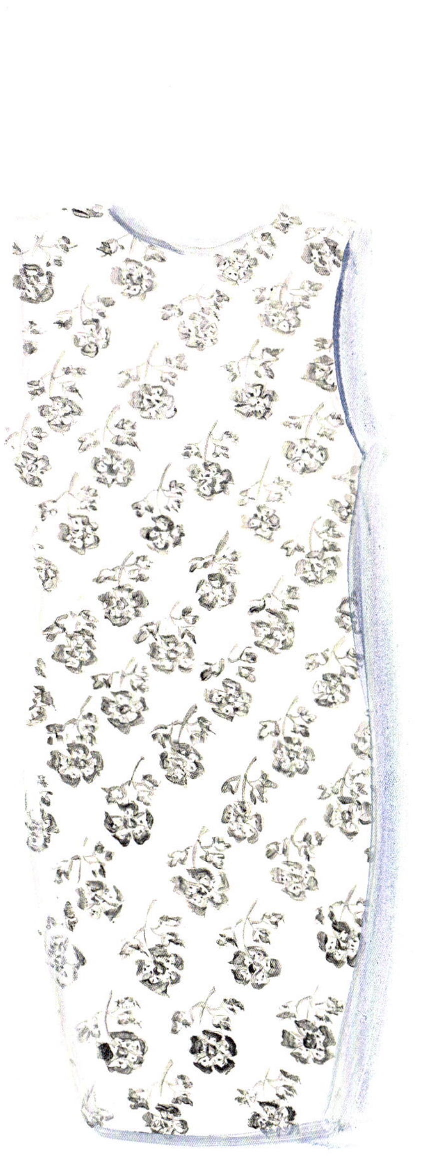

Professor Dhruva Mistry CBE RA (b. 1957)

Head, 2012

Watercolour and gouache

50.9 x 65.9 cm

RCIN 212767

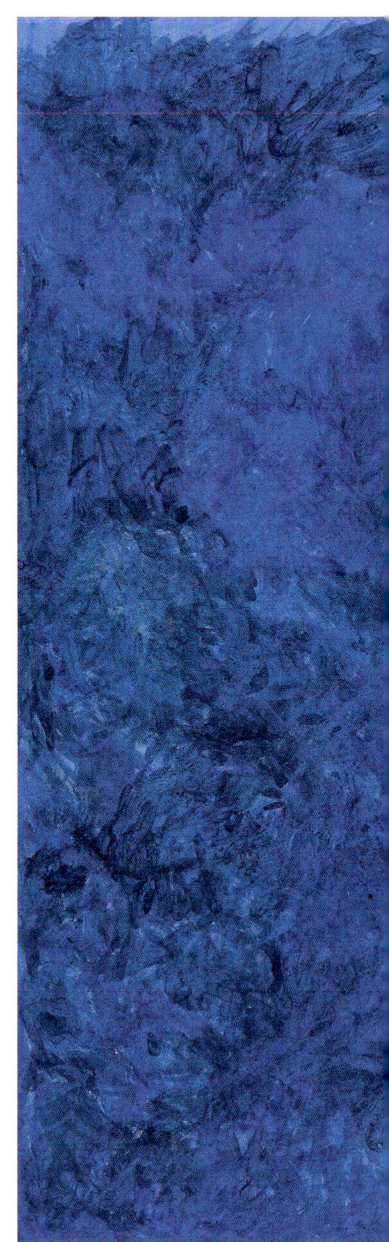

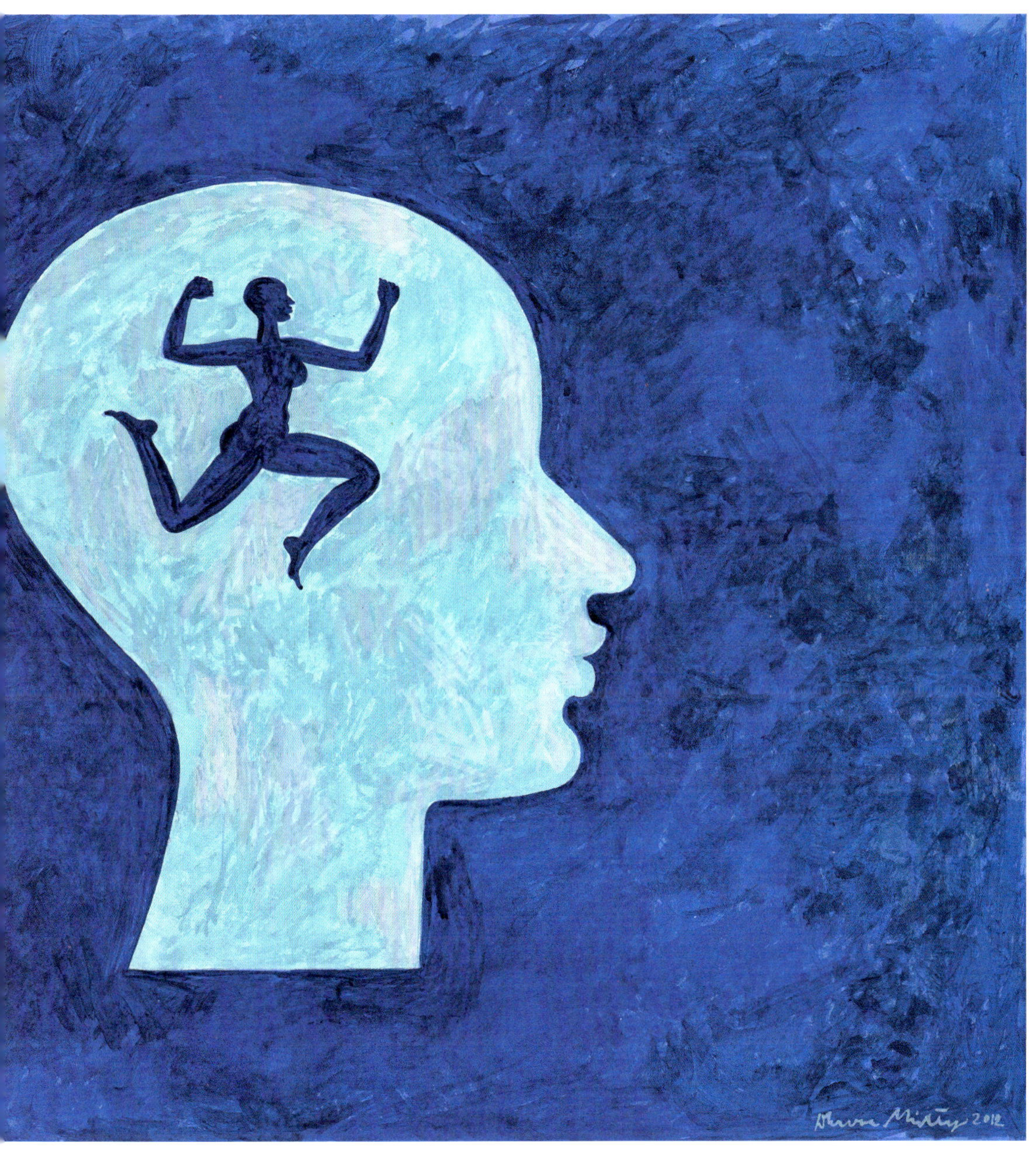

Mali Morris RA (b. 1945)
Landing Light/Golden Corner, 2012
Acrylic
30.0 x 36.5 cm
RCIN 212768

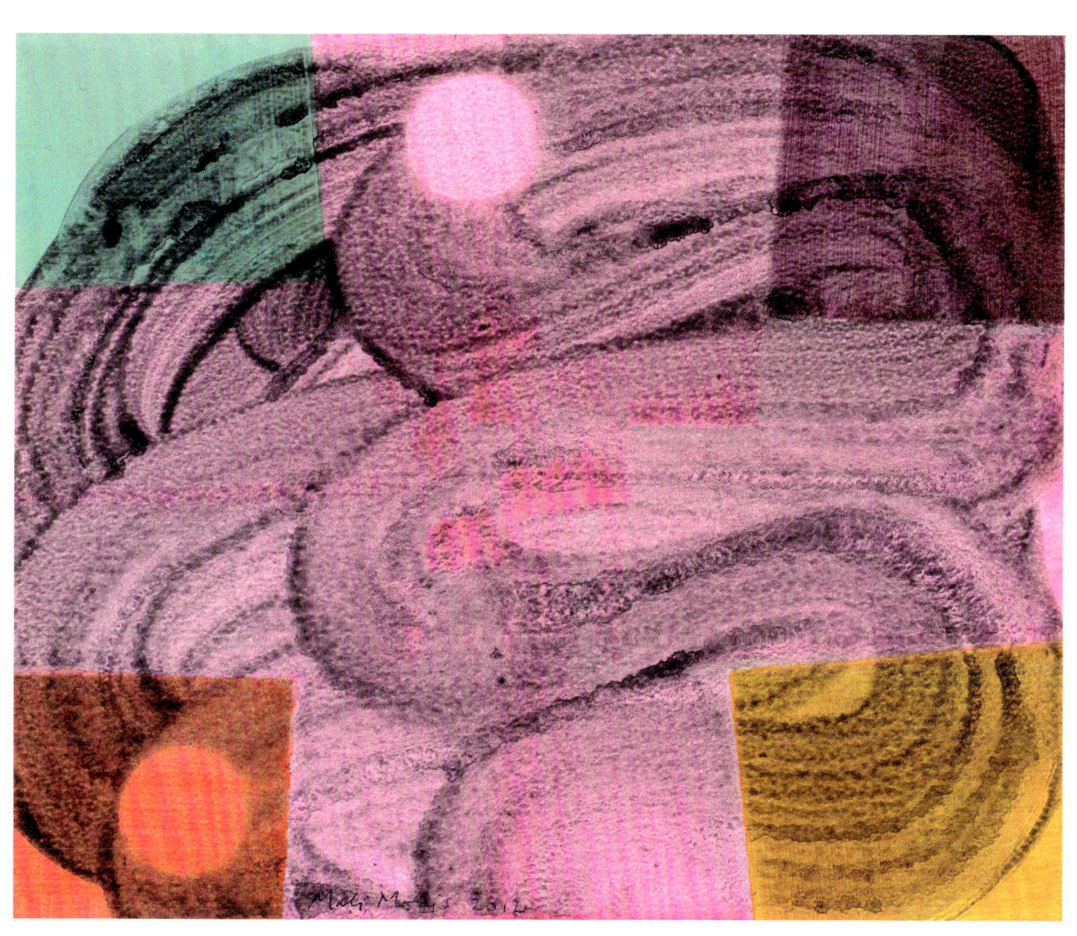

David Nash OBE RA (b. 1945)

Yellow, 2012

Pastel

53.4 x 37.2 cm

RCIN 212769

Three prime shapes: triangle, circle, square; as forms: pyramid, sphere, cube. The triangle has dynamism and a sense of action; the circle has a sense of movement and timeless singularity; the square is balanced, static and material.

Three prime colours: yellow, red, blue. Yellow is most potent in the shape of a triangle; blue brings depth and space to the circle; red brings immediacy and power to the square.

'Yellow' is made by rubbing yellow pigment into the paper surface with diagonal movements using a fleece cloth. The triangle is applied using the same yellow rubbed through a stencil to make the clean edges that defines the shape within the loose yellow area.

I remember seeing The Queen wearing a yellow coat with a yellow hat and being very impressed by the boldness and liveliness that the colour brought to the occasion.

'Yellow'

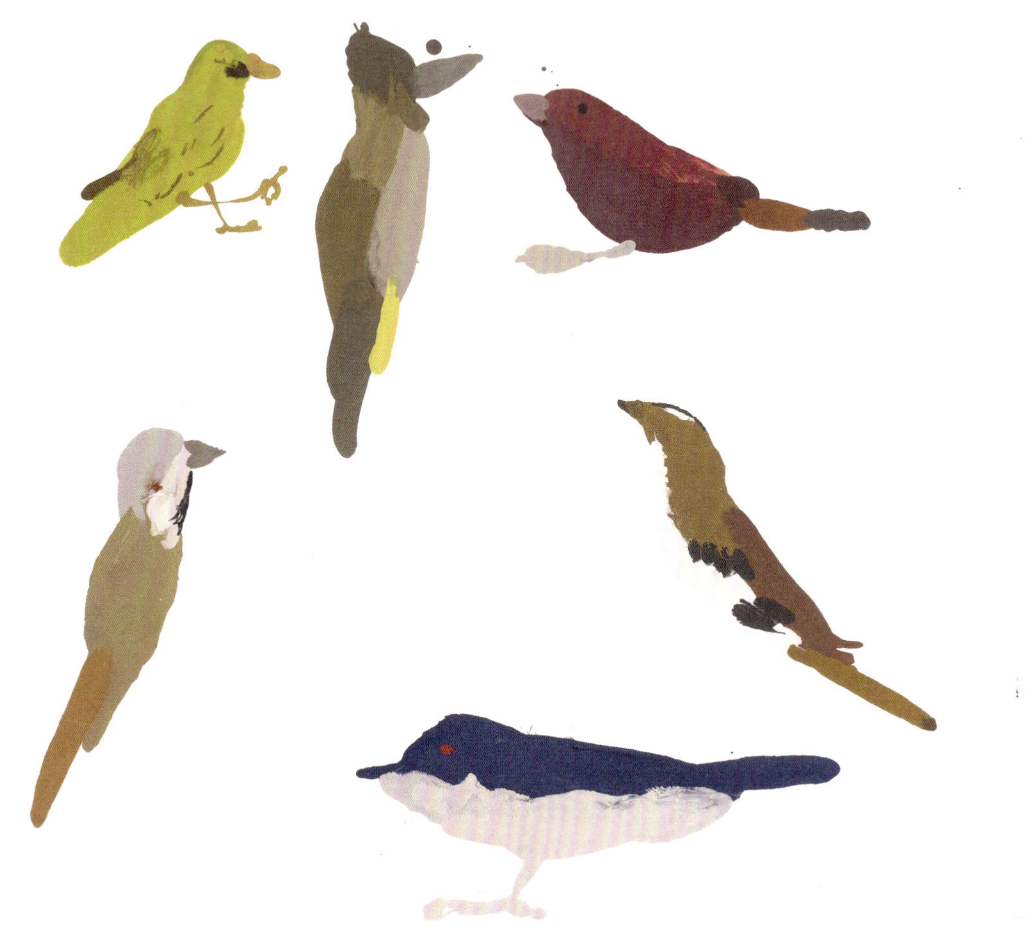

Humphrey Ocean RA (b. 1951)
Birds at Ngong, 2012
Gouache
44.0 x 55.2 cm
RCIN 212770

These are birds I saw near Ngong racecourse, just outside Nairobi, up the road from where my sister Rachel lives. They are local, a bit like our garden birds so nothing overly exotic, but of course to me they are. Clockwise from top left: African Citril, Mousebird, Red-billed Firefinch, White-browed Sparrow Weaver, Black-throated Wattle Eye, House Sparrow.

I go and stay with my sister in Kenya about every five years. She has been an Assumption nun since she was 20 and I stay in her small community. We spend our days doing all sorts of things – we go for walks, an English concept; this makes the African nuns laugh like a drain. They will walk 15 miles for a sack of flour. In the evening everyone is generally asleep by 9pm to be up early for Mass, but not me so I go to my room, listen to my iPod, write and paint things I've seen in the day into an A6 book. The book extends my brief time there when I come back to England.

The birds in my Jubilee painting are almost a page from my book. It occurred to me Kenya is where The Queen was when her life changed.

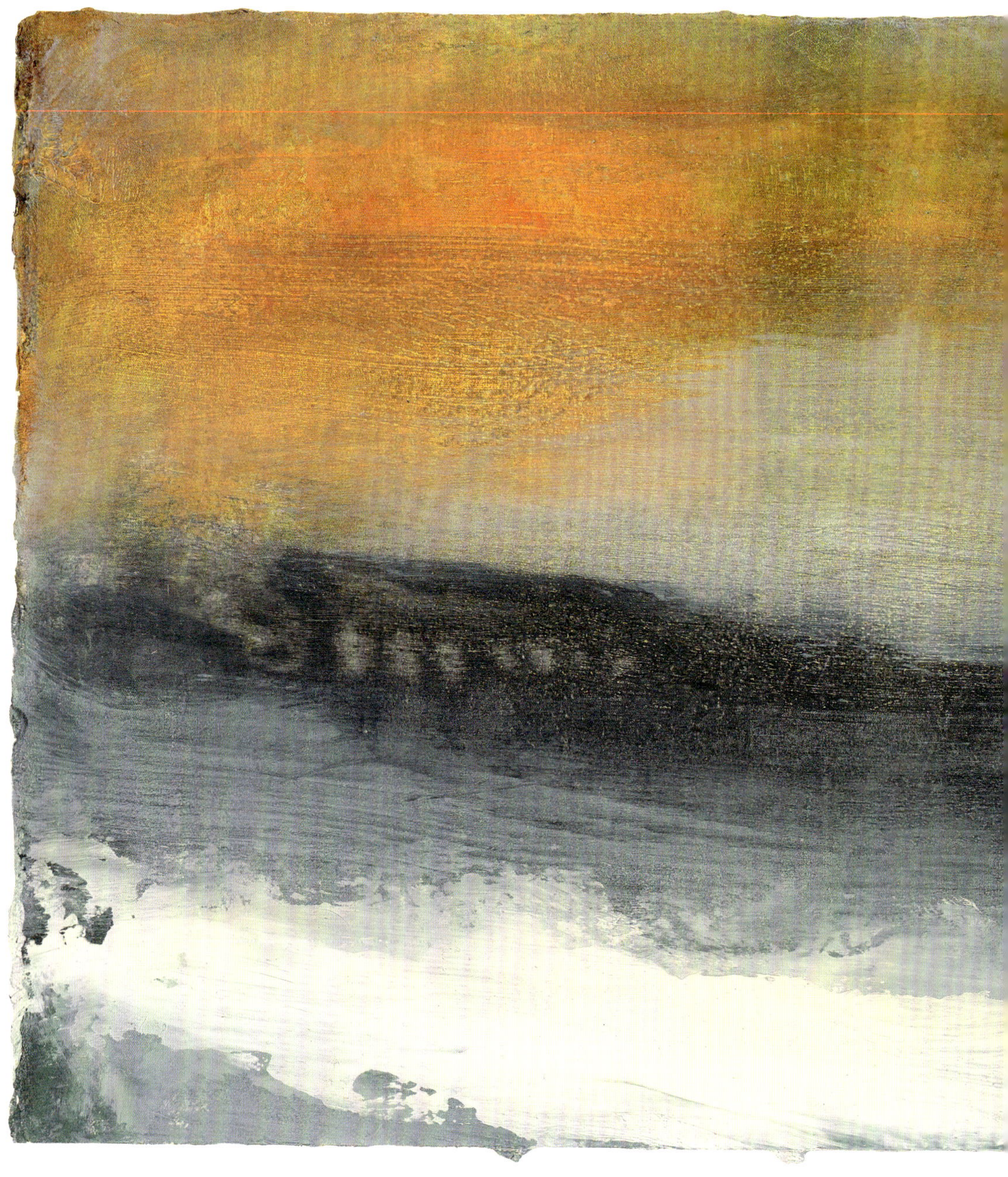

'The wreck of the Plassy is on the little island of Inis Oirr. I have been visiting it since 1962, and it has appeared in many of my paintings.'

Hughie O'Donoghue RA (b. 1953)
Voyage of the Plassy, c.2009/10
Oil
39.0 x 57.7 cm
RCIN 212771

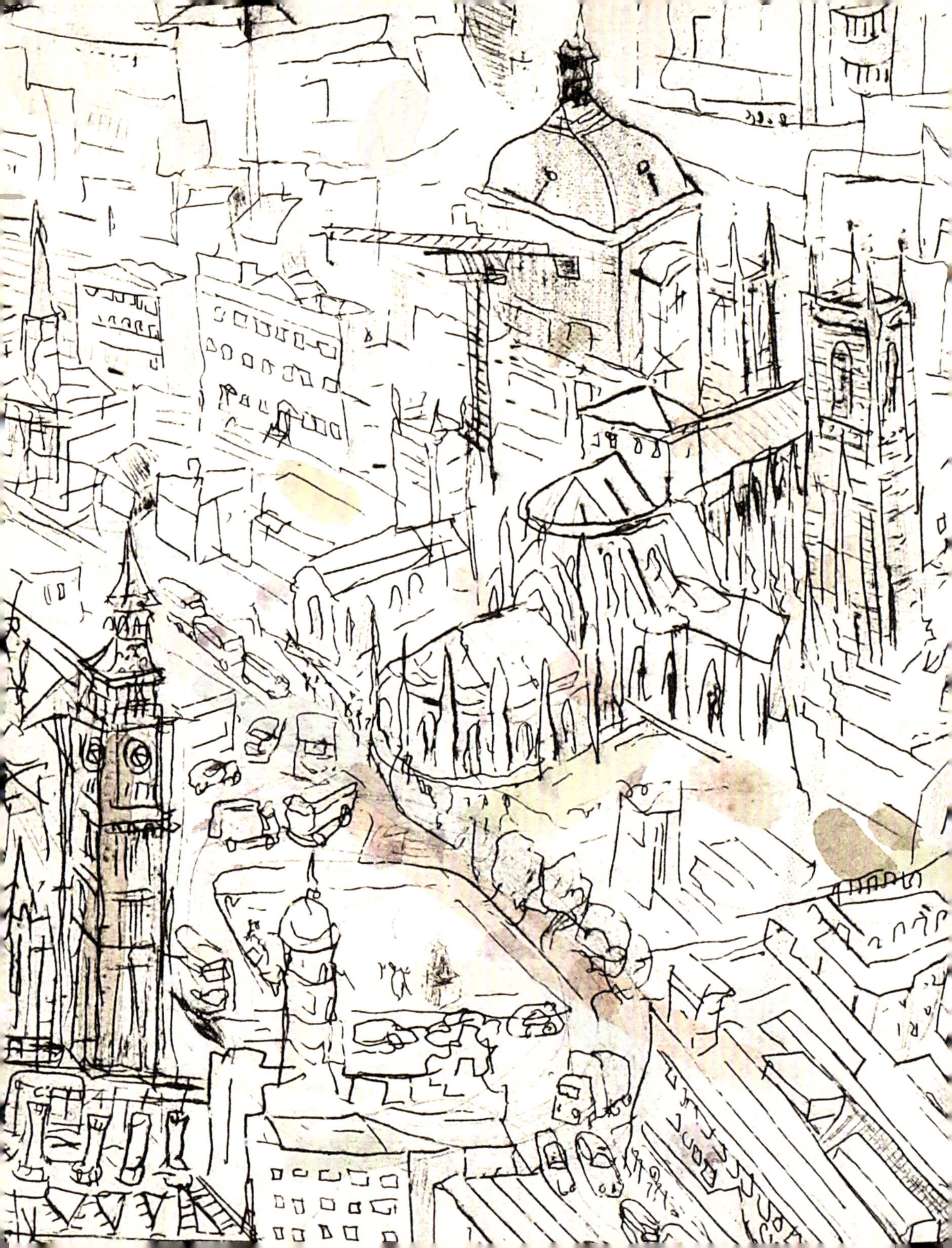

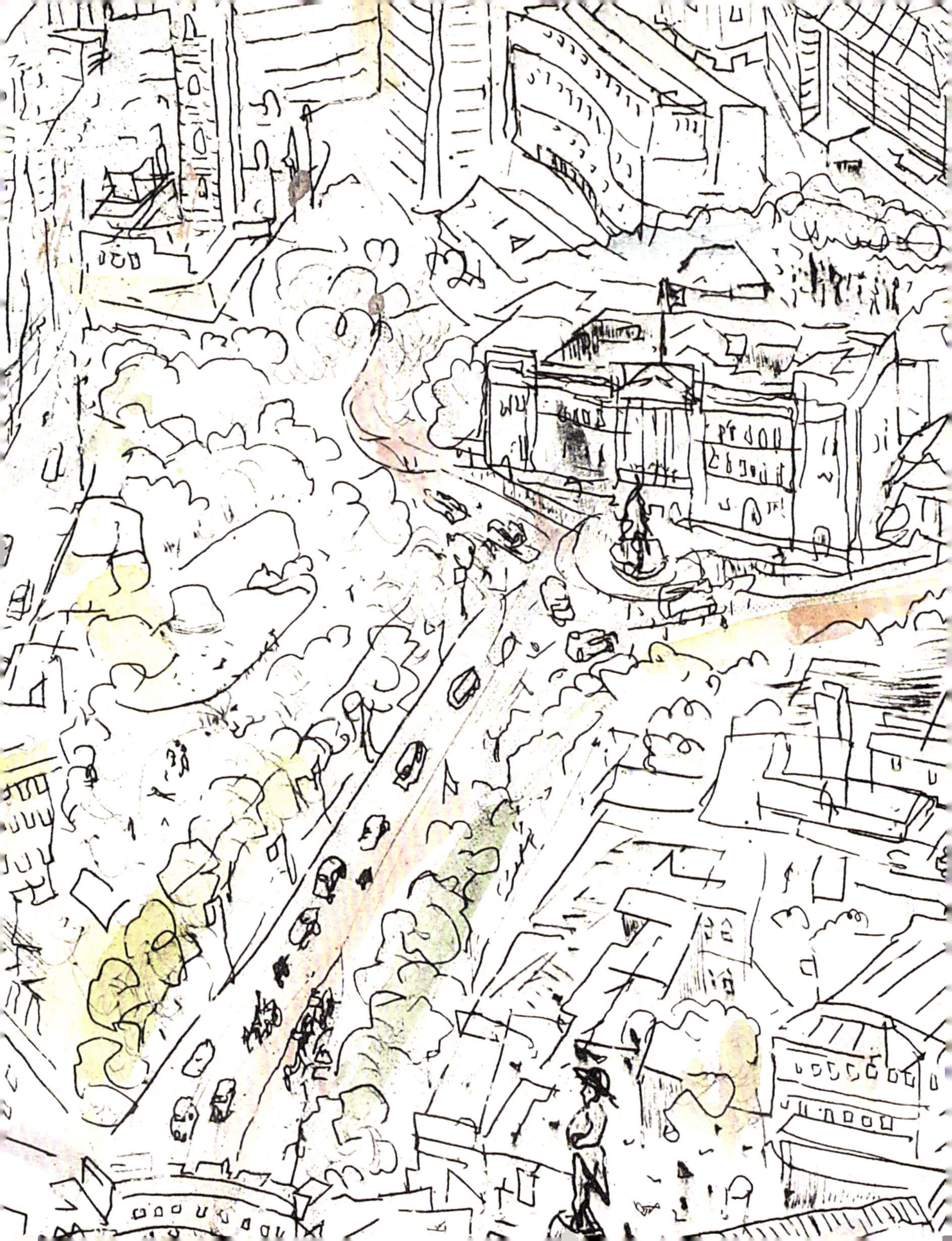

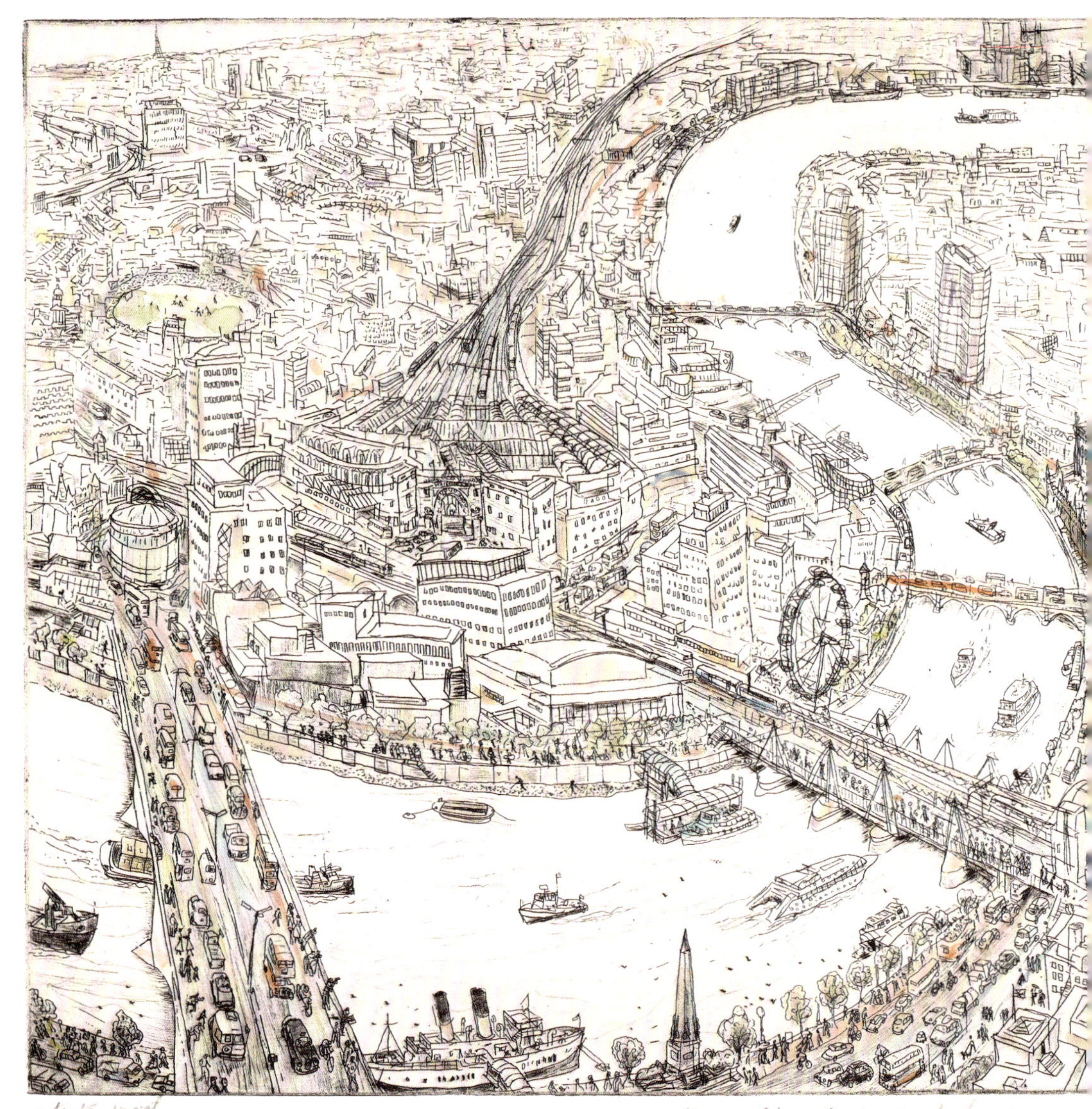

artist's proof

From Cleopatra's point of view

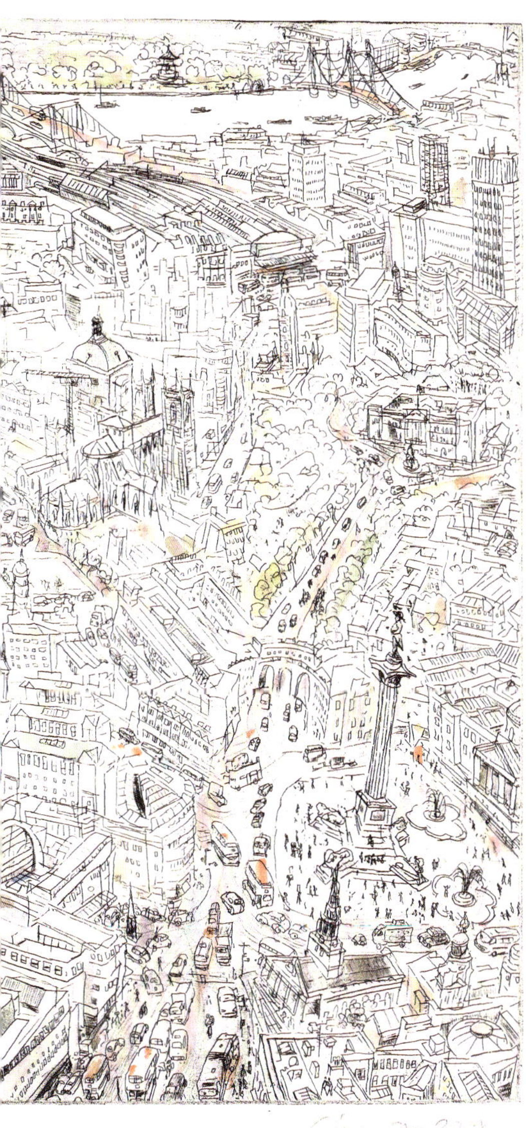

'The picture tries to give a grand imaginative sweep to London, embracing all sorts of incidents such as cricket at the Oval to throngs of people crossing Waterloo Bridge. Her Majesty appears on the balcony of Buckingham Palace (admittedly as just a dot).'

Professor Chris Orr MBE RA (b. 1943)
From Cleopatra's Point of View, 2004
Etching and drypoint with watercolour
53.4 x 74.3 cm (sheet)
37.4 x 60.6 cm (plate)
RCIN 212772

Cornelia Parker OBE RA (b. 1956)
Spitting Sugar, 2003
Sugar-lift aquatint
56.9 x 55.9 cm (sheet)
20.7 x 27.6 cm (plate)
RCIN 212773

Eric Parry RA (b. 1952)

Proposal for 212–14 Piccadilly, 2008

Pen and ink wash on detail paper

30.0 x 49.9 cm

RCIN 212774

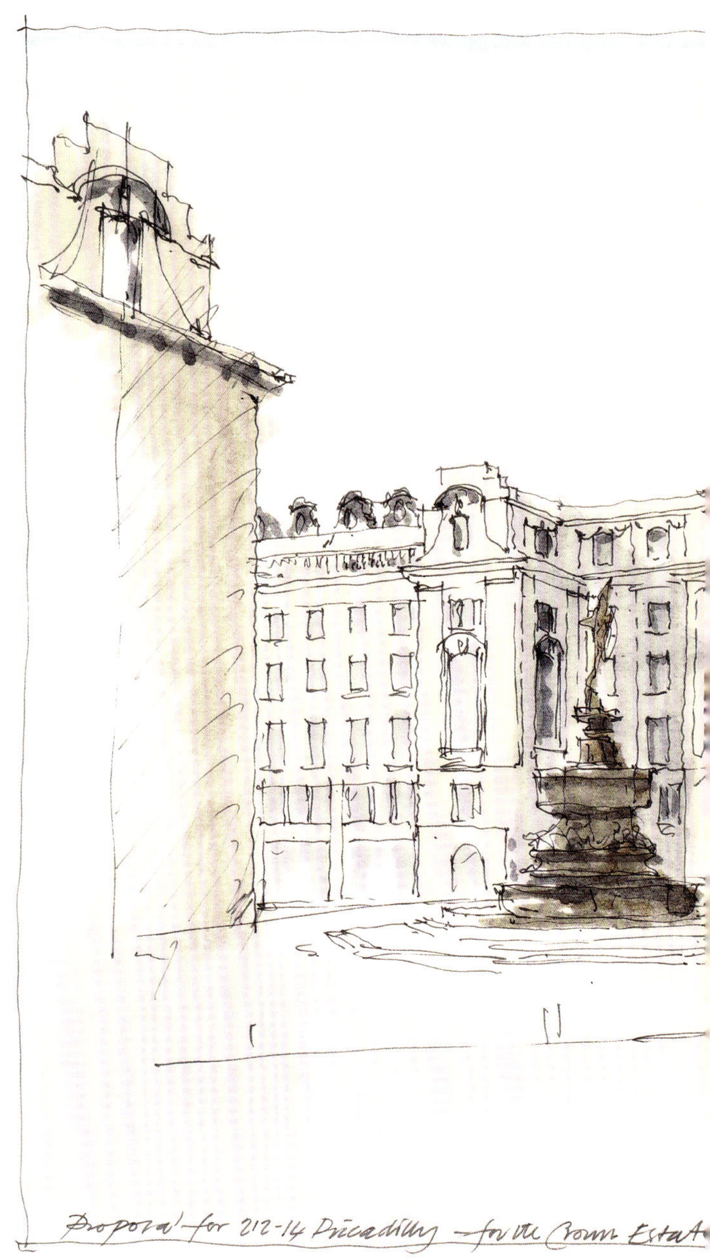

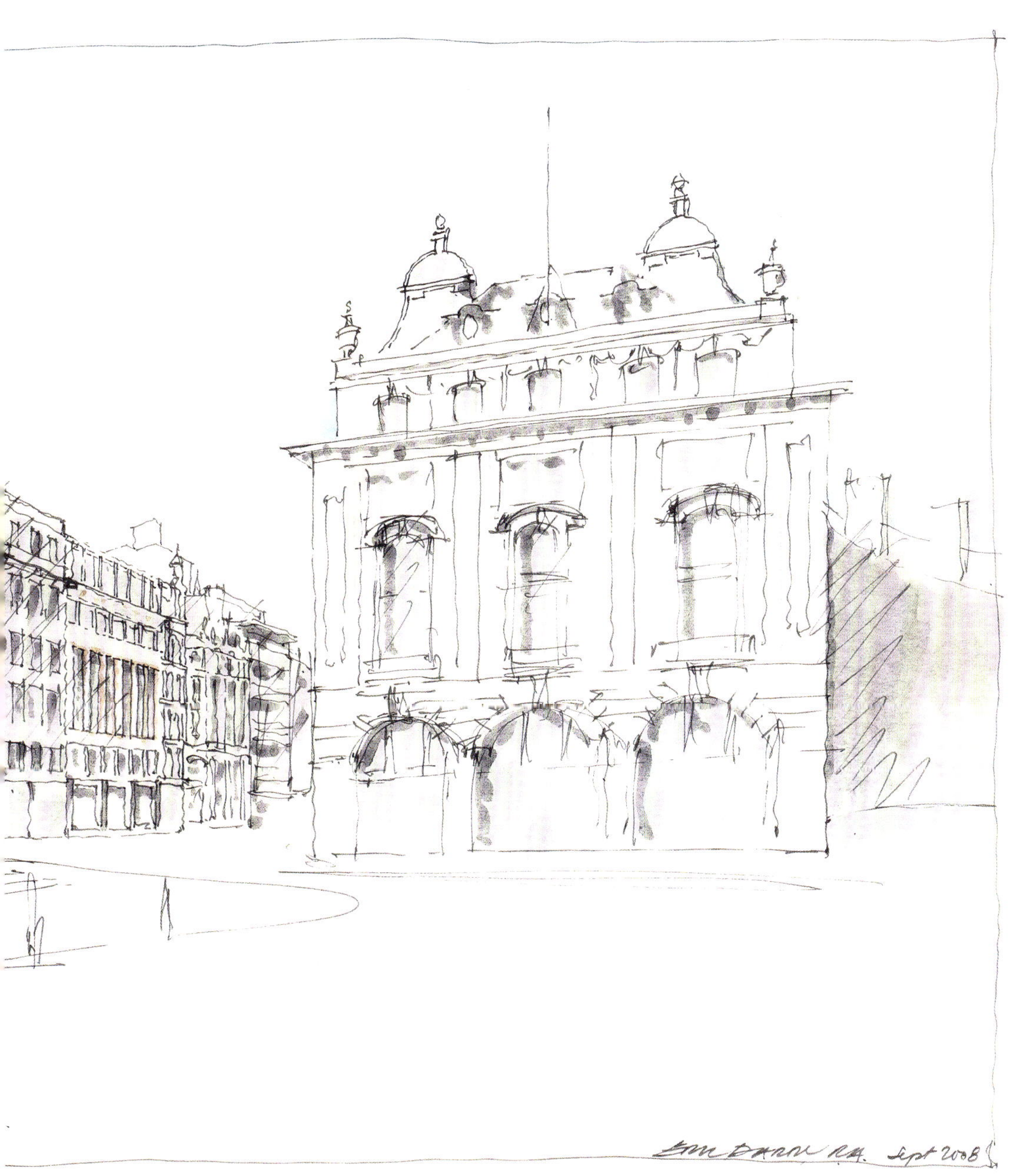
Sept 2008

John Partridge CBE RA (b. 1924)

Japanese University College, Canterbury, 1991

Inkjet print

28.9 x 37.7 cm

RCIN 212775

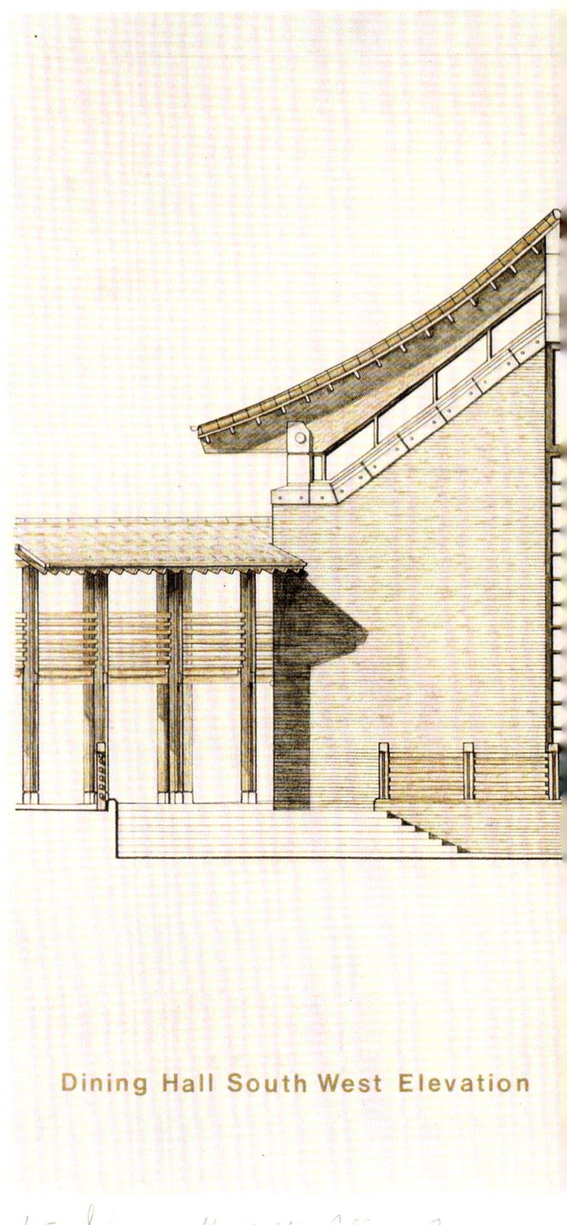

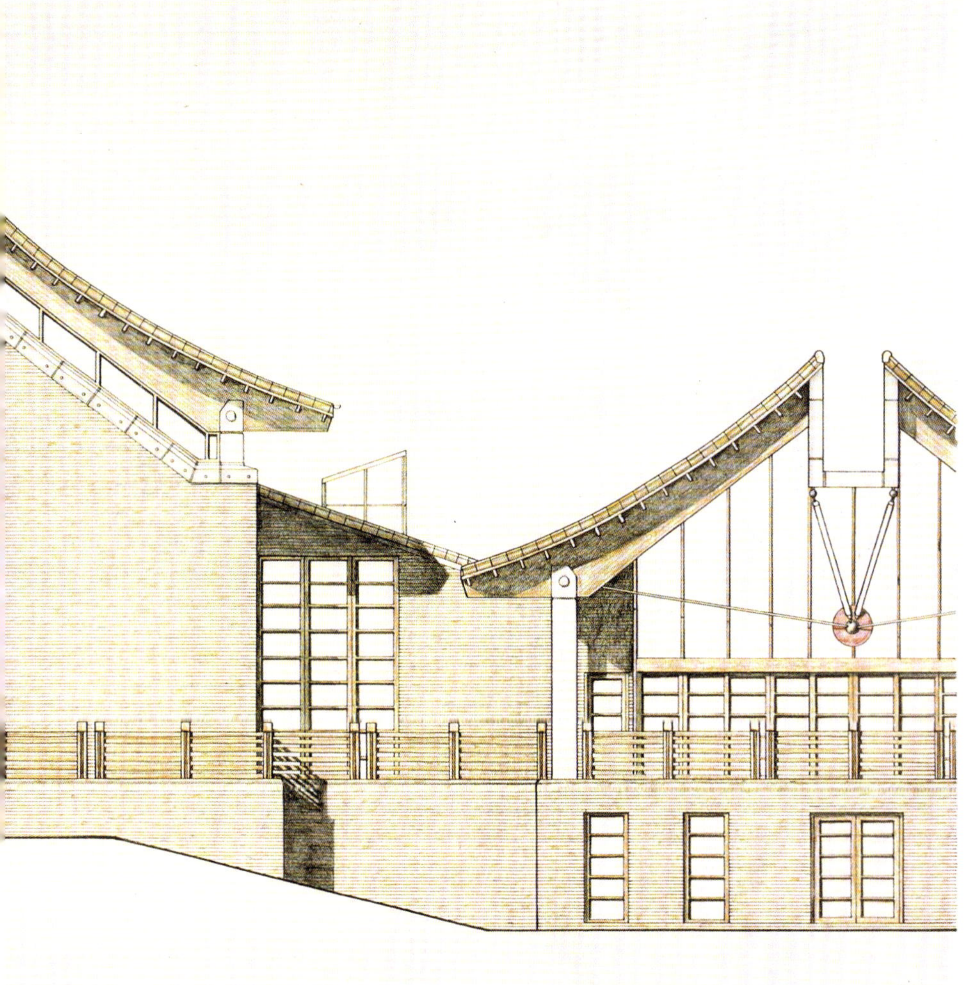

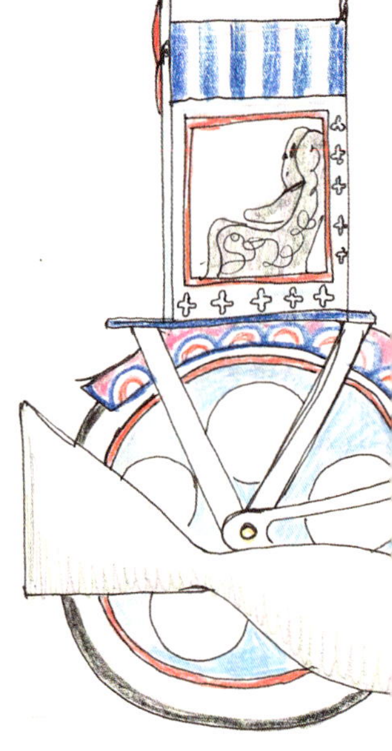

Grayson Perry CBE RA (b. 1960)
Design for Kenilworth AM1, 2010
Pencil, pen and ink and crayon
29.6 x 41.9 cm
RCIN 212776

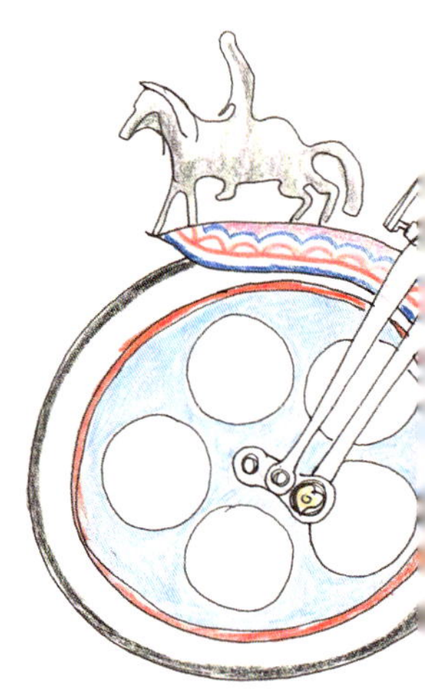

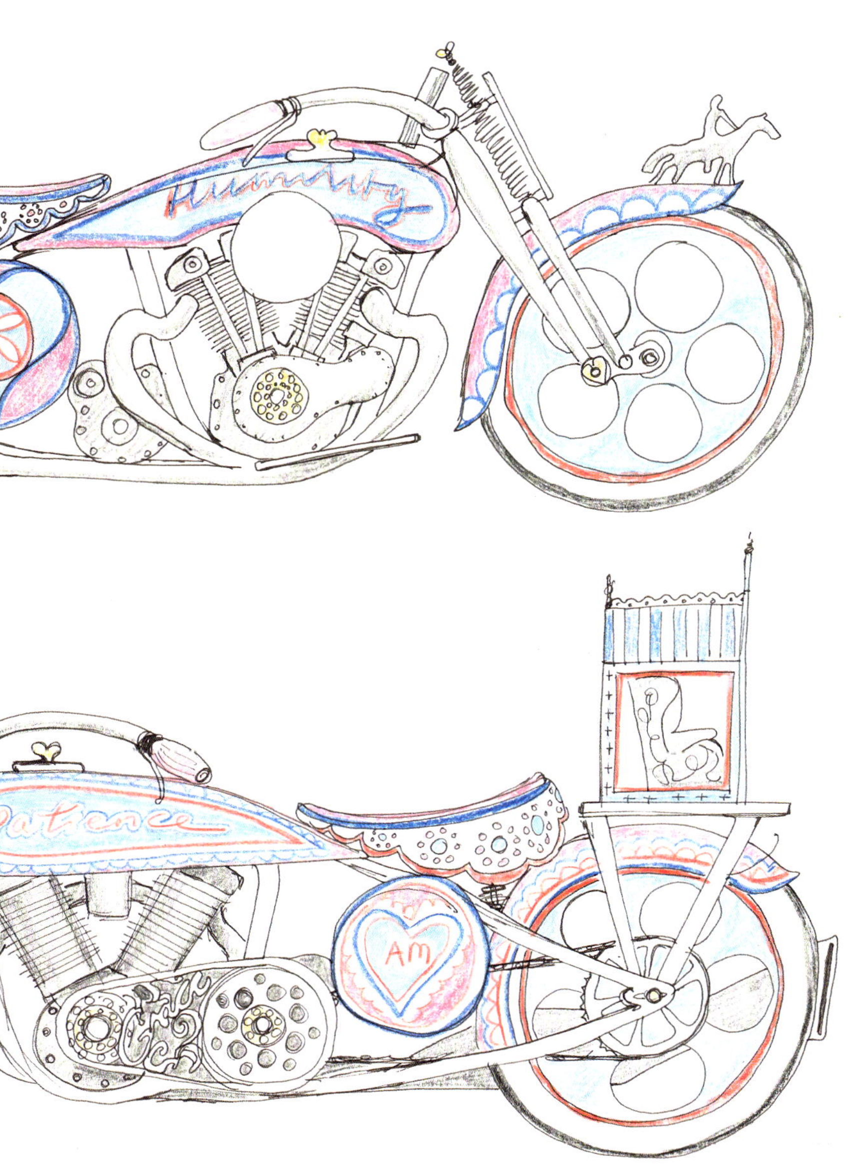
Humility
Patience
AM

Tom Phillips CBE RA (b. 1937)

Sixteen Appearances of the Union Jack, 1974

Screenprint

44.0 x 61.5 cm

RCIN 212777

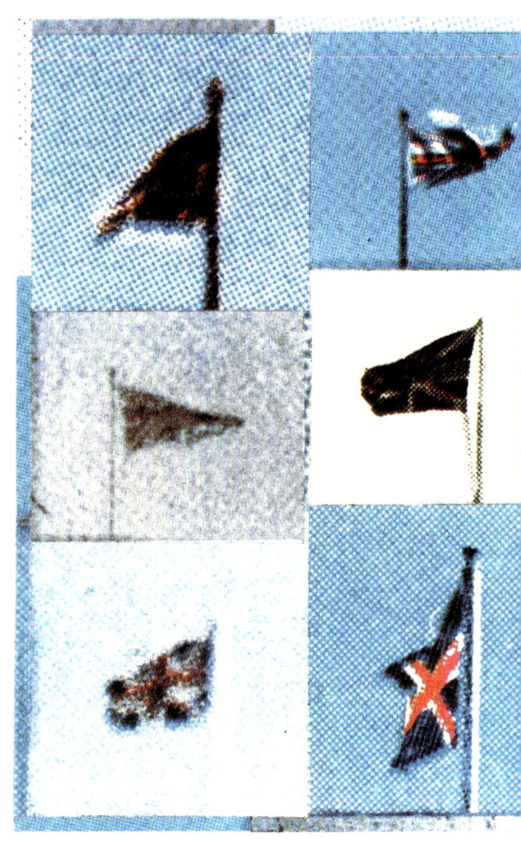

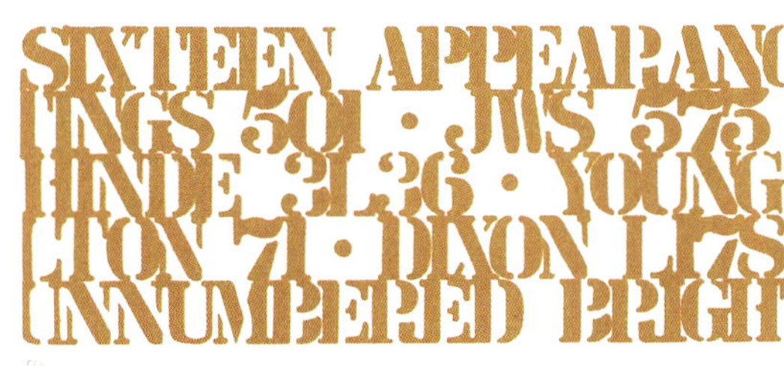

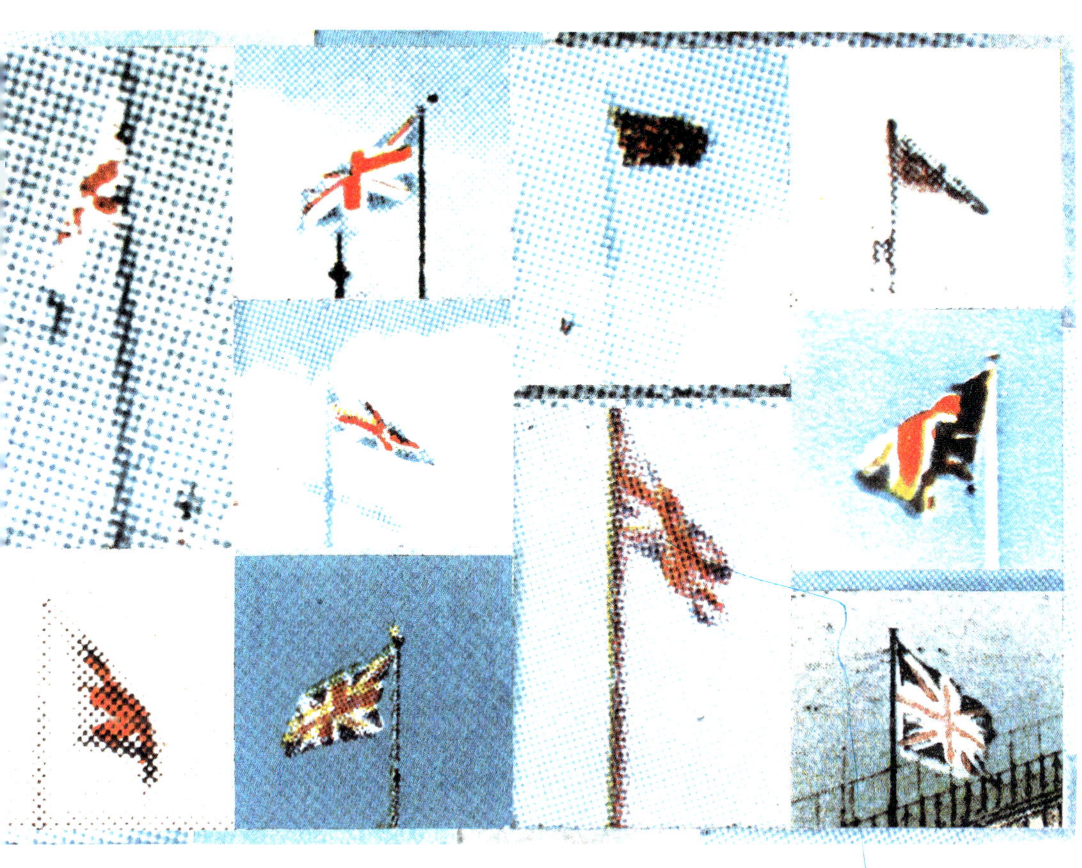
OF THE UNION JACK : AFTER PHOTO GREE
ON LONG65 · SKILTON 9552 · PP60 · JOHN
7 · ANON 142 · JH 3 LS · PG 162 & 430 · SKI
· WILPRO · HARVEY BARTON 3022 · ANON
TOM PHILLIPS . XXVIII · III · MCMLXXIV

Dr Barbara Rae CBE RA (b. 1943)
Bealach na Bà – West, 2011
Acrylic
37.9 x 57.6 cm
RCIN 212778

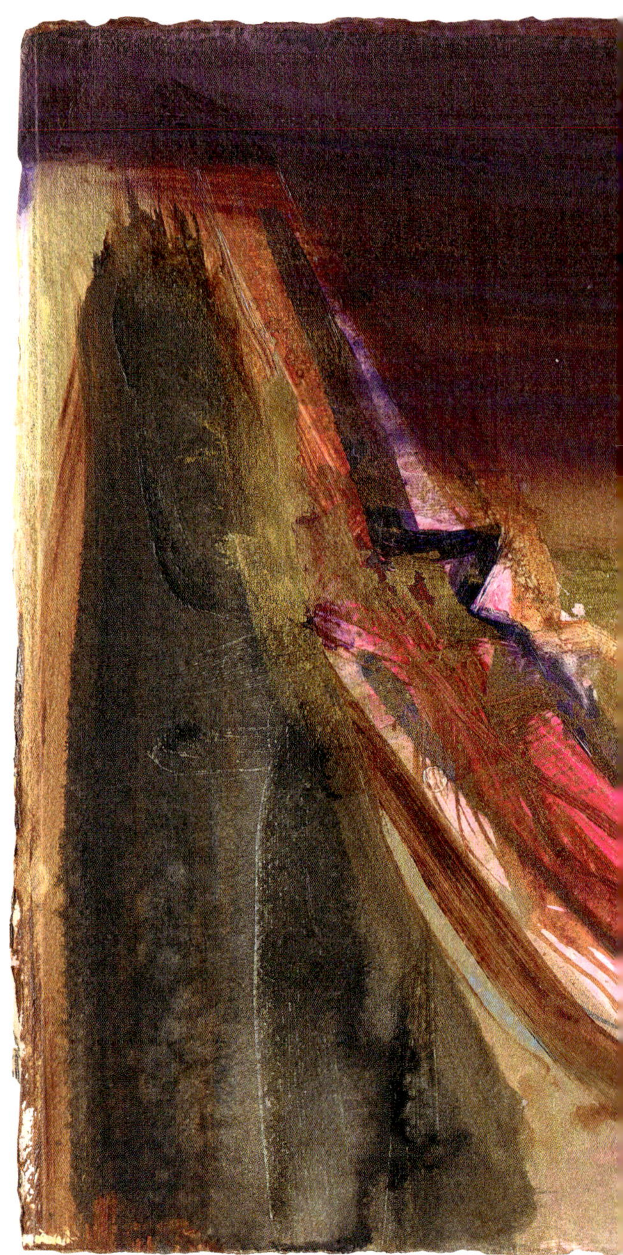

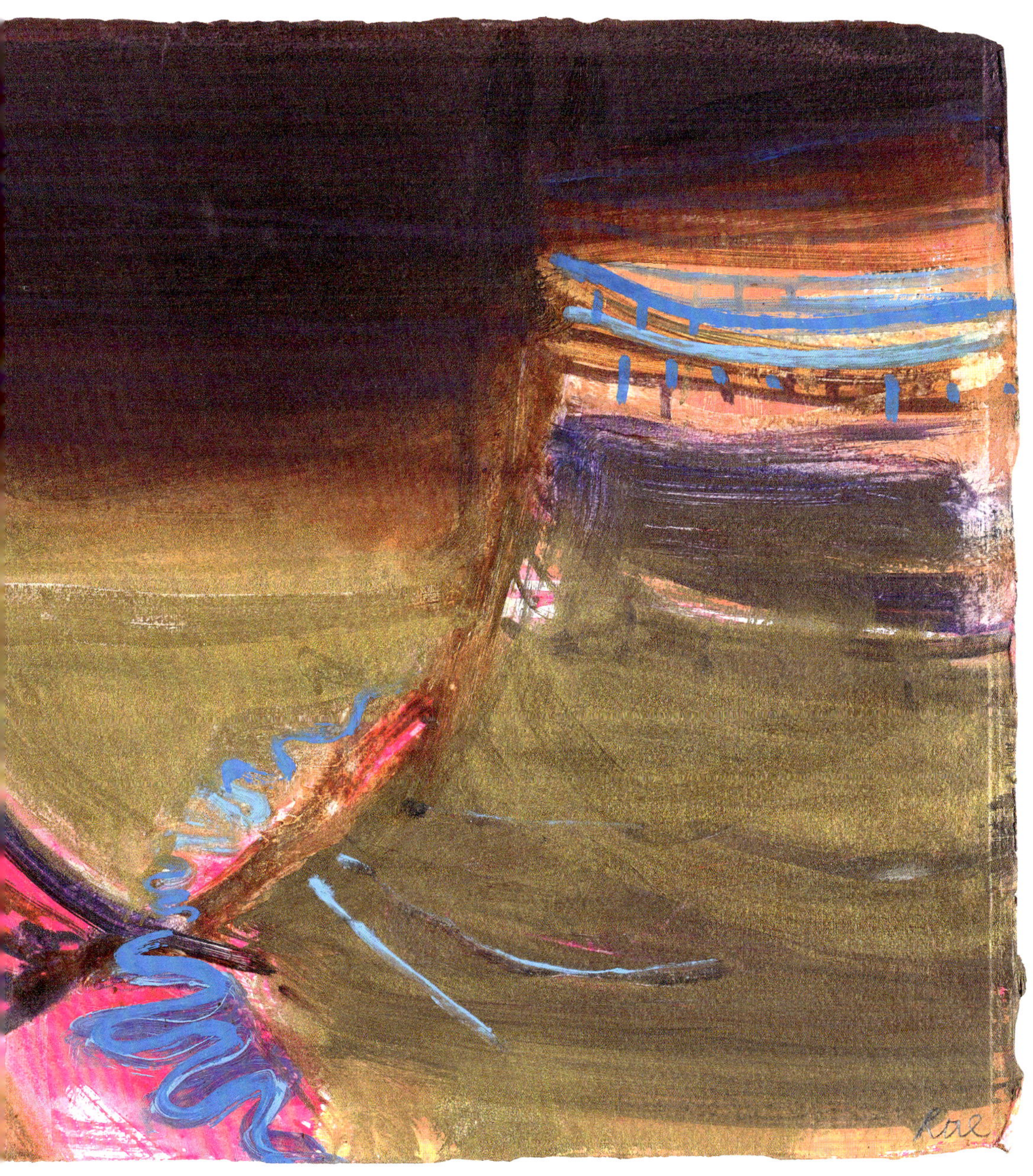

David Remfry MBE RA (b. 1942)
Havana Dancers, 2004
Pencil and watercolour
51.3 x 33.9 cm
RCIN 212779

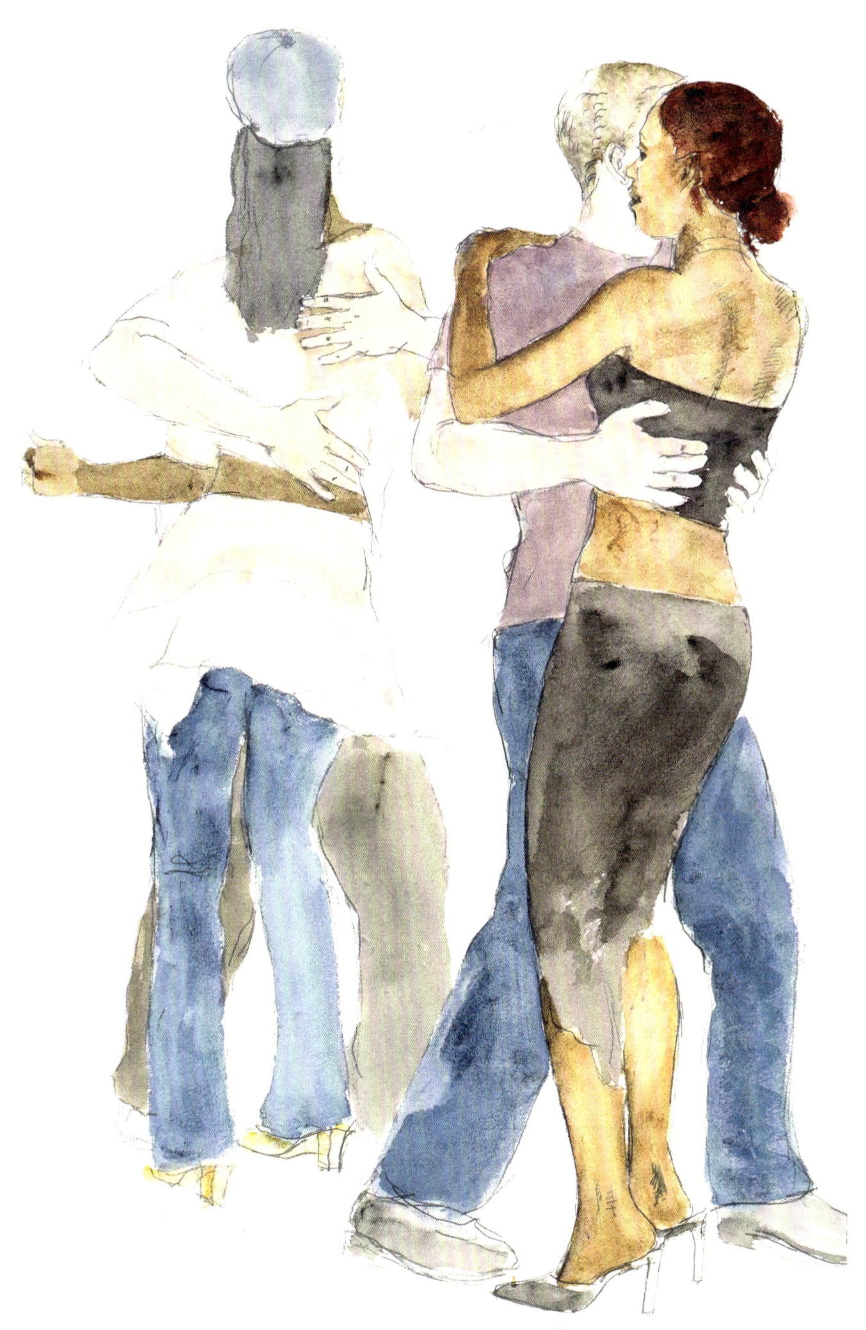

Professor Ian Ritchie CBE RA (b. 1947)
RSC Courtyard Theatre, 2005
Aquatint and red pencil
28.7 x 31.3 cm (sheet)
20.0 x 23.4 cm (plate)
RCIN 212780

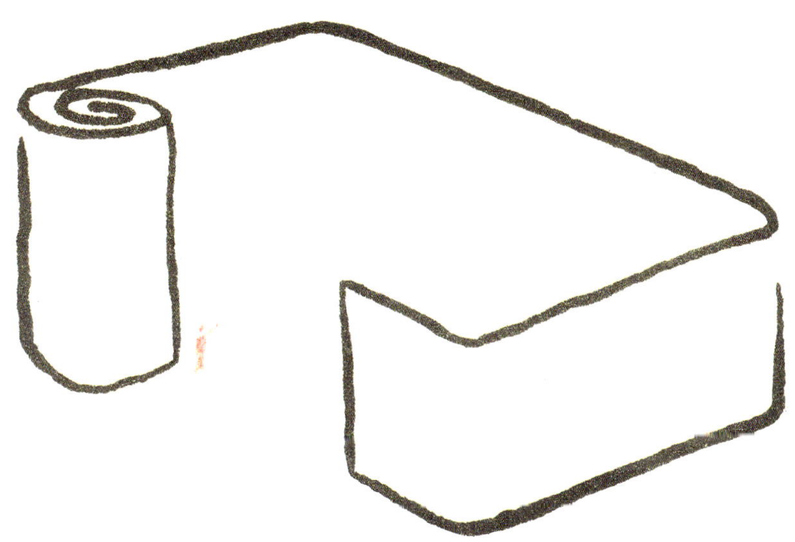

Mick Rooney RA (b. 1944)

All Quiet in the Yard, 2012

Gouache and tempera

24.9 x 15.4 cm

RCIN 212781

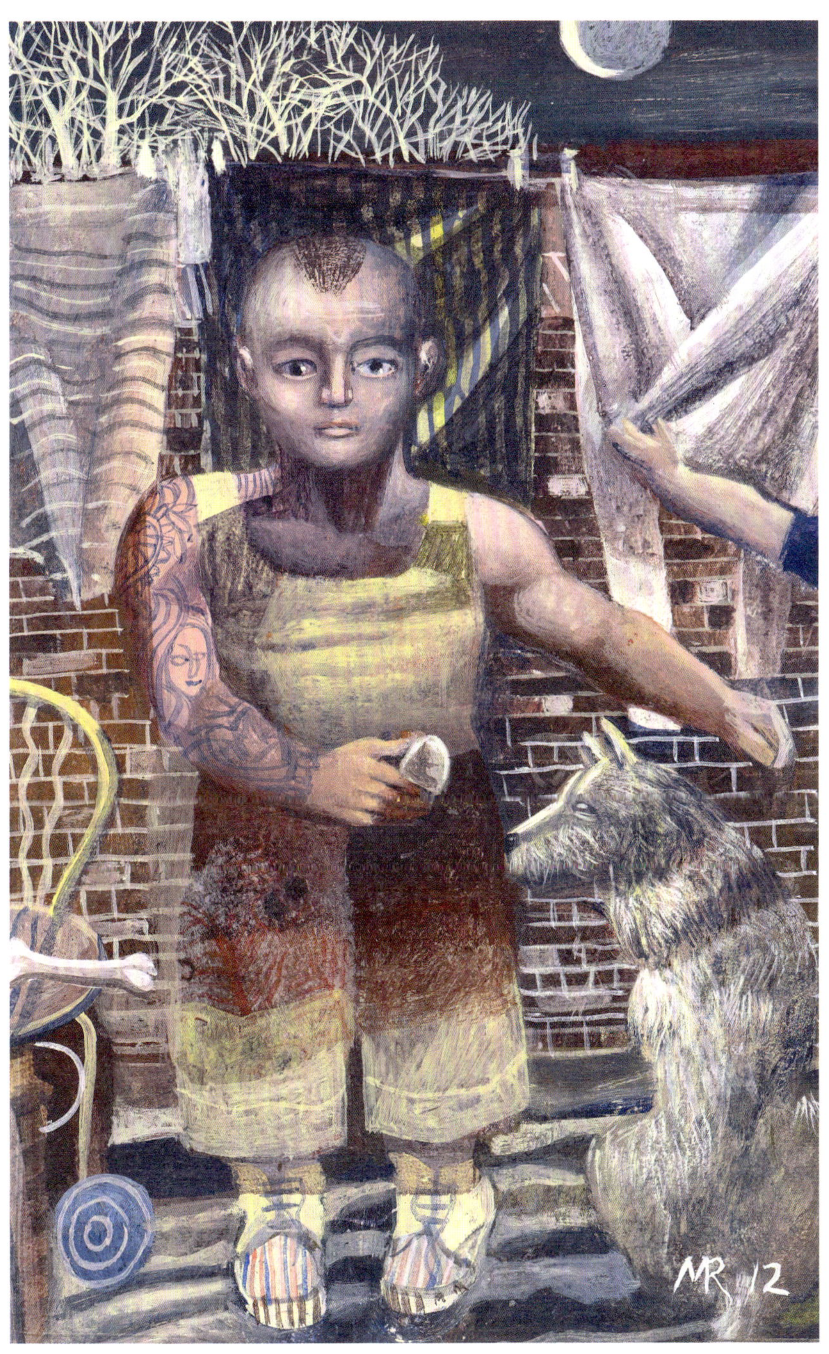
NR 12

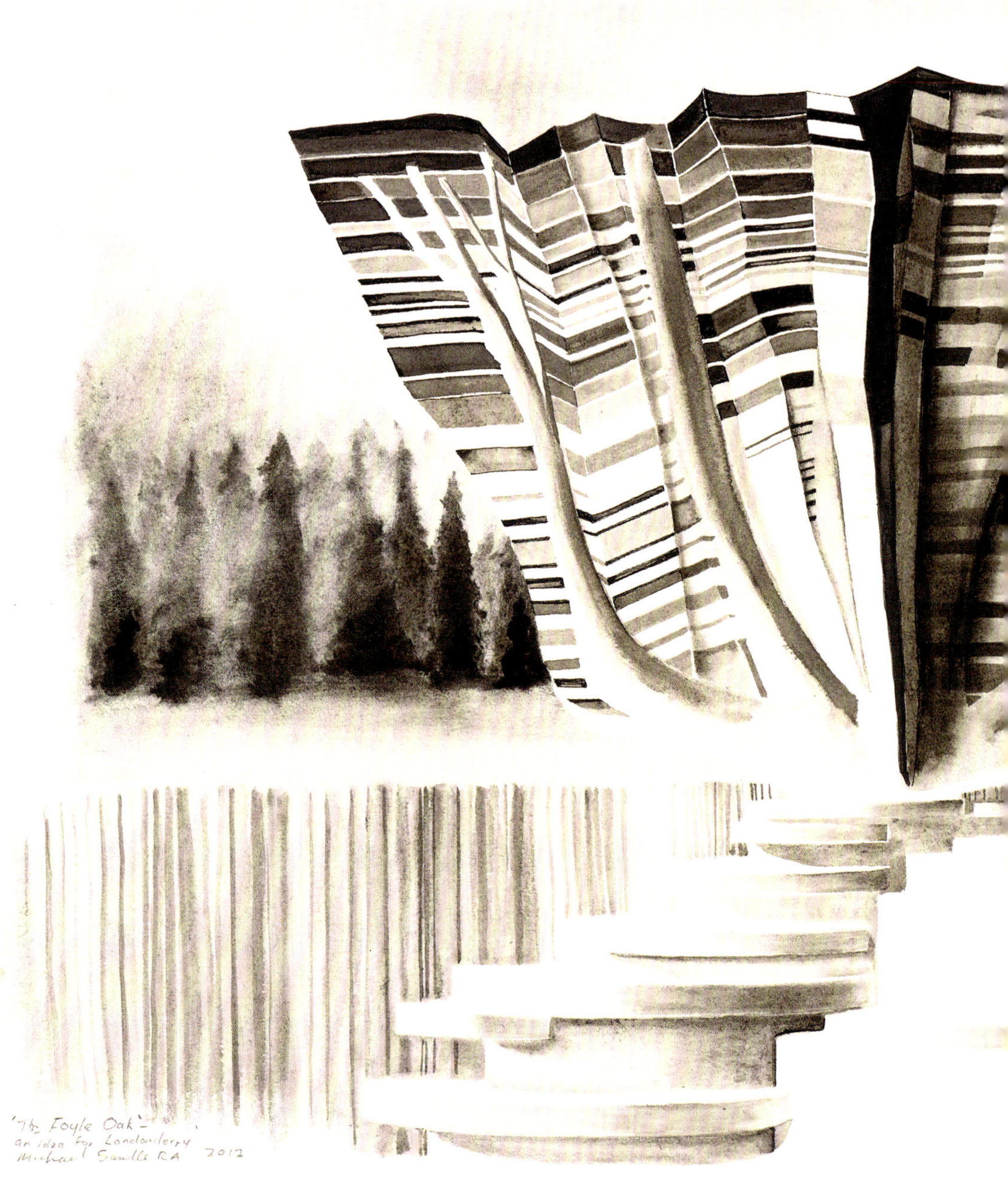
'The Foyle Oak' –
an idea for Londonderry
Michael Sandle RA 2012

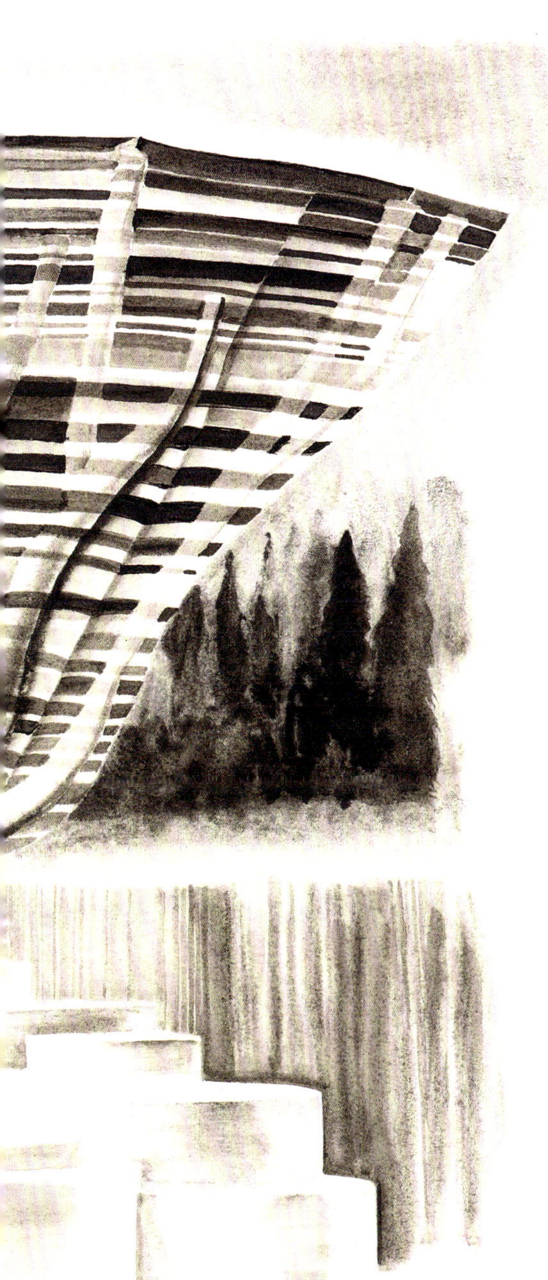

Professor Michael Sandle RA (b. 1936)
'The Foyle Oak' – an Idea for Londonderry, 2012
Pencil, pen and ink and wash
51.2 x 68.3 cm
RCIN 212782

Terry Setch RA (b. 1936)
Steep Holm, 2012
Watercolour, oil and wax
23.1 x 29.1 cm
RCIN 212783

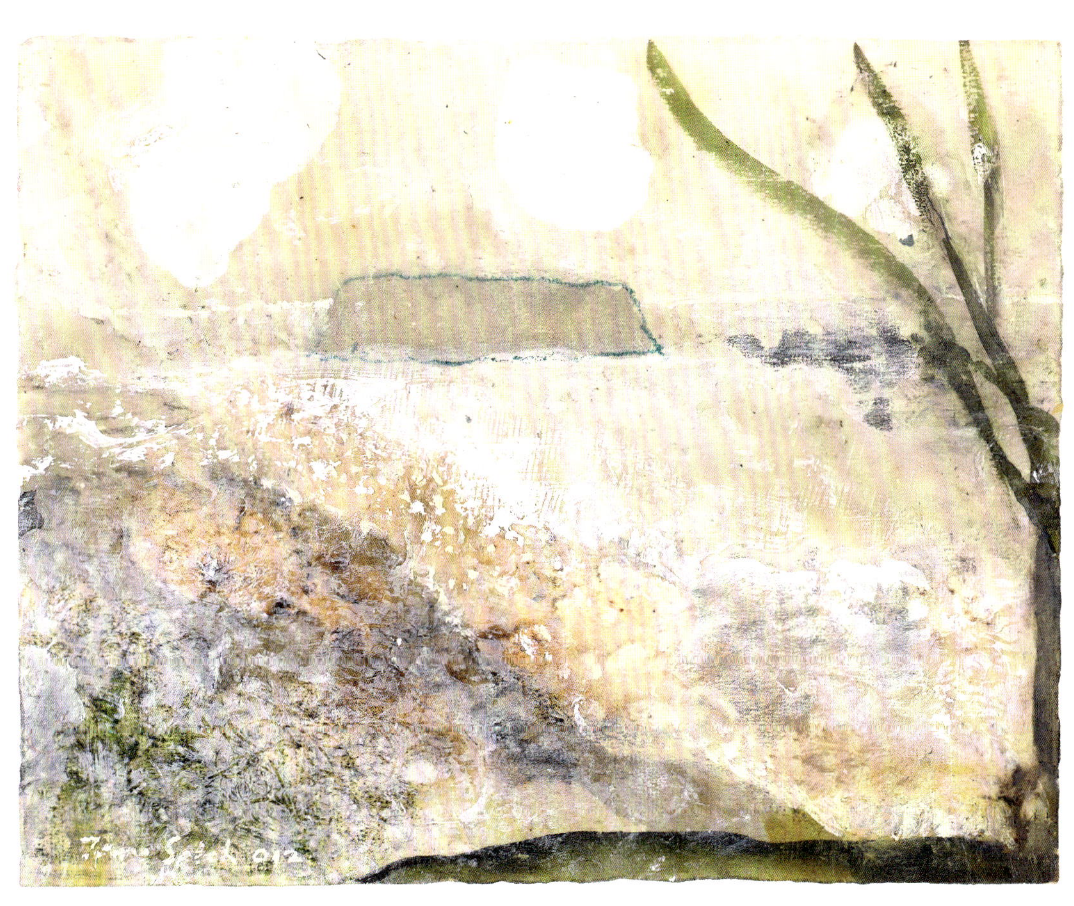

Alan Stanton RA RDI RIBA (b. 1944)

Belgrade Theatre, 2010

Inkjet print

52.1 x 39.8 cm

RCIN 212784

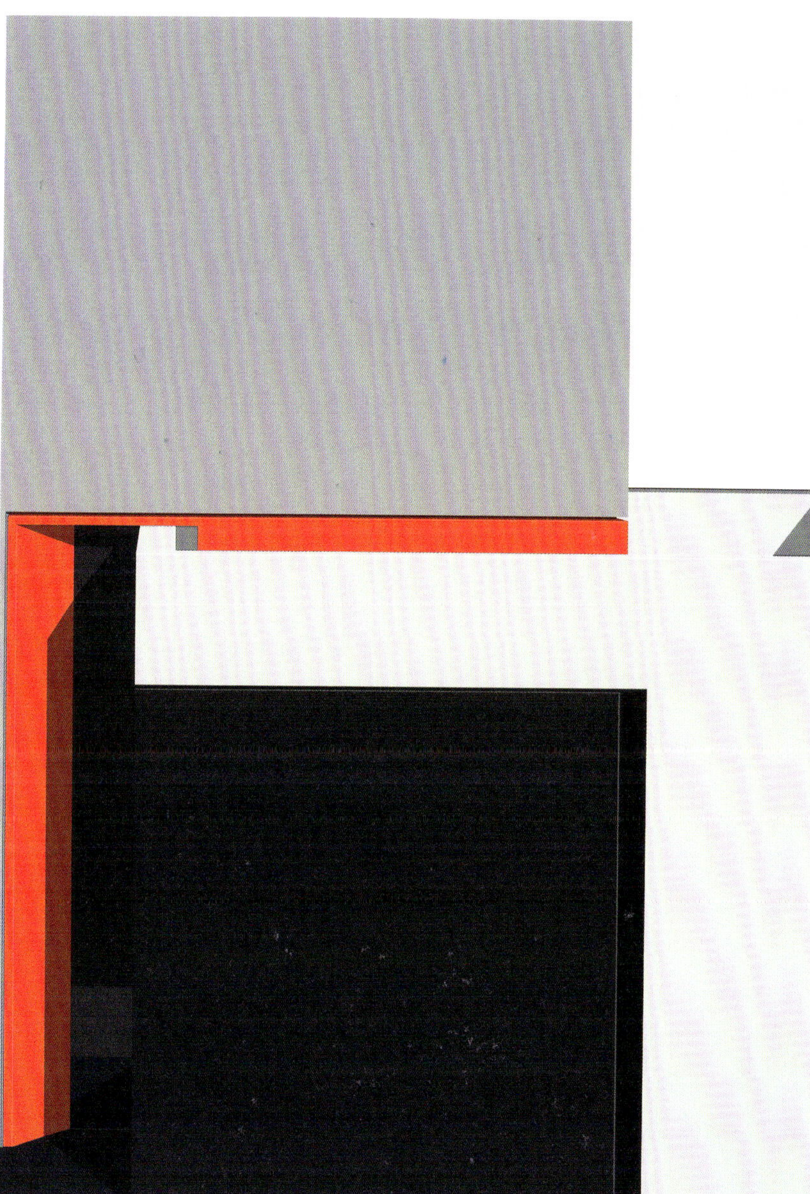

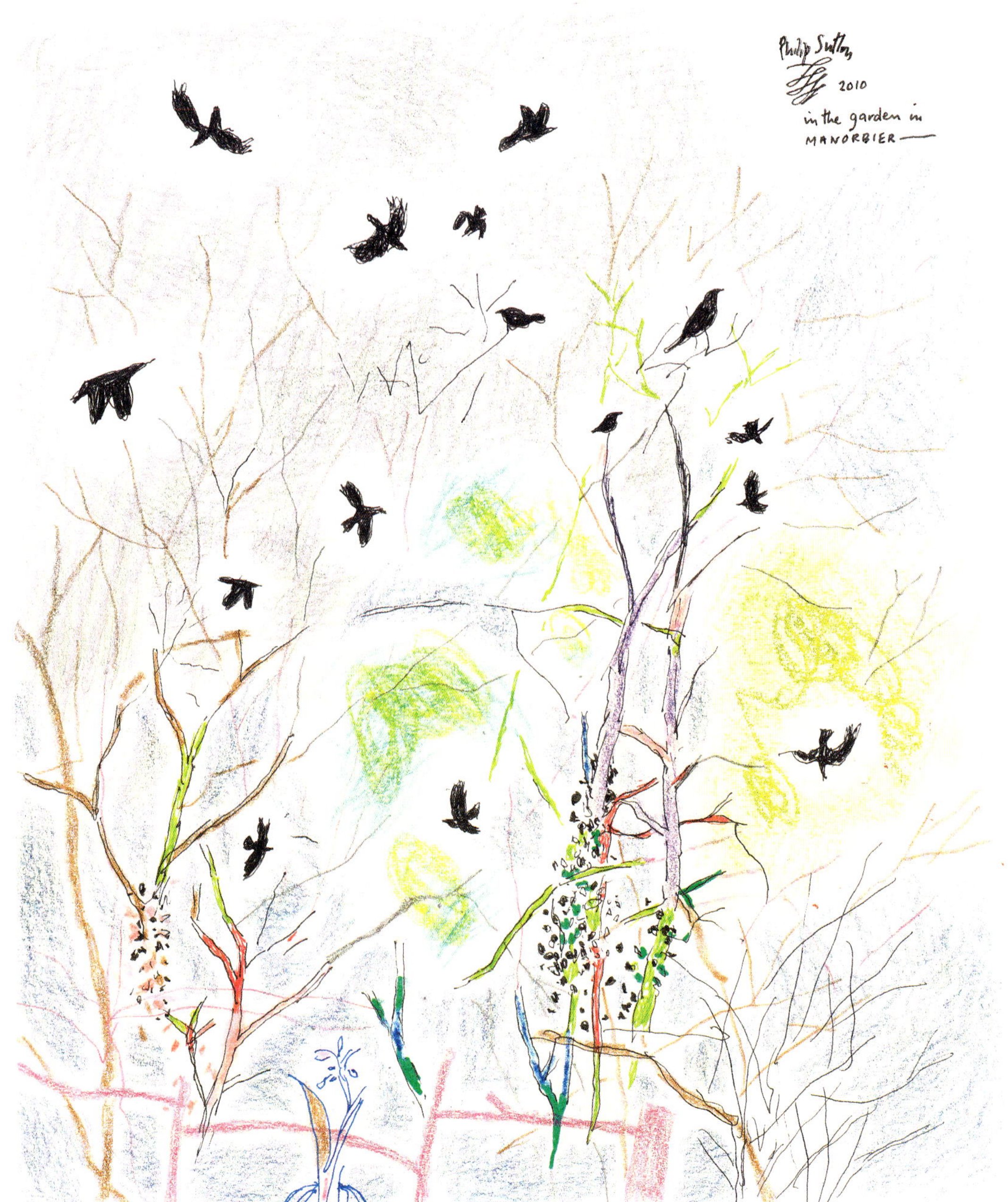
Philip Sutton
2010
in the garden in
MANORBIER —

Philip Sutton RA (b. 1928)
In the Garden in Manorbier, 2010
Pen and ink and coloured pencils
24.8 x 21.0 cm
RCIN 212785

Joe Tilson RA (b. 1928)

For Her Majesty the Queen a P.C. from Venice, 2012

Screenprint and collage

70.0 x 50.4 cm

RCIN 212786

a P.C. from Venice

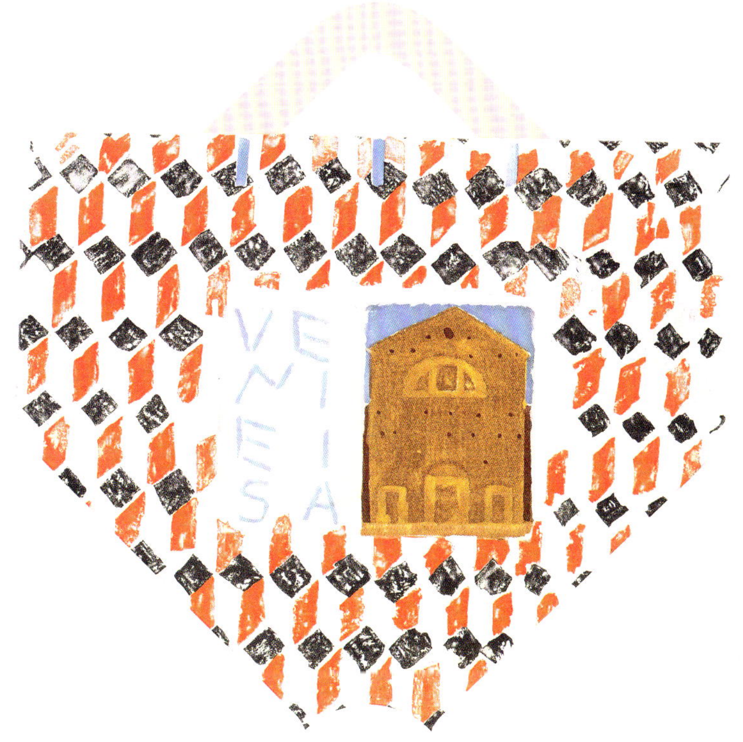

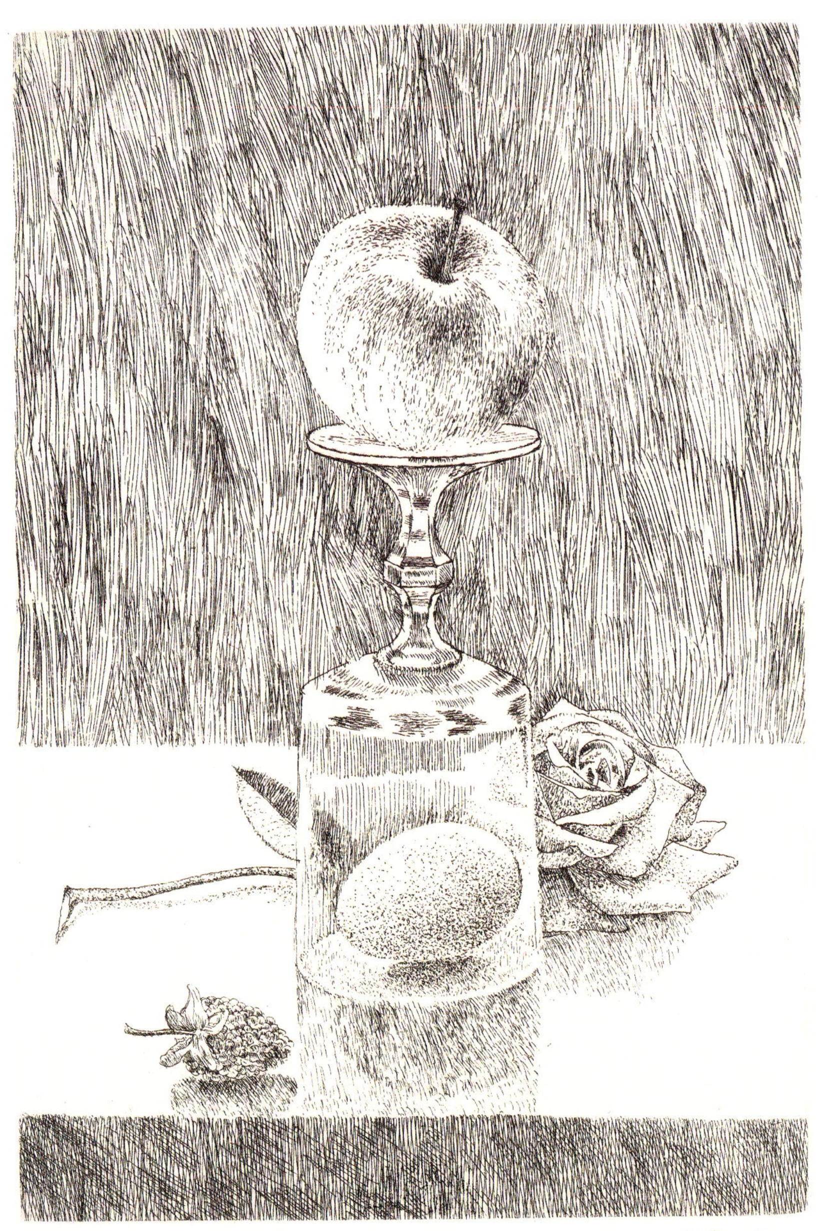

Dr David Tindle RA (b. 1932)
Still Life with Apple, 1996
Etching
35.9 x 27.7 cm (sheet)
19.8 x 13.5 cm (plate)
RCIN 212787

William Tucker RA (b. 1935)
Limb 5, 2011
Monotype with charcoal
38.2 x 28.3 cm
RCIN 212788

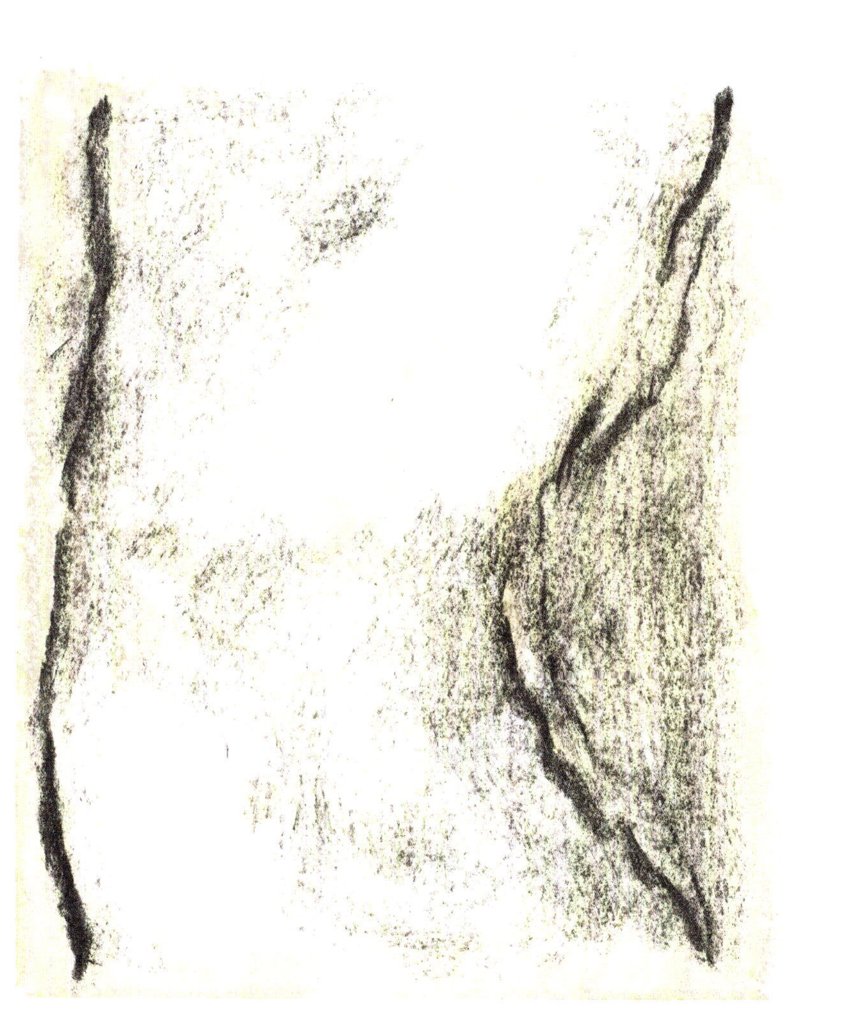

Anthony Whishaw RA Hon RWA ARCA (b. 1930)

Seated Woman on Sofa/Bed, 1993–4

Acrylic and collage

31.4 x 42.6 cm

RCIN 212789

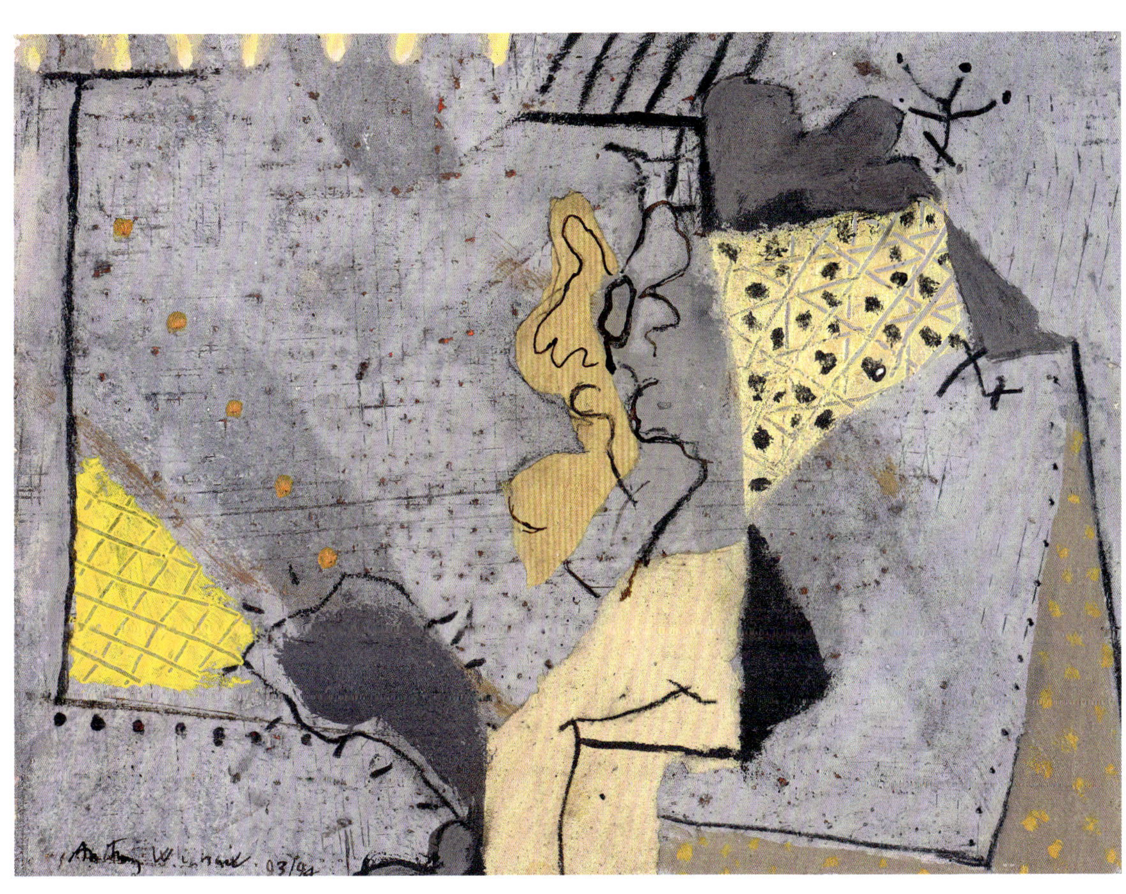

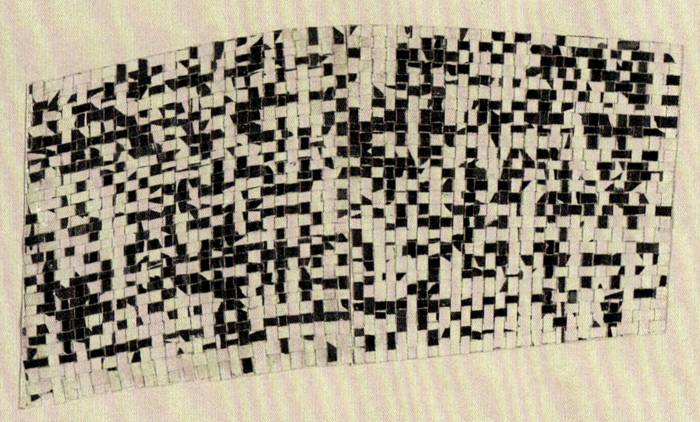
An Anagram

Alison Wilding RA (b. 1948)
An Anagram, 2012
Collage and ink
42.6 x 53.1 cm
RCIN 212790

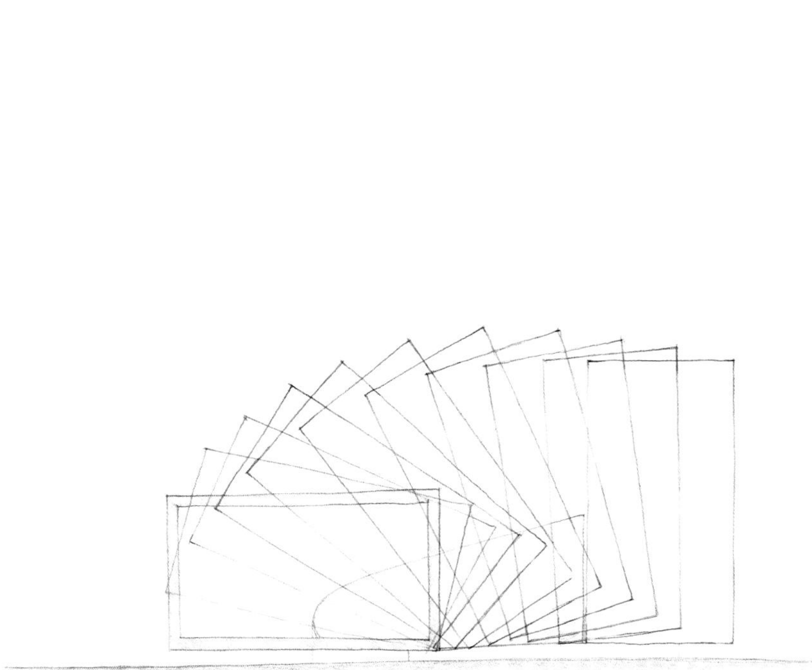

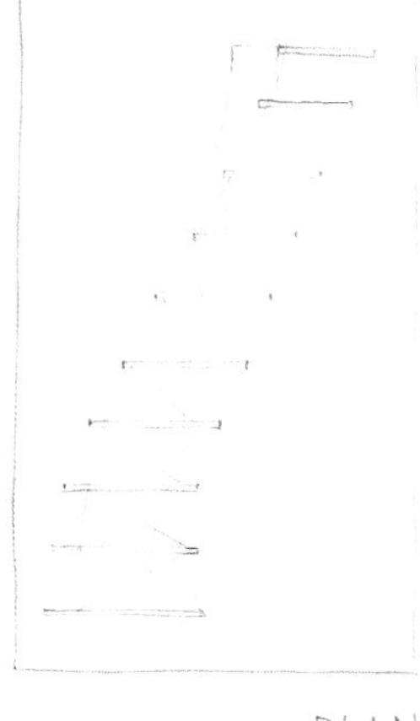

FROM LANDSCAPE TO PORTRAIT

AN ARCHITECTURAL INSTALLATION AT THE ROYAL ACADEMY IN 2012

CHRIS WILKINSON RA

Chris Wilkinson OBE RA (b. 1945)
From Landscape to Portrait, 2012
Pencil
49.9 x 70.6 cm
RCIN 212791

Professor Richard Wilson RA (b. 1953)
Hang on a minute lads, I've got a great idea!, 2012
Collage
56.1 x 42.0 cm
RCIN 212792

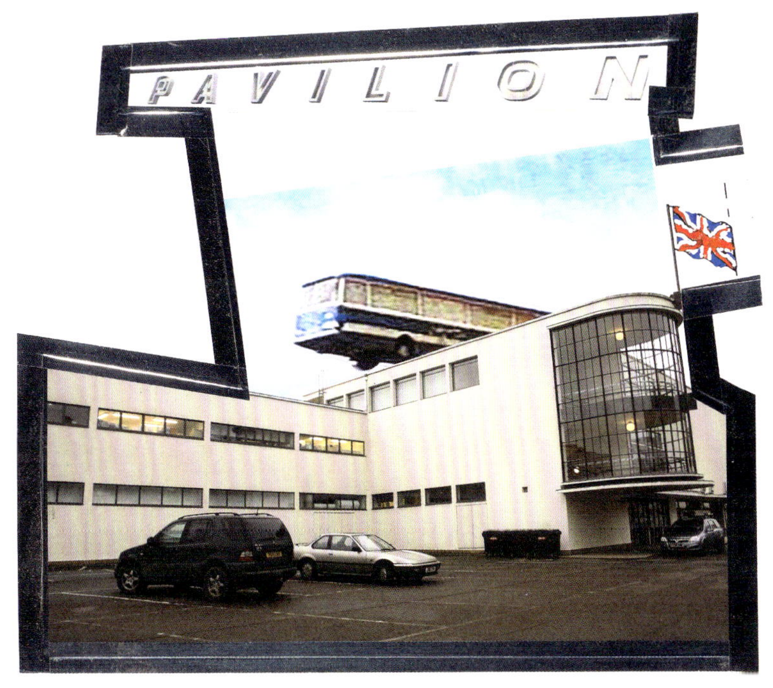

HANG ON A MINUTE LADS, I'VE GOT A GREAT IDEA !

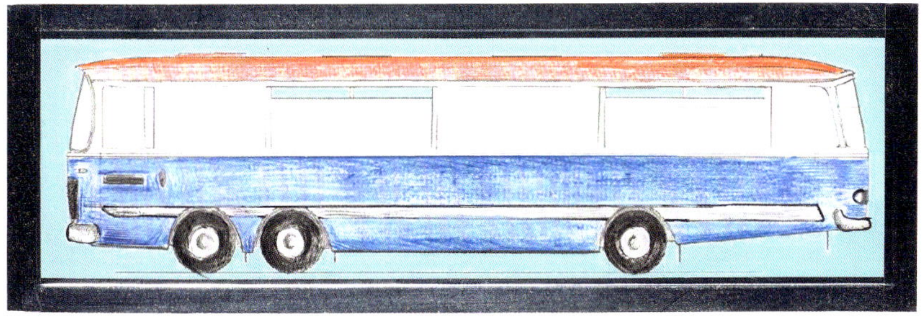

Bill Woodrow RA (b. 1948)
Untitled, 1999
Pen and ink
23.1 x 31.1 cm
RCIN 212793

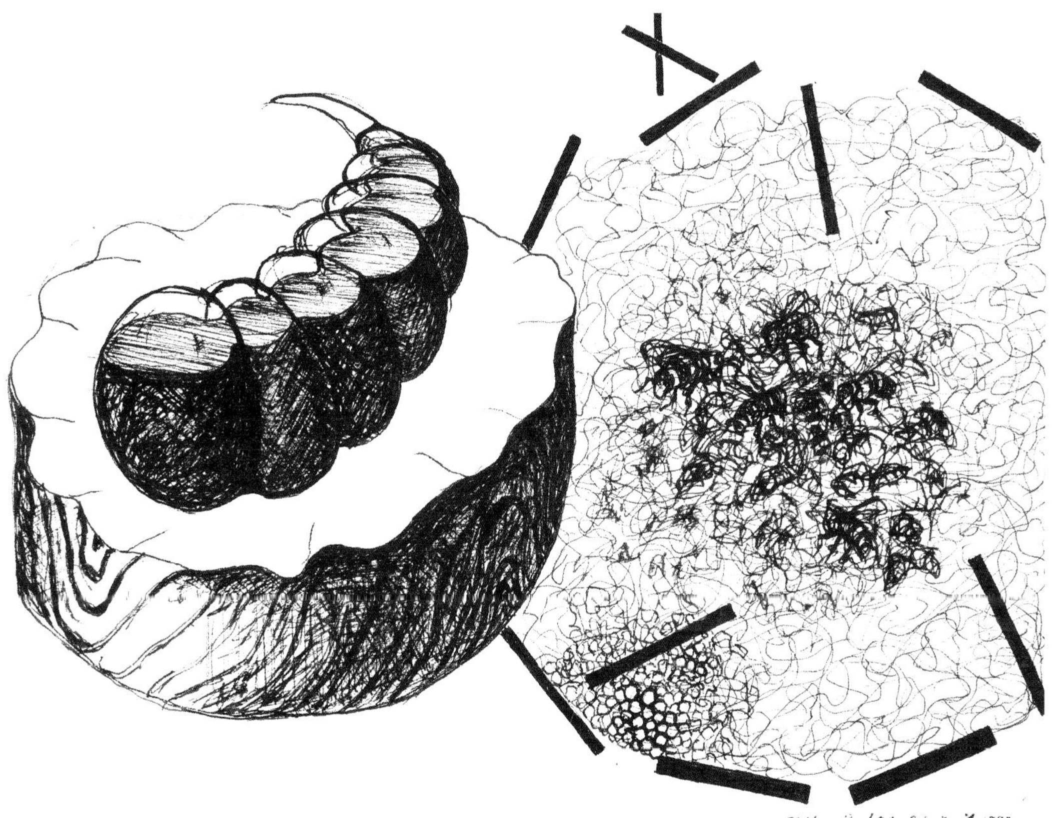
Bill Woodrow 26 April 1997

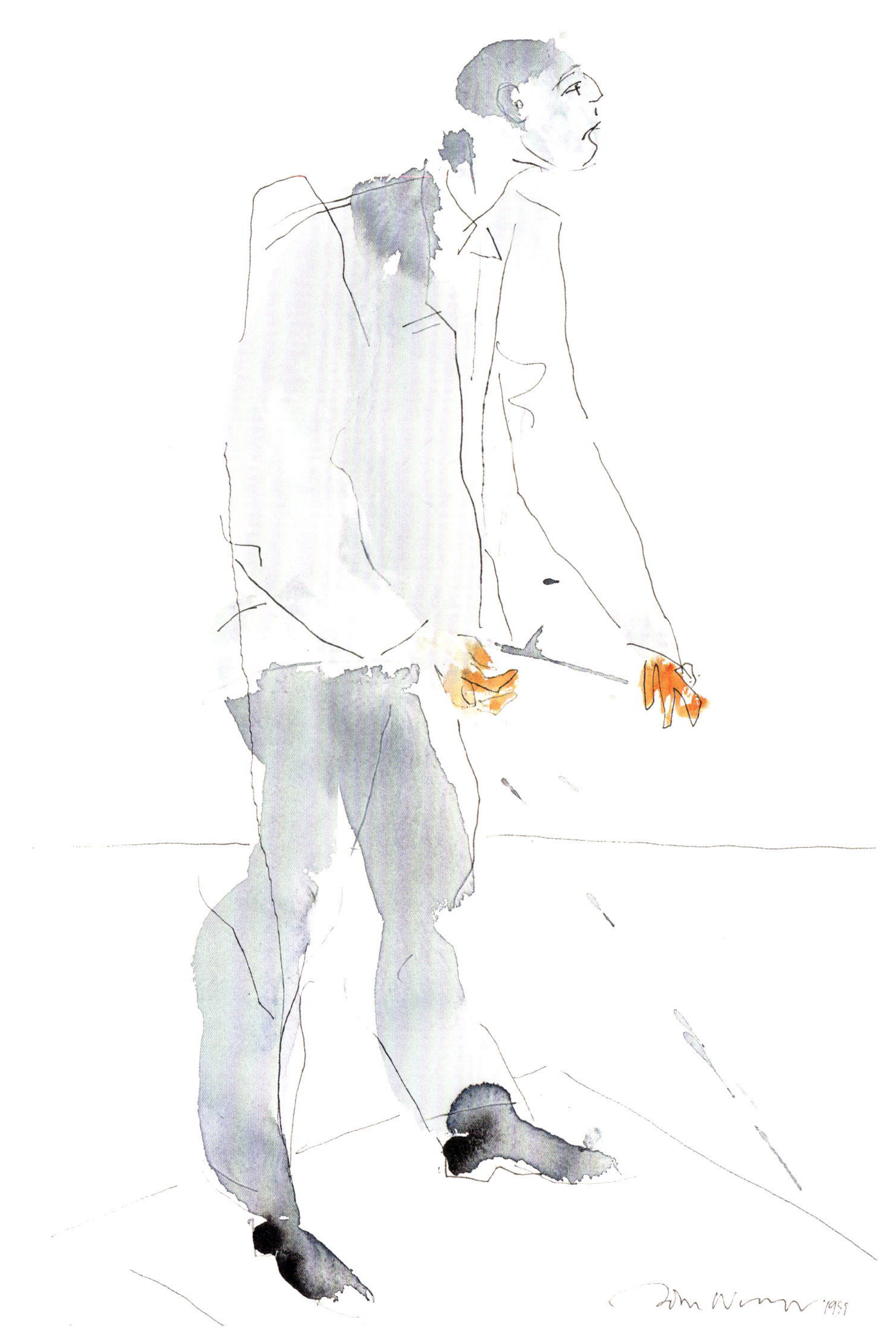

John Wragg RA (b. 1937)
Nervous Man, 1999
Pen and ink and watercolour
55.7 x 39.8 cm
RCIN 212794

Gifted
From the Royal Academy to The Queen

Written by Martin Clayton. Published by Royal Collection Trust.

Find out more about the Royal Collection at www.royalcollection.org.uk

ISBN 978 1 909741 06 5
014694

British Library Cataloguing in Publication Data: A catalogue record for this book is available from the British Library.

Designed by Anne Brady, Vermillion Design
Production management by Debbie Wayment
Typeset in Myriad Pro
Printed on 170gsm Arctic The Volume
Colour reproduction by Altaimage, London
Printed and bound in the UK by Butler Tanner and Dennis